ObamaScare

Philip J. Berg

ObamaScare

Philip J. Berg

obamacrimes.com

Philip J. Berg

Visit our website at http://www.obamacrimes.com/

ISBN-10: 0996157425
ISBN-13: 978-0-9961574-2-1
Kindle ASIN: B00U4W3YX4
Printed in the United States of America
Published by: Shecktor Enterprises, Inc, Berwick PA

Contents

Philip J. Berg

Preface

What Obama and his propaganda have done to this country is *very scary*. As the title of this book, **ObamaScare** represents frightening events that have taken place. His divisive movement will continue if we do not stop him. It is *scary* that an unknown man with sealed records about every aspect of his entire existence became President of the United States. Ask yourself and friends... just how close are we to a Socialist Nation since Obama nation took over. I fear for this country if we do not take action... *now!*

I want a future for our citizens, our children and grandchildren, and future generations, based upon the successes that have been accomplished prior to Obama taking office. The direction that Obama has taken this country is far beyond frightening- *this is really scary!*

We must open our eyes to the facts and truth of the Obama movement. We must unite Democrats, Republicans and Independents and demand that "our" United States Congress and "our" supposed Free Press expose Obama for the fraud he is. We must *seal our borders* now; and *repeal ObamaCare* or major changes now. We must insist on the truth about Benghazi, IRS, VA and Fast & Furious.

Given his association with communists & terrorists, a military background check would have long ago disqualified Barack Hussein Obama a/k/a Barry Soetoro for the job of President of the United

States. With his associations, the Chicago Police Department or hundreds of other agencies could not employ Obama. Yet, he became president - *something is very wrong with our focus!*

Barack Obama a/k/a Barry Soetoro would not be authorized for security clearance for access to the White House toilet *much less access for the codes for US nuclear weapons.* The USA has surrendered to an enemy within. A divisive America has accepted *fiction as fact and lies as truth.* A secret war rages across America, killing Americans via medical proxy & plundering the country's wealth with impunity.

And I found the 'missing link' – proof that Obama was born in Kenya! My interview with film producer Bettina Viviano discloses that Bill Clinton knew that Obama was and is ineligible to be President.

And the Election of November 4, 2014 was devastating to the Democrats because voters indicated their dissatisfaction with Obama. The question is, "What will occur between now and January 20, 2016 with the Republicans in control of both Chambers of Congress and what Obama does, as he says, "on his own."

Why I use "president Obama" with a small "p."

Please note that I refer to Obama/Soetoro as "president Obama" with a lowercase 'p' because Obama is a total fraud and not "Constitutionally Eligible" to be President of the United States. The facts prove that to be true.

Obama was never vetted by "our" supposed "Free Press" or by any government entity or agency, and regretfully not required. Eligibility issues and questions were raised regarding his eligibility beginning in 2007.

When Obama was a candidate and elected as United States Senator for Illinois, the headlines read that Obama was a candidate from "Kenya, Africa," yes, "Kenya."

I do not just make allegations; I follow through!

I filed a *"Qui Tam"* [False Claim Action] or 'Whistleblower' lawsuit against Obama on November 7, 2008 in the U.S. District Court for the District of Columbia in Washington, D.C., with the caption of the case, *Philip J. Berg, Esq., on his own Behalf and on Behalf of the Government of the United States of America, Relator v. Barack Hussein Obama, Jr., Defendant* and was assigned Case Number 1:08-cv-01933 before the Honorable Richard W. Roberts.

My position or allegations in my lawsuit were:

1) That Obama was not only not a "natural born" citizen, but he was not even a "naturalized" citizen and therefore, not a United States "citizen" as required to be a United States Senator [*U.S. Constitution, Article 1, section 3, clause 3*].

2) That the salary and benefits Obama received as a U.S. Senator for Illinois were fraudulently received and therefore, all of those funds shall be returned to the U.S. Treasury.

The case was filed under "seal" [meaning no one is allowed to discuss the case or release any pleadings or press] as required pursuant to statute and served upon the U.S. Attorney's Office and the U.S. Department of Justice.

Subsequently, after a Court Hearing, the case was dismissed. I believe and explain in Chapter VII – that there was a major "Conflict-of-Interest" because the U.S. Attorney and the U.S. Department of Justice was requested by Judge Roberts for their position on my case with three [3] options: [1] For the U.S. Attorney and the U.S. Department of Justice to proceed or take-over my case; [2] Allow me, as the *"Relator"* to proceed with my case; or [3] Dismiss the case. Guess what their position was? To DISMISS my case.

Realize, if Obama was not "Constitutionally Eligible" to be a U.S. Senator, he was not "Constitutionally Eligible" to be President of the United States.

And I filed other lawsuits against Obama regarding my questioning Obama's Constitutional Eligibility, dismissed by the Courts as they too, were protecting Obama. The first case I filed against Obama was before he was nominated by the Democratic National Committee at their Convention in August 2008 in Denver, Colorado. The case was dismissed stating I did not have "Standing" or the right to bring the lawsuit. The U.S. Constitution begins with the following three [3] fabulous words: "*We The People*." My position is that all of us, all U.S. Citizens have "Standing."

Therefore, my designation of Obama as "president Obama."

ObamaScare covers Obama's birth; his parents' divorce; his mother's remarriage; Obama's adoption in Indonesia where his name became Barry Soetoro; his illegal terms as U.S. Senator for Illinois and President of the United States; Obama's actions to take away y[our] 1st & 2nd Amendment rights guaranteed by "our" U.S. Constitution; Obama's lies and all of his scandals; his actions that must be reviewed regarding Treason and Impeachment; and what "WE THE PEOPLE" must do now. It's *scary*... when people fear their government. Please help put common sense back in American government.

Change! It is time to make it happen!

Phil
Philip J. Berg
Author & Activist

DEDICATIONS

*I dedicate **ObamaScare…***

To "our" forefathers; who fought and won our fight for independence; and came forth with *"our"* U.S. Constitution, *"our"* Declaration of Independence; and *"our"* Bill of Rights; that guided "our" United States and its citizens to a prosperous country that has led our nation to one of strength and leadership around the world, until Obama.

To my late father, Sidney Bernard Berg, Esquire, and my late mother, Rebecca Fishbein Berg Nissenbaum.

To my three [3] children and their significant others and my four [4] grandchildren.

To my loving fiancée, Carol, who has always supported and guided my efforts. She wants America to once again be respected, at home and throughout the world, as it has been during her lifetime.

To all of the people in "our" United States and around the world who LOVE "our" country, The United States Of America!

Letters and comments across America:

The following comments are by the individuals indicated. There are millions of people that want the truth and facts to come out. These are but a few of them.

"Phil Berg has survived the slings and arrows of the stormy political atmosphere we American's are living through. In 2008, Phil had the courage to tell the truth he had discovered. Mainstream media and P*rogressive "Obamobots"* have attacked him ever since then. Now, in this great book, Phil Berg further exposes Obama and his criminal administration."
Tina Trenner, *President*
Pahrump Valley Tea Party / TV Host NEWSMAX

....

"Barry Soetoro/Obama will *"NOT"* be exposed before his term is out. However, the failure of the media, "traditional" Democrats, Independents, and cowardly Republicans to impeach this illegal, lawless, evil man will be paid by all Americans over the next couple of decades. History will eventually confirm that the greatest act of treason that has ever occurred in America was the misrepresentation of fact by the American media. Media's failure to report the truth, and in many cases intentionally misrepresenting the truth, will be the reason the greatest Nation on earth joined the trash heap of another failed culture. Barry is just our Hitler."

"I have followed Phil's efforts to override the abysmal failure of the media (and other responsible parties) to expose Barry for what he is: a fraud, liar, traitor, the most lawless man to ever hold the office of President of the United States. Phil has surrendered everything that is dear to any business person or person in general who seeks to have a piece of the American dream, so that those who refused to speak-up could hide their heads in the sand and avoid the risk that face all who are willing to stand up against a corrupt/tyrannical government. For that, Phil should be applauded."

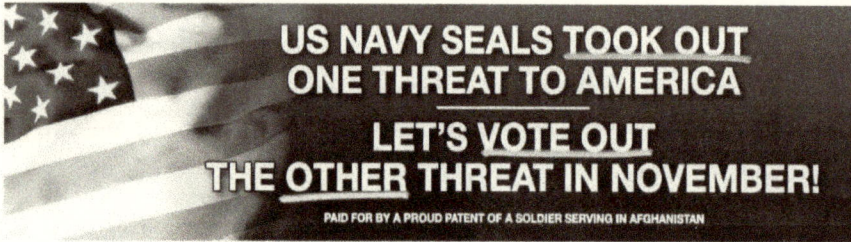

US NAVY SEALS TOOK OUT ONE THREAT TO AMERICA

LET'S VOTE OUT THE OTHER THREAT IN NOVEMBER!

PAID FOR BY A PROUD PATENT OF A SOLDIER SERVING IN AFGHANISTAN

Dane Fulmer, Christian, Traditional American / Proud parent of two [2] American Soldiers.

Dane Fulmer put his money behind his words. He purchased four [4] Billboard locations and placed anti-Obama signs thereon. One of them is above and one follows and another photo shows Dane with me at my Rally at the U.S. Capitol in Washington, DC:

"It has been my pleasure in knowing and working with Phil Berg for over twenty-four [24] years, having joined his campaign for Governor of Pennsylvania in 1990. Phil is a very determined individual and politician. He speaks what he believes, but he is open for input and has changed his opinion over the years. An example: Phil was very anti-gun, but after intense discussions with him, he now is a paid-up Life Member of the NRA. What a change for a Democrat, but Phil finally agreed with the principle that 'guns do not kill people, people kill people and he is now a strong proponent of the 2nd Amendment.

The Democratic Party for major positions has not endorsed Phil, in his many campaigns for political office because he is too independent versus party officials who want candidates to kiss their ass.

ObamaScare took Phil a long time to write because of the detail he presents and the delay in releasing the book has been caused by the additional information that has been forthcoming about pending scandals and the new scandals. The Obama administration has been and remains a nightmare.

"ObamaScare is a must read."

Eric Bradway
    Former Constable
    Democratic Committeeperson
    Former Candidate for State Legislature
    Advisor & Friend of Phil Berg

....

I am writing regarding my friend, Phil Berg, who I had the pleasure of listening to Phil speak on several occasions. He spoke at Freedompalooza in 2011, 2013 & 2014, held in Kintnersville, PA every July 4th. I first heard Phil speak on the lawn of the United States Capitol in Washington DC a few years ago. He had great delivery; held the audience; always staying on topic; and very interesting. It was my pleasure to hear Phil speak at our annual first amendment event.

Phil focused on is his efforts to expose Obama for the fraud he is; his ongoing efforts by filing several lawsuits against Obama and going to the United States Supreme Court in 2008 & 2009 four [4] times seeking Injunctions regarding Obama's election.

ObamaScare covers Obama's life from birth, to adoption, to his illegal terms as president, to the scandals, and what America must do to stop Obama.

Respectfully yours,
Paul Topete

....

"Phil, it is my pleasure knowing you as you deserve all the credit for pursuing Obama. God is using you to persevere to reveal the truth for the sake of this nation and beyond. You are standing for what is the truth! May the LORD uphold and strengthen you. I am praying for you and Israel. Your book is needed now more than ever. Thank you; many are behind you because your dedication is of the Lord! May Almighty God give you the fortitude to go to press!"

In Jesus name,
K. Kelly

....

This is from a special friend who has supported me from the outset of my efforts to expose Obama.

"It has been my pleasure to have been able to speak with Phil over the years as he has been very understanding and willing to discuss all of my ideas, some of which he adopted. Phil is a true patriot; a dedicated American; who has and continues to fight for the truth; a rare individual, who deserves the respect of our nation."

Roy Callahan

Rupert, Georgia

....

Like sheep to the slaughter the Holocaust again begins. I have often wondered why the Jews (and others considered "undesirable") in Nazi Germany and its occupied territories allowed their captors to take them, essentially without a fight. Now, in the United States we are facing a similar fate.

Lead by quasi dictator Barack Hussein Obama the "sheeple" are permitting our rights to be exchanged for handouts. Thanks to the likes of NAFTA and CAFTA, and liberal rebates for companies that open and operate overseas facilities, the majority of our population is either unemployed or underemployed or works for the government.

Government welfare (and no, don't even think about giving it a softer name) is at an all-time high and the gap between welfare payments and a low paid retail job is so great that there is no incentive to return to work – which is exactly what the ruling class wants, control of its citizens.

And now the federal government controls the health of the population as well. Once again the citizens hand over their cash, their guns, and their lives to a government that is bent on total control. Yet, it is interesting to note that if you poll a random selection of people, virtually ALL are opposed to this control – yet none will rise up against it.

They are lured by the small and unimportant personal interests – does gay marriage or legalization of marijuana usurp our general freedoms and the ability to work at a job that actually pays the bills and keeps people off welfare.

This is what we have become – a nation that wastes every waking minute watching sitcoms and stories about adultery and naked people roaming on an island trying to "survive." A nation of texts and tweets rather than personal interaction.

A nation where the media (in bed with the government and big business) controls the flow of information. A nation whose "leaders" sign bills into law without reading them. A nation where every small town is slowly being equipped with para-military equipment, not for controlling terrorists, but for controlling its citizens. This is our present and our future under Barack Obama and his cronies in D.C.

And then there is the ruse that Hillary Clinton is a fallen angel. Hillary Clinton was used to assist in the creation of the "Affordable Health Care Act" (which has done nothing to control health care cost) and then was dumped as a martyr by the Democratic Party.

She never was pleased that she could not enact her plan to control the people when her husband was President, and was happy to finally able to get her way. Now, she is free to run for President on the guise that she was ousted by Obama and can reject the current regime. Yet, she is not divorced from Obama – she is part of the bigger plan to continue the oppression begun by Obama. This evil and deadly plan must end, and it must end now. Obama must be stopped, as must Hillary Clinton.

There are precious few people in this country who are willing to speak out against this oppression, Phil Berg being one of them. I have given up the fight, but not the cause – everyone wants to listen but no one is willing to act. Those who refuse to stand up for their rights and stand up against oppression deserve what they get. I can only hope that in the end the will of David triumphs over the power of Goliath, for if not, our fate is sealed, and we too will suffer, as did the victims of the Nazi's.

Written by Andrew M. Shecktor, CR 2014, all rights reserved
Local political leader and author of "Centralia PA, Devils Fire"
....

From a longtime friend:

"Without getting into the politics regarding Obama, I want to express my feelings regarding the economy during Obama's Administration. It is not good; my business is down; customers do not have money for extras, only necessities. When one drives throughout the area, you see empty stores in strip malls and in shopping centers; and commercial building after commercial building that are for rent/sale as tenants/owners have closed down."

"I have known Phil for years and I have seen excerpts from *ObamaScare* and Phil has prepared a thorough book that should be read to open people's eyes as to problems that our country is facing."

Anonymous

....

It has been my pleasure watching the ongoing efforts of Phil Berg in his determination to uncover the truth about Obama. I know he has spent an enormous amount of time writing this book, and in discussing with him the content of **ObamaScare**, I know that the readers eyes will open as Phil has dealt with scandal after scandal and recent nightmares that have been revealed and developed, many directly the responsibility of Obama.

As for economics, the whole bailout after the first election of president Obama was completely wrong. While I understand that as President, Obama did not want to let the auto industries fail completely, thus creating the loss of more jobs. The fact is that he had a tremendous opportunity to turn the auto industry around and make the United States the global leader in auto sales both domestically, but more importantly, as an exporter.

All financial banks and lenders make demands on their borrowers. These are terms, responsibilities, and conditions about how the borrowed money will be used and paid back. Had Obama demanded that all automakers receiving bailout money produce vehicles that would get 150 miles to the gallon, had a bumper to bumper warranty of six years, and 100,000 miles, and sold for under $30K; not only would he have turned the consumers from purchasing imports to purchasing domestic vehicles, but he would have been able to increase the demand to export these vehicles globally.

The effect Detroit would have had would force all international auto manufacturers to follow. In addition, this would have created more wealth for U.S. citizens having more monies to spend on other items than just gas. In the end, we the consumers and citizens would have seen increased exports of U.S. autos, a tremendous rise in our GNP, strengthening of the dollar, increases in jobs, decreases in taxes and most importantly, a significant decrease in our dependence on the importation of oil as well! Had Obama made such a demand he would have restored the economy to full employment simply by fixing the auto industry and decreasing the number of dollars sent overseas daily purchasing and importing fossil fuels. In addition, many other opportunities were overlooked. As a man who ran his campaign on "change," he would have been the first President since John F. Kennedy to challenge our nation to become completely green and self-sufficient as a nation, no longer having a dependence on the importation of fossil fuels.

Why didn't Obama set a goal to be independent of all nations for our energy needs and provide a challenge that we as a nation would no longer be an importer of fossil fuels by the end of the decade? Why didn't he support a policy to be completely self-sufficient using new technology, such as perpetual motion harnessing wave action from oceans and inland lakes (The Great Lakes), hydro-electric, wind, solar, hydrogen, etc. Obama would have literally opened the job market to new companies, increased our scientific base with more people entering science and engineering. Combined, those two policies alone would have significantly decreased the outflow of American dollars leaving our economy to OPEC.

Obama overlooked or ignored numerous opportunities at his fingertips to bring back jobs, manufacturing, and rebuild our economy and improve employment. Again, had Obama done nothing more than take a Keynesian Economics approach to fix our economy and realize that our nation's infrastructure is in a drastic state of disrepair and in need of a major federally sponsored national overhaul of unprecedented scale to the likes that would have rivaled FDR or even China's Three Gorges Dam Project. Had Obama addressed the rebuilding of our nation's levees, dams, bridges, tunnels, highways, power grids and infrastructure, again he would have created millions of jobs and new wealth as FDR had done with his great public works programs during the great depression.

Marc D. Swartz

Obama and Our Modern Don Quixote de la Mancha
Phil Berg by Paul J. Landis

"Don Quixote de la Mancha" is part of classic Spanish literature. Written by Miguel de Cervantes Saavedra it tells of its hero, Don Quixote, who decides to set out to revive chivalry, and perceives a windmill as threatening giants and single handedly with lance and trusty horse proceeds to challenge them.

As editor of "Wethepeoplewethemedia.com," I was introduced to possible issues of Barack Obama as a U.S. Presidential candidate by Phil Berg, our modern, heroic Don Quixote de la Mancha. This time, the windmills really are monsters.

Having met and spoken with Phil concerning other issues, I had very little doubts that there would be significant substance to his endeavors to show that Barack Obama lacked the required credentials to run for U. S. President.

Briefly, Phil secured sworn Affidavits by ministers, statement of a Barack relative as to his Kenya birth, Obama's promotion literature from U.S. Senate in 2005 stating he was born in Kenya and the Kenyan government announcing work of a monument to their Kenyan born U.S. Senator.

In August 2008, Phil filed papers in the U.S. District Court, Eastern District of Pennsylvania and asked that Obama and the DNC respond to his allegations that Obama was not Constitutionally Eligible to be President.

The papers were served and they denied everything and Obama failed to answer Request for Admissions directed to him.

Rather than be concerned with the real issues of Obama's "Constitutional Eligibility," the Court took hard positions against Phil and dismissed the case based upon "Standing," that is the right to bring an action.

When there are/were questions about this, or any U.S. Government candidate, do not the American people have the right to judge, ask questions?

Why did the mainstream media not ensure a fair dialog before the U.S Presidential election process including whether Barack Obama was allowed to continue based upon his eligibility?

Even more important, this author suggests who gains and or sought gain by having a treasonous shill in the White House.

How about those who have worked to ensure there is "Corporate control" of our media.

Obama authorized the use of Drones that killed many civilians worldwide, without Congress approval. Also, without Congress or approval of the American People, he authorized troops for Afghanistan and many other locations, including Somalia, around the world, where our soldiers are being killed and maimed.

With such poor media coverage, you are probably not familiar with "Death by China," a documentary by Peter Navarro.

This vital work tells how Communist China, who joined the World Trade Organization (WTO) in 2000, is NOT playing by the rules. They have outsourced over 24 million U.S. jobs and are responsible of the majority of 57,000 U.S. factories gone.

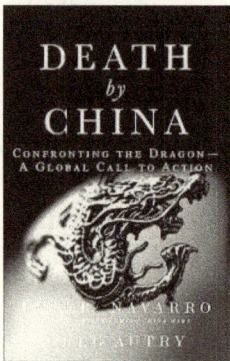

Is this not an issue for a U.S. President who is sworn to protect and defend the American People and the U.S. Constitution?

How many people must get ill (both in the U.S. and worldwide) before this hollow man and Congress close down the deadly pesticide producer Monsanto?

And the tragic, over-riding objectives of the Obama shill: Government not by *We the People*... but rather by "Them, the greedy criminal corporations," corporations who are willing to put, and have put, innocent civilians in harm's way in wars: to make money.

Lastly, Trans-Pacific Partnership (TPP): Job Loss, Lower Wages, and Higher Drug Prices

http://www.citizen.org/tpp

Have you heard? The TPP is a massive, controversial "free trade" agreement currently being pushed by big corporations and negotiated behind closed doors by officials from the United States and 11 other countries – Australia, Brunei, Canada, Chile, Japan, Malaysia, Mexico, New Zealand, Peru, Singapore, and Vietnam.

In one fell swoop, this secretive deal could:

Roll back Wall Street reforms,
Sneak in SOPA-like threats to Internet freedom,
Ban Buy American policies needed to create green jobs,
Jack up the cost of medicines,
Expose the U.S. to unsafe food and products,
and empower corporations to attack our environmental and health safeguards.

Although it is called a "free trade" agreement, the TPP is not mainly about trade. One chapter would provide incentives to offshore jobs to low-wage countries. Many would impose limits on government policies that we rely on in our daily lives for safe food, a clean environment, and more. Our domestic federal, state, and local policies would be required to comply with TPP rules.

The TPP would even elevate individual foreign firms to equal status with sovereign nations, empowering them to privately enforce new rights and privileges, provided by the pact, by dragging governments to foreign tribunals to demand taxpayer compensation over policies that they claim undermine their expected future profits.

We only know about the TPP's threats thanks to leaks – the public is not allowed to see the draft TPP text. Even members of Congress, after being denied the text for years, are now only provided limited access. Meanwhile, more than 600 official corporate "trade advisors" have special access.

And who has worked to keep TTP secret from Americans AND wants to sign it in 2014:

The TPP has been under negotiation for five years, and the Obama administration wants to sign the deal by early 2015.

End Media Consolidations;
Impeach Obama and charge his conspirators with Treason;
End and Reverse Outsourcing;
Bring back the 57,000 companies;
Demand Congress pass laws prohibiting Outsourcing and or Factory sales without Americans' Approval;
Import duties for all China imports; and
Outlaw secret deals like TTP and prosecute those involved.

Paul J. Landis
www.wethepeoplewethemedia.com

From Where I Stand

"We will keep this promise to the American people: If you like your doctor you will be able to keep your doctor. Period. If you like your healthcare plan, you will be able to keep your healthcare plan. Period." (Barack Obama, June 15, 2009)

Today, any American who is not deaf or blind knows this "promise" was *a very big lie. Most doctors that have patients know it was a lie.* A lie deliberately told because if the truth were widely known at that time, The Affordable Care Act would never have become law.

It is another ***ObamaScare*** lie. A lie so obvious the media and free press cannot easily ignore it or cover it up. In fact, the media and free press now seem more willing to shed light on Obama, not just on the ObamaCare lie, but also on some of Obama's other lies.

Perhaps they will eventually revisit and take another look at the biggest lie of all on April 27, 2011. The lie that is central to Barack Obama's identity. The lie not only glossed over, but for which they ostracized everyone who brought forth facts to point out it was a lie. *More on this later.*

The words "blind" and "trust" are both useful and important words used separately. They should never be used together, in a manner that represents *the peoples* approach to our government. When that happens... it is time for Americans to wake-up. There is an old saying in politics: "What's old is new."

Today, I stand by my original statement in 2008:

"Obama is a fraud, phony and an imposter and has put forth the greatest 'HOAX' against the United States of America in over two hundred and thirty years."

Anyone that doesn't accept *the lies sold as truth* or raises questions about Obama's background is called a "Right-Wing" conspiracist, racist, out-of touch and just out to destroy the Obama administration. *Wrong!* I am a life-long Democrat. I registered on

03/29/1965 in the City & County of Philadelphia, Pennsylvania. People ask, "How can a Democrat sue a Democrat?" My response. "The U.S. Constitution is more important than any political party." I have been on thousands of radio shows, and some people comment.... "You are a racist!" *Wrong again!* "You cannot see me, I am white and a paid-up Life Member of the NAACP, so what is your next question." Critics do not know what to do with me. My response is simple and straightforward, "I just want the truth!" However, Obama does not want me *or you* to have the truth or the facts. They know full disclosure of the truth and it is not in *their* best interest.

ObamaScare is timely and even more *scary* because new information surfaces weekly about new scandals and lies come out about old scandals that will not go away. Benghazi, IRS, VA, Iraq, foreign policy (mostly - lack thereof), ISIS/ISSL, Radical Islam, illegal immigration, ACORN, ObamaCare, Cuba and many others failures continue to show the incompetence of the Obama Administration. *ObamaScare is real.* Other Obama nightmares include but not limited to; children being sent illegally to the United States through our southern border from South America; the terrifying missile that brought down Malaysia MH17; and ISIS/ISSL infiltration in the United States. We... the people should require truthful and factual disclosure. The *truth* is not different for each skin color, political party line, or socio-economic level. However, the truth and facts remain hidden in the Obama agenda.

A lawsuit against president Obama will help. Actually, the answer to finding the truth requires action from each of you.

As an American, I am frightened that Obama replies to the important questions and opposition with sound bites instead of facts. Sound bites that would have America believe there are no scandals. Sound bites that would have America believe that people who believe in the Constitution just make up scandals because they are racist.

More on racism. Barack Obama was supposed to bring us together... Remember? His campaign was about unity, promise, and peace. Can we all come together with cooler heads to solve the nation's problems? "Yes We Can!" he shouted from between Greek columns, in town halls and on network television interviews.

Well that promise, that dream, has not simply fizzled or faded. It has been shattered into pieces by the direct hands of president Obama and Attorney General Eric Holder, and in historic fashion.

A recent example is the "fanning of the flames" approach taken by the White House to the "trending" drama in Ferguson, Missouri, where a young black man, Michael Brown, was shot and killed by a white police officer, Darren Wilson, on August 9, 2014. In the beginning, we did not know the facts but that does not stop the race-baiters in the Obama administration and its allies from undermining the rule of law by drawing their own conclusions and rushing to the scene of the next..."hate crime." Yes, both of the "Reverends" Sharpton and Jackson were immediately on the scene... playing the race card. All of this grandstanding, including by president Obama and Attorney General Holder did what it always does: undermine justice, encourage racial division, and tacitly encourage the appearance of racial divisiveness. *Can anyone tell me what Al Sharpton really does?*

Obama further tells *"we... the people,"* there is nothing wrong with the; *what, how, and why of his actions.* His *magic pen* will sign executive orders in order to bypass and ignore Congress *as he damn well chooses.* If he is not accountable to anyone... that puts him in the same class as Hitler and every other dictator. Beware of *blind trust in government.* America needs you to have 20-20 vision for her to survive.

Recent facts and truths make it apparent that "cover-up" runs rampant in the Obama administration. From Benghazi, to the outright lies regarding the IRS and the VA-deathgate and many other cover-ups, Obama does as he pleases. As a result of the failure of Obama's foreign policy; Iraq is unraveling (again); ISIS/ISSL remains unchecked; Iran is a step away from having nuclear weapons and what is Obama doing – negotiating with Iran [would you negotiate with someone who wants to destroy Israel and the United States ?]; immigration laws are ignored; and forty thousand children from South America were invited to illegally [and politically motivated] to enter our borders [many bringing diseases]. Do you find these major threats to our security just a little *scary...as in **ObamaScare**?*

Obama continues to undermine the United States of America that we all have known and loved. Obama was determined to change the United States and he has done so, to the detriment of all of us. Not to mention that Freedom of Speech has an asterisk placed behind it... *it's called political correctness.* Control the speech controls the narrative and the people. I remind you again of Nazi Germany!

I have a Chapter regarding what Obama has done and tried to do to limit y[our] 1st and 2nd Amendment rights guaranteed by "our" U.S. Constitution. Also, how the Democrats attempt to force Rush Limbaugh off the airwaves. This is not only *scary*, but also frightening!

Hopefully, I will open the eyes of many: "our" supposed Free Press; Congress; and more important, the citizens of the United States who must raise their voices and demand action and/or do something, to stop Obama before he does further damage to y[our] United States of America!

The detrimental change in U.S. foreign policy started in 2009 with *Obama's apology tour* to the Middle East to the Arab nations. He did not bother to stop in Israel... the United States closest ally. Don't you find that *scary* that Obama ran around the world apologizing for your country?

Obama has not led; has no foreign policy; has placed the United States in a vulnerable position in the world. Our allies realize the United States will not support them. Other countries know we have no backbone. Obama has cut back our military to pre-World War II levels. Won't that make it easier for ISIS/ISSL, Radical Islam and other terrorists to infiltrate the United States and other countries? I find that *scary*.

I recently watched the movie "42," not Clinton President # 42, but the Jackie Robinson movie. In 1946, he broke into the ranks of major league baseball as a talented and determined man who stood up against the racial barriers of that time. Although the movie was made in 2013, it dealt with our country at a time when racial differences prevailed.

I mention the movie because it is apparent when people question decisions made by president Obama, invariably issues of racism become the topic and not the decision. The major reason people question Obama has nothing to do with race, but about his incompetence as a leader of y[our] country. They see racism where there is not racism because it is an easy sell that supports their agenda.

ObamaScare sets forth the facts of how Obama has disgraced and hurt y[our] country. The damage caused by the Obama hoax, fraud and lack of leadership will take a long time to straighten out, *if at all possible.*

Why are people growing more and more concerned? Because, when the facts are analyzed about Obama's life, they realize it has all been one big Lie! *Remember this: the fine print is always more important than the selling price.*

Unfortunately, our so called… *"Free Press"* gave Obama a free pass and free ride without due diligence and investigative journalism. The press accepted and reported Obama *fiction and fantasy as fact.* They report *sound bites as policy* and allow incidents/scandals to blend right into the next scandal without digging below the surface for the facts or truth. The news media has treated Obama with blind trust and rock star status. Don't you find that *scary*!

A Wall Street Journal article *"Wall Street Journal Sizes up Obama"* on July 17, 2014 by Alan Caruba, discussed… "When anyone else would quickly and easily produce a birth certificate, this man [Obama] spent over a million dollars to deny access to his. Most other documents, the paper trail we all leave in our wake, have been sequestered from review. He has lived a make-believe life whose true facts remain hidden.

We laugh at the ventriloquist's dummy, but what do you do **when the dummy is President of the United States.**" [Emphasis added by me] It should be no surprise Obama lied to the American people about

ObamaCare. It is what he does best. His entire life is a lie, from his birth to the present day. It is *scary* that people believe lie after lie.

Question: If Obama has nothing to hide, why then are his records "sealed"? Records are sealed because someone does not want the facts and truth disclosed to the masses... *for obvious reasons!* That reason is not difficult to figure out. And Obama has spent over Three Million [$3] Dollars to keep his records sealed.

Obama's records are "sealed" because he is hiding important facts and details about his life. The *"transparency"* he campaigned on in 2008 needed to begin with "un-sealing" the hidden facts... he does not want you to know. I know the facts, he knows the facts, and his grandmother knew the facts... and you have a right to know the facts. The question is... can you deal with the facts when they are revealed and exposed?

I cannot tell you of one major accomplishment of Obama that has benefitted all of the citizens of the United States.

The release date of **ObamaScare** became later and later because of the constant new facts regarding Obama scandals. Meanwhile Obama golfs and attends expensive fundraiser dinners and events.

The newest **ObamaScare** nightmare... **ISIS**. Islamic terrorist groups are operating in the Mexican border city of Ciudad Juarez while planning to attack the United States with car bombs or other *vehicle borne improvised explosive devices* (VBIED). High-level federal law enforcement, intelligence and other sources confirmed that a warning bulletin for an imminent terrorist attack on the border had been issued. Agents across Homeland Security, Justice and Defense agencies have been placed on alert and instructed to aggressively work all possible leads and sources concerning an imminent terrorist threat. I find that *scary*... I hope you do too and do something about it.

Specifically, the government sources reveal that the militant group Islamic State of Iraq and Greater Syria [ISIS] is confirmed to now be operating in Juarez, a famously crime-infested narcotics hotbed situated across from El Paso, Texas. Violent crimes are so rampant in Juarez that the U.S. State Department issued a number of travel warnings for anyone planning to go there.

Intelligence officials have picked up radio talk and chatter indicating that the terrorist groups are going to "carry out an attack on the border," according to one Judicial Watch source. "It's coming very soon," according to another high-level source, who clearly identified the groups planning the plots as "ISIS and Al Qaeda." An attack is so imminent that the commanding general at Ft. Bliss, the U.S. Army post in El Paso, is being briefed.

This isn't a Halloween spook story... this is real and should scare the hell of out of you to do something about it. There are numerous low profile stories that get lost in the free press. Here are a few.

DOJ gives Leftist Obama supporters' cash.

The Department of Justice (DOJ) keeps giving radical leftist groups that support president Obama huge amounts of cash collected from big banks to settle discrimination and mortgage abuse lawsuits filed by the government. Judicial Watch first reported the scheme two years ago when Countrywide Financial Corporation doled out $335 million...

Muslim activists demand overhaul of all U.S. Law enforcement training.

Islamic activists that strong-armed the FBI to purge anti-terrorism training material considered "offensive" to Muslims have made their next wave of demands, which include an overhaul in the way all law enforcement officers are trained in the United States. The coalition of influential and politically-connected Muslim rights groups is demanding that the Obama administration implement a mandatory retraining program for all federal, state and local law enforcement officials who may have been subjected to materials they deem "biased and discriminatory" against Muslims. There must also be an audit of all federal law enforcement and intelligence gathering training.

Furthermore... Council on American-Islamic Relations (CAIR) got several police departments in president Obama's home state of Illinois to cancel essential counterterrorism courses over accusations that the instructor was anti-Muslim. The course was called "Islamic Awareness as a Counter-Terrorist Strategy" and departments in Lombard, Elmhurst, and Highland Park caved into CAIR's demands. The group responded with a statement commending officials for their "swift action in addressing the Muslim community's concerns." CAIR has wielded its power in a number of other cases during the Obama presidency, including blocking an FBI probe involving the radicalization of young Somali men in the U.S. and pressuring the government to file discrimination lawsuits against employers who do not accommodate Muslims in the workplace. America is one-step closer to implementation of Sharia Law. *Can you say... good-bye Constitution it was nice knowing you.*

Kids and adults sent to cross the U.S. borders

The illegal... yes illegal immigration of tens of thousands of children rushing our border. Some use the sound bite... 'humanitarian crisis at the border', from South America, many of whom are bringing diseases with them. And what is Obama's response? Obama is claiming the Republicans in Congress have not done anything regarding Immigration, so he plans to act alone and in the summer of 2014 he asked Congress for Three Hundred Seventy-Five [$375] Billion Dollars to set up procedures to care for the illegal immigrants and very little for our border protection. Congress did not authorize that amount.

Most of us realize that the mainstream media is no longer a true and viable news source... so where do we get the news and facts? *Scary* thought isn't it! Here is a novel idea... since they are so supportive of the illegal invasion, let them offer to take several home and care for them, school them, see to their medical needs. Let's see how many of them take any of them home.

Of course, that's not their job. Their job is to *report* the news in the manner that Obama wants. They no longer care for the truth nor do they report it.

Side bar note: See if they mention how many of these men, women, and children are over 18. The *scary* part is... we have no way of knowing how old they are. They arrive with only a piece of paper with detailed instructions about what to do once they cross the U.S. border.

HOWEVER, Obama failed to tell the American people that he let it be known in South America that if... children illegally entered the United States they could stay. That is what is called buying "future" party line votes.

In a later chapter, I set forth what Congress must do along with our "so-called" Free Press.

Obama has lost the support of "our" citizens and his polls have plummeted. Obama has lead "our" nation down a path of Big Brother and Big Government and if we don't take action at the ballot box, it will continue to destroy y[our] country. Obama is a lame duck president; Obama's presidency is over. We must concentrate on... what is next?

ObamaScare exposes Obama's background from birth to presidency... and his lies, *yes, lies*. Don't act shocked. The questions were raised and the facts ignored. But proper evidence, truth, scrutiny, due diligence and logic was never applied. Feel-good sound bites and lies are continually presented by Obama as truth. America bought it. America bought "used oats" while believing they were buying fresh oats. You know - the slightly used oat variety from the backside of the horse and not the fresh oats in the bucket.

My book, **_ObamaScare_**, exposes Obama's birth in Africa; his lies about birth in Hawaii; his adoption in Indonesia, attendance in Jakarta at Besuki Public School and Fransiskus Assisi School and more. I have his school records secured by TV show *Inside Edition* indicating Obama's name is "Barry Soetoro," his nationality "Indonesia" and his religion "Islam." He was raised Muslim. Indonesia is very significant because the adoption controls Obama's life; there is no documentation to support his legal change of name or his applying to be a "naturalized" citizen; therefore, his legal name still is "Barry Soetoro" and his nationality is "Indonesia."

Obama/Barry Soetoro returned to Hawaii at the age of ten [10] without his mother and he used his Indonesian Passport; at the age of twenty [20], in 1981, Soetoro/Obama went to visit Pakistan with two [2] of his friends; prior thereto, he stopped in Indonesia to renew his Indonesian passport.

When Soetoro/Obama went to Occidental College in California people called Obama, "Barry" and the reason they called him "Barry" was that his legal name at that time and still is "Barry Soetoro." Soetoro then illegally changed his name back to Obama. Yes, one can use an alias, but "not" for fraudulent purposes.

Side bar note: Before Soetoro/Obama sealed all of his records; a FOIA [Freedom of Information Act] inquiry was made requesting a copy of Obama's passport. It was returned, indicating there is no such passport on record. This reinforces the position that Obama used his Indonesian passport until he became a United States Senator from Illinois; at that time he used a government or diplomatic passport; and as president he used a government or diplomatic passport.

Obama/Soetoro's lack luster term as a State Senator in Illinois, where he voted "present" many times, thus "not" taking positions on major issues; being an "illegal" U.S. Senator from Illinois, as one must be a U.S. citizen and Obama is a citizen of Indonesia; to not being vetted by the United States "Free Press" and media regarding his not being a U.S. citizen and "not" being "natural born" and therefore, "not" permitted to be a President of the United States.

Remember... Presidential candidate Obama did "not" salute the American flag, while the other candidates paid respect to our country and American flag during the singing of the National Anthem at a Tom Harkin fundraiser in Iowa in 2008.

Jonchristianryter.com/2008/080621

That was another clue something was wrong with the whole Obama story. He choose "not" to wear an American flag pin on his lapel for years:

Scaredmonkeys.com/2007/10/05

And Obama's campaign issues including cleaning-up the VA so that "our" military personnel received timely medical treatment and then not following through.

Obama "not" being "Constitutionally Eligible" to be president; to his two [2] terms as the worst president in the history of the United States; worst because of his determination to change the United States from a Super Power to a country that has lost respect around the world; a president who has scandal, after scandal, after scandal, including but not limited to IRS, AP, border security, VA and Bergdahl prisoner exchange; and now the deteriorating situation in Iraq and throughout the Middle East with Radical Islam, that Obama will not confirm; with Benghazi, IRS and ObamaCare [Affordable Health Care] that will probably be his downfall.

Question: With the allegations regarding the VA of mismanagement, lack of prompt and necessary treatment for those who have served "our" nation, by the established and long standing VA, how can we expect ObamaCare to work? It cannot work!

Then, I discuss what we, as American citizens must do to prevent Obama from continuing to undermine "our" country.

Donald Trump: When Obama released his so called "long form birth certificate" on April 27, 2011 in the White House Press Room from pressure from Donald Trump, I, and many others, knew that this "long form birth certificate" was another phony from just looking at the document. [I discuss later in **Chapter VII** but most glaring is Obama's father's race – "African" – in 1961 no one was African; you were either "Negro" or "Black"]. What member of the White House Press Contingent or their respective affiliates questioned/examined it – unfortunately, none of them. Again, "our" so called "Free Press" covered for Obama."

I credit Donald Trump for bringing Obama's Birth Certificate issue to the national attention it deserved; too bad he did not continue his efforts after Obama produced his latest fraudulent birth certificate.

Oprah Winfrey: Read the two [2] letters that I, as author Philip J.

Berg, wrote to Oprah in 2008 and 2009 as I believed Oprah was the only person that could convince Obama to be truthful and withdraw from his campaign for and being president. Read the letters and outcome in Chapter XIII.

And the truth prevails, year after year, at Freedompalooza, an annual festival on July 4th committed to the fight for freedom by exposing the truth by means of music, speakers, and vendors. I proudly say that I have been a regular featured speaker with my last appearance this past July 4, 2014. Read further in Chapter XIX.

Glenn Beck: And why did Glenn Beck place my picture on his "Black Board" several times and call me a "provocateur" – Beck was questioning why I was pursuing Obama. Whose side is Glenn Beck really on, other than just wanting to make controversy, to make money? Read Chapter XIV.

Obama supposedly wrote two [2] books, *Dreams from My Father*: a Story of Race and Inheritance (1995) and *The Audacity of Hope* (2006). These books boxed Obama in on several issues, most important, his adoption in Indonesia.

In 2013, PolitiFacts "Biggest lie of the year" belonged to Obama for his lie, "If you like your health plan, you can keep it" – about the Affordable Care Act [ObamaCare].

BENGHAZI - I was right and confirmed on 01/14/2014 that Obama knew about Benghazi and therefore, there was and is a massive "COVER-UP." It was disclosed that Obama was made aware of a "terrorist attack" on Benghazi on 09/11/2012 within one & one-half [1 ½] hours after the attack began. Further, Obama spoke with then Secretary of State Hillary Rodham Clinton around 10:00 p.m. on 09/11/2012; yet he allowed his National Security Advisor Susan Rice to go on five [5] Sunday morning TV shows five [5] days later on 09/16/2012 claiming it was from a spontaneous event, arising from a little-known anti-Muslim video on the internet.

More significant, Obama lied about it when he appeared on The

David Letterman Show and for at least fourteen [14] days as specifically, on the fourteenth [14th] day, 09/25/2012, Obama addressed the United Nations and five [5] times in his speech, yes, five [5] times, Obama said that the attack at Benghazi was caused by the internet movie [what a lie and an ongoing cover-up]! **For additional details, read Chapter XI.**

I set forth chapters on Treason [Chapter XVII] and Impeachment [Chapter XVIII] and lists of those events that Obama has done that can be used if Congress has the guts to proceed to save "our" country. Time will tell, but I doubt it. Also, a poll in July 2014 stated that the majority of people in the United States do not want Impeachment.

ObamaScare ends with a call to understand what is really happening in y[our] country with the lack of leadership and Obama's determination to *change* our country to the detriment of "our" citizens that is frightening and *scary*. Remember... he promised to... change America, but he didn't tell us what he was going to change it into. He kept his promise, to y[our] detriment!

Can our country and Constitution survive?

It is time for our citizens to wake-up and do our part to stop Obama from destroying our country as he has about two [2] more years, as he says, "to use my pen."

Chapter XII lists just a few of Soetoro/Obama's Lies, a must read.

Judge Jeanine Pirro – She Tells It Like It Is:

I have to compliment Judge Jeanine Pirro as she says it like it is. I look forward to her weekly show, *"JUSTICE with Judge Jeanine"* on Fox News Network, especially her "Opening Statement" as she speaks the truth about issues of the day, especially about president Obama with his ongoing disregard for "our" U.S. Constitution. A must watch on her

Saturday night show at 9:00 p.m. ET.

We need more people like Judge Jeanine Pirro to speak out regarding the misgivings of government and to rally the rest of us.

And, the best way I can describe Obama's present actions as president, is to quote Eric Bradway, a good friend and political advisor of mine for years, saying, "... the Middle East is Melting Down and Obama is Voting 'Present' and doing nothing else to Lead."

CHAPTER I

Philip J. Berg - a Life Long Democrat

I was a candidate for Governor and United States Senate. In Pennsylvania I served as a Deputy Attorney General of Pennsylvania for eight [8] years. I have fought for the rights of others all my life. As a life-long Democrat, I was the Pro-Choice candidate in the 1990 Democratic Primary for Governor. I lost to incumbent Robert Casey.

During the 1990 campaign, one of my ideas changed politics forever. I traveled the Commonwealth of Pennsylvania with my political advisor and friend, Eric Bradway, in a motor home called the "**BERGMOBILE**." Casey's Campaign Manager was James Carville. They were concerned about the widespread TV and Newspaper coverage I was receiving, with the very visible "BERGMOBILE" as it traveled thousands of miles throughout Pennsylvania. With a budget of $120,000, I received twenty-three [23%] percent of the vote against the most popular Governor in Pennsylvania's history. I attributed it to the issues and the "BERGMOBILE."

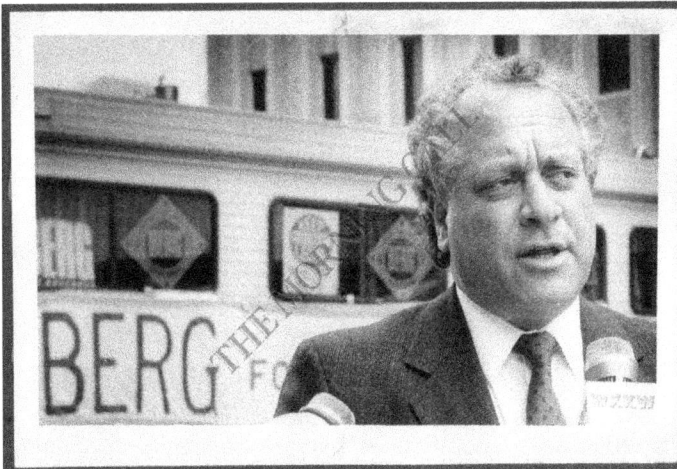

Philip J. Berg in 1990 campaigning for Governor of Pennsylvania in front of his BERGMOBILE

1990

**14th WARD
DEMOCRATIC CLUB**
OFFICIAL VOTERS GUIDE

GOVERNOR
PHILIP J. BERG   1A

U.S. HOUSE of REPRESENTATIVES
WILLIAM COYNE   5A

STATE REPRESENTATIVE 23rd DISTRICT
IVAN ITKIN   9A

STATE REPRESENTATIVE 34th DISTRICT
RON COWELL   9A

STATE DEMOCRATIC COMMITTEE
Joyce Lee ITKIN   13A
Beatrice Bicky GOLDSZER 14A
Avery ABRAMS   15A
Michael F. COYNE   21A
William A. SEIFERT   22A

Don't neglect the vital
importance of *Real*
neighborhood representation -
be sure to vote for your
COUNTY DEMOCRATIC COMMITTEE

ERIC MARCHBEIN
CLAIRE STAPLES

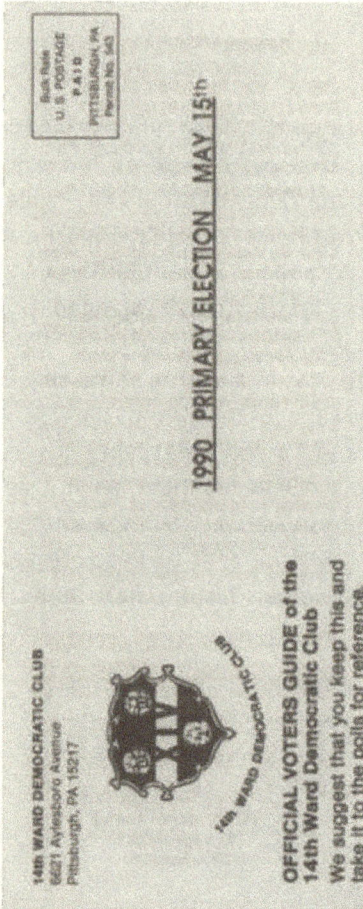

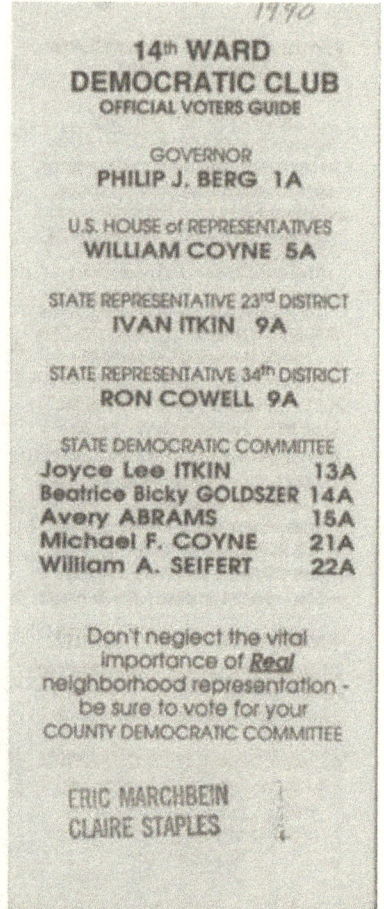

Philip J. Berg endorsed for Governor of Pennsylvania in 1990 by 14th Ward Democratic Club in Pittsburgh, PA, one of the most liberal organizations in Pennsylvania.

Two [2] years later, in 1992, James Carville was Campaign Manager for Bill Clinton. After the Democratic National Convention in New York City, Carville put Clinton in a fancy Campaign Bus and traveled through several states. I changed politics and campaigning forever. I smile every time I see a campaign bus.

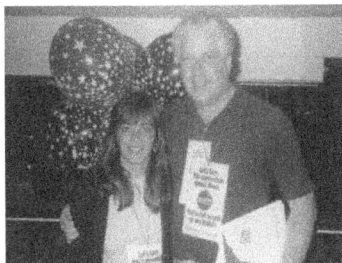

Philip J. Berg at 1992 Democratic National Convention in New York with Carol Miller.

Philip J. Berg at 1992 Democratic National Convention in New York being interviewed by Philadelphia TV Channel 6 regarding his Demand that Governor Robert Casey be allowed to speak at the convention

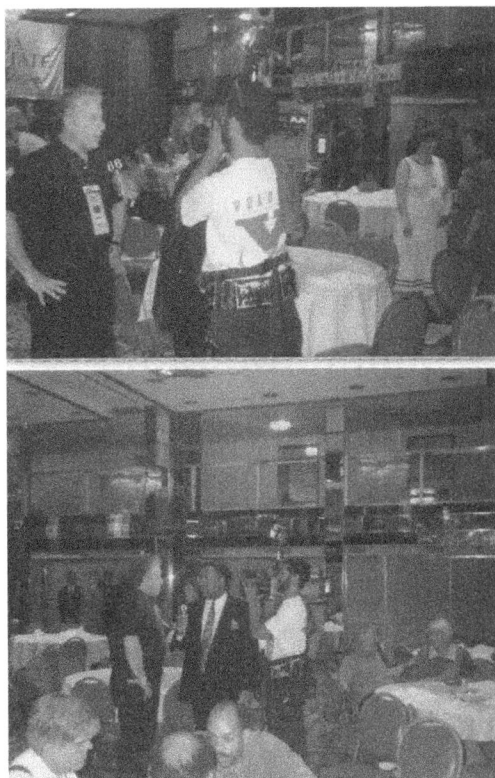

In 1992, I was a Delegate from Pennsylvania to the Democratic National Convention. I am proud to say that I was the only Democrat in the Pennsylvania delegation to stand up to the DNC and I issued a Press Release and held a Press Conference and called for the Convention to permit Governor Robert Casey to address the Convention. Remember, I was the Pro-Choice candidate against Governor Casey in the 1990 Democratic Primary; and Casey was a strong Pro-Life individual. The Convention would not allow Casey to speak.

My pressure and effort was successful. Governor Casey was *finally*

going to be allowed to address the Convention although not at prime-time TV. There was no internet.

Philip J. Berg with Senator Joe Biden [D-Delaware]

Philip J. Berg with Governor Jerry Brown [D-California]

Philip J. Berg with Senator Ted Kennedy [D-Massachusetts] (below) - I attended the Inauguration of President Clinton.

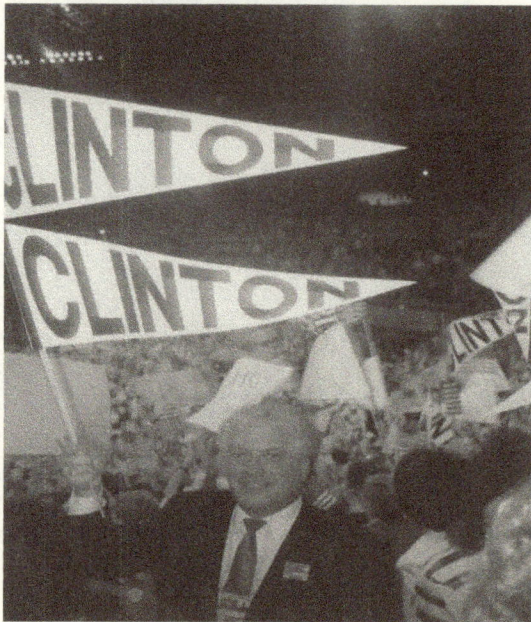

I include My Democratic political background as I am accused of being part of a *"Right Wing Conspiracy against Obama."* That theory is ridiculous because I was... and am a life-long Democrat in Pennsylvania:

Chair, Montgomery County Democratic Committee 1986 - 1988
Member, PA Democratic State Committee - 8 yrs. 1978 - 1990
Advance Staff, Vice Pres. Hubert H. Humphrey 1968
Campaign Manager – Congressman Thomas Ludlow Ashley - 1970
Committeeperson, Philadelphia County 1971 - 1977
Committeeperson, Montgomery County 1977 - 2002
Delegate - Democratic National Mini-Convention
   Memphis, Tennessee /13th PA Congressional District 1978
Secretary - Pennsylvania Delegation to the
   Democratic National Mini-Convention/Memphis, Tennessee 1978
Democratic National Convention Platform
   Advisory Committee on Government Reform 1980
   [One of only (2) Pennsylvanians elected]
Democratic Candidate for Governor – Primary 1990
Delegate - Democratic National Convention
   New York, New York, 13th PA Congressional District 1992
Democratic Candidate for United States Senate – Primary 2000

In addition, I have held many campaign positions for candidates in the Democratic Party.

Side bar note: I was born April 13th, the same day as President Thomas Jefferson who said: "For here we are not afraid to follow truth wherever it may lead." That statement has inspired me over the years and especially when Obama came on the scene.

My general law practice of thirty-three [33] years was in Lafayette Hill, Montgomery County, Pennsylvania before retiring in July 2013. I remain a Volunteer, as I have for the past 34 years, with the Barren

Hill Volunteer Fire Department in Whitemarsh Township, as a Fire Police Officer, having served as a Sergeant and Lieutenant. In 2014, I was honored by being Fire Police Officer for the year and promoted again to Sergeant.

I am the only Attorney to ever file lawsuits against two [2] standing Presidents of the United States. I am a true American patriot. I have never been afraid to ask hard questions or address unpopular issues, others fear to raise.

On behalf of William Rodriquez, a janitor working in the World Trade Center during 911, I filed a law suit under the Racketeering Influenced by Corrupt Organizations [RICO] Act against President Bush.

Rodriquez testified before the 911 Commission that: he was in the basement of the WTC and witnessed a bomb going off before a plane hit the building and witnessed a man coming from the area of the explosion with burns on his body and skin coming off his body; it must be noted that the 911 Commission Report made no mention of Rodriquez's testimony. Still to this day, I believe the 911 attack could have been prevented and President Bush just ignored the supporting statements, documentation and facts.

My ongoing statement regarding 911 since 2001:

"Bush and his cronies either made 911 happen or let it happen. If they let it happen, then they made it happen; and they must be held accountable."

I was invited and joined multi-millionaire Jimmy Walter in 2005 on a month long, seven [7] country, eight [8] city European Tour to spread the word of an effort to Re-Open the 911 Investigations. To this day, there are Architects & Engineers working diligently on the facts and evidence to prove that 911 could not have occurred the way the stated findings of the 911 Commission Report.

I supported all United States Veterans in 2013 when I started the web site: *fondaisatraitor.com*, to protest Jane Fonda [a/k/a "Hanoi

Jane"] sitting on a tank facing our U.S. military while smiling as she was surrounded by Communist North Viet Cong. More in Chapter XX "Berg Helps Veterans Protesting Jane Fonda."

In or about the end of 2006, early 2007, an assistant [hereinafter at times "Ms. X"] began donating her time and working with me. The two [2] of us worked well together. We understood each other's thoughts in terms of the law and the different cases we worked on together.

My assistant and I never discussed politics. In fact, she was never political; but always was very supportive of me and my choices in the political arena.

During the 2008 Presidential campaign, Ms. X sent jokes she received via Email regarding Hillary Clinton. Although Ms. X and I had worked together for some time, she was unaware that I was voting for Hillary Clinton. Again, we did not discuss our political views. I never took offense, instead, after a while, I stated, "you know I'm voting for Hillary, don't you." Ms. X said, "Phil, I had no idea but you have to admit, the jokes are funny. I agreed and we both chuckled.

My office work was very sporadic. One minute it was quiet, but the next, look out, the phones were ringing off the hook; clients appearing; all in all, it was a fast paced busy law firm. Rest assured, there was never a dull moment.

I handled a lot of pro bono legal work. I had returning clients that I represented for years. I also fought issues and filed cases that I strongly believed in. When it comes to the United States Constitution, I will never back down.

I have very strong ties with my family. Unfortunately, my father, Sidney Bernard Berg, Esquire, passed away in 1960 when I was fifteen [15]; however I assisted him before his death when he was a candidate for Judge for the Court of Common Pleas of Philadelphia; this early political involvement was the beginning of my political career.

My Mom, Rebecca, and my brother, Norman, worked with my at my law firm. My Mom was my office manager/bookkeeper for years, greatly assisting me and also a huge supporter of whatever I was involved with, that being my political candidacies, my volunteer endeavors and the groups/issues I supported. These included: The Wellness Community of Philadelphia, now Cancer Support Community Greater Philadelphia [CSCGP], where I was a Founding Member in 1991 and I served as President in 1992 with the purpose "Cancer Support for Life" and The Terri Lynne Lokoff Child Care Foundation,

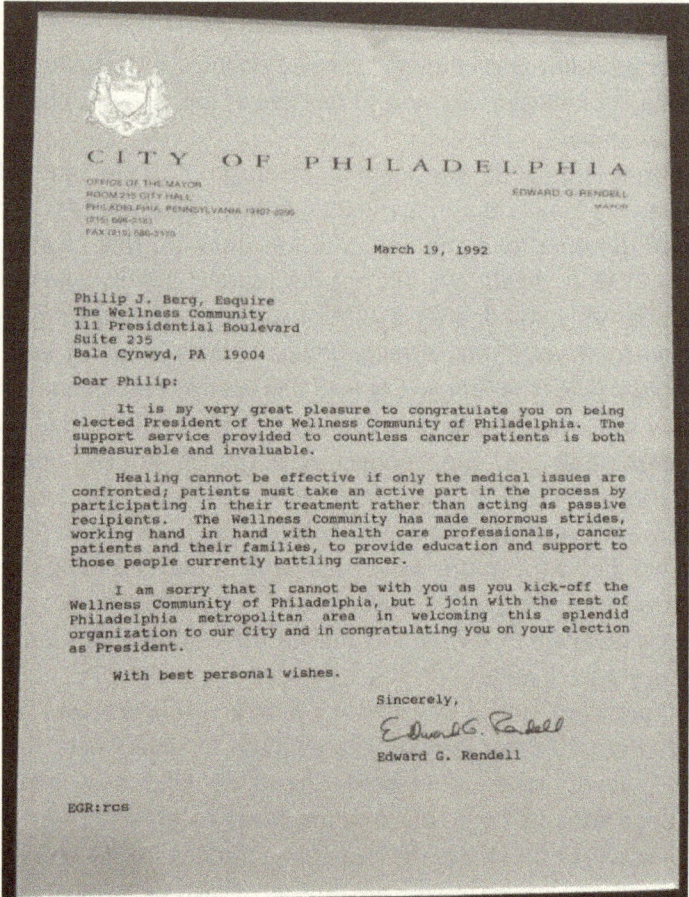

CITY OF PHILADELPHIA

OFFICE OF THE MAYOR
ROOM 215 CITY HALL
PHILADELPHIA, PENNSYLVANIA 19107-3295
(215) 686-2181
FAX (215) 580-2333

EDWARD G. RENDELL
MAYOR

March 19, 1992

Philip J. Berg, Esquire
The Wellness Community
111 Presidential Boulevard
Suite 235
Bala Cynwyd, PA 19004

Dear Philip:

It is my very great pleasure to congratulate you on being elected President of the Wellness Community of Philadelphia. The support service provided to countless cancer patients is both immeasurable and invaluable.

Healing cannot be effective if only the medical issues are confronted; patients must take an active part in the process by participating in their treatment rather than acting as passive recipients. The Wellness Community has made enormous strides, working hand in hand with health care professionals, cancer patients and their families, to provide education and support to those people currently battling cancer.

I am sorry that I cannot be with you as you kick-off the Wellness Community of Philadelphia, but I join with the rest of Philadelphia metropolitan area in welcoming this splendid organization to our City and in congratulating you on your election as President.

With best personal wishes.

Sincerely,

Edward G. Rendell

EGR:rcs

where I was a Board Member.

My brother, Norman, was a para-legal in my office and I always admired his intellectual abilities. He knew and spoke seven [7] languages; had graduated from Central High School in Philadelphia and received a Mayor's Scholarship to the University of Pennsylvania for full tuition, room, board and books; he was a teacher and an employee of the United States. Norman passed away in December 2008 from Cancer. Prior to Norman's death, I always made it a point to take him to his doctor appointments; chemotherapy and radiation at The Hospital of the University of Pennsylvania where he received excellent care. After surgery, Norman was given four [4] months to live, but lived for seven [7] years. On a specific medication, he was the longest person in the world on it, for three and one-half [3 ½] years. And we ate dinner at Norman's favorite Chinese restaurant, King Buffet in Plymouth Meeting, PA, frequently.

I assisted my wonderful loving mother, Rebecca, until she passed in July 2013, at the age of 96.

My long time fiancée, Carol, teaches at a local school. We were engaged on the TV show _American Journal_ with Nancy Glass on Valentine's Day years ago when twenty [20] of her five [5] year old students surprised her by saying, "Phil wants to marry you" and as her mouth dropped, I came into the room with two [2] dozen roses and kneeled, proposed and gave her a diamond engagement ring; Carol said, "yes."

I have three [3] children and four [4] grandchildren.

Above I am closing the road in 2014 for a motorcycle accident while being a member of the Fire Police of Barren Hill Volunteer Fire Company [whose 100 year anniversary is in 2015], in Whitemarsh Township, Montgomery County, Pennsylvania, where I am serving in my 34th year, having served as a Lieutenant and Sergeant. I was very honored to be recognized with the Fire Police Award in 2014 and promoted to Sergeant.

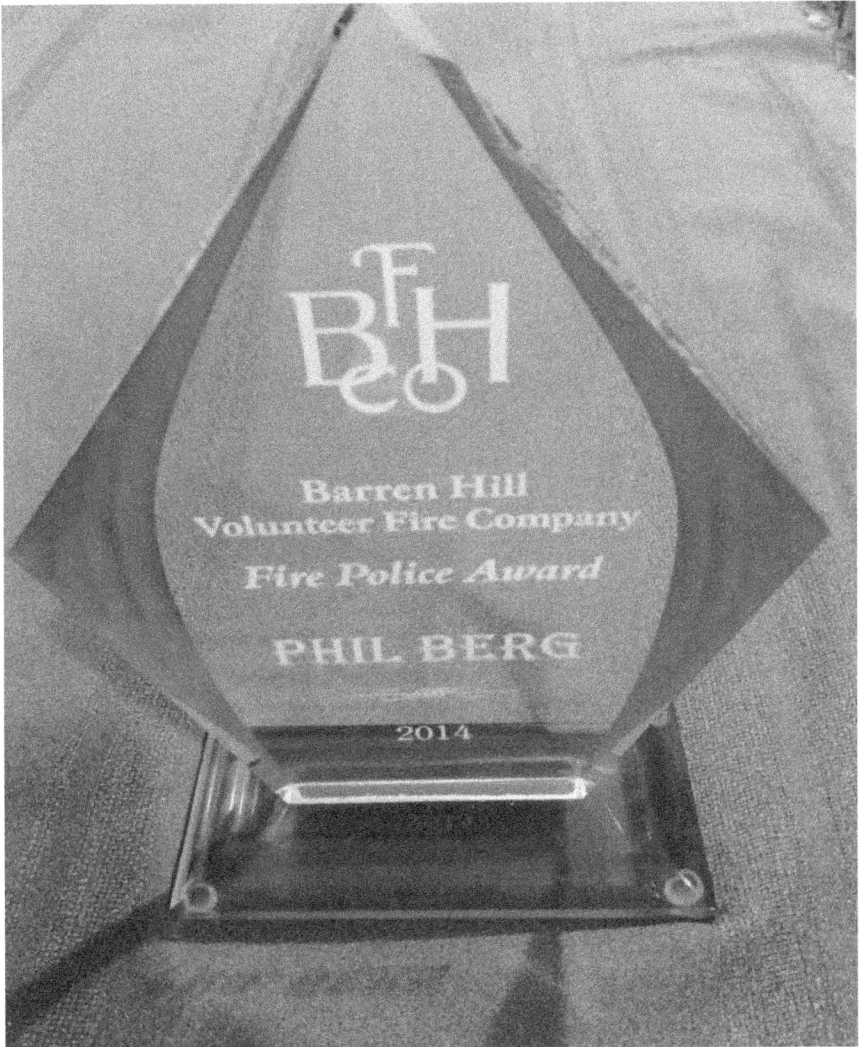

CHAPTER II

Barack H. Obama's DoubleSpeak

Obama's Citizenship Status came to my Law Firm

The following dialogue reveals my efforts to expose Obama for the fraud he is. I believed it then... and even more so now. I refer to "Obama DoubleSpeak" because with "all" of his records "sealed," he said he is natural born citizen and therefore, eligible to be President of the United States. Obama, if you have nothing to hide, release "all of your records." Why in God's name would he not open them to public scrutiny? *Oh... wait...* he doesn't want you to see the truth.

This is how it all began. On a busy afternoon, the first week of August 2008 I received a phone call.

Berg: Hello, this is Phil Berg.

Caller: Hi Phil, Have you heard about the issues involving Barack Obama?

Berg: What issues?

Caller: Surrounding his birth... Obama is not a "natural born" citizen as defined by the U.S. Constitution. You are the only attorney that I know that is not afraid to go up against the political status quo and has "brass balls and brave enough" to challenge Obama's citizenship status.

Berg: What evidence do you have?

Caller: I don't have anything. Well, Phil, do what you do and call me back.

I hang up and start thinking what to do, how to research the issue, as these are serious Constitutional issues. I immediately said to Ms. X, "I just received a call telling me that Barack Obama is not a "natural born" citizen. You know if he is not a "natural born" American citizen, he cannot hold the Office of President."

Ms. X: "That's correct Phil, but do we have anything substantiating it?"

Berg: No, but we are supposed to receive a phone call with information."

Ms. X's phone rings at her home.

Caller: Hi, I am a friend of Phil's. Phil stated he discussed with you the birth issues regarding Barack Obama.

Ms. X: Yes, he did. However, what is there that proves this allegation?

Caller: We don't have anything; can't you just file a lawsuit?

Ms. X: No, it does not work like that. If you have something that questions or substantiates the position that Barack Obama was not born in the United States and is not a United States "natural born" citizen, then you can file a lawsuit. See what you can find and I will do the same.

Ms. X to Berg: I found this Indonesian School Record where Barack Obama went to school. The School Record was obtained from Jack Robinson, a Reporter for a television show, *Inside Edition*. But, Barack Obama went to school under the name of Barry Soetoro and his father is listed as Lolo Soetoro. What bothers me more Phil is the fact, his citizenship status is listed as "Indonesian." What is your take on this?

Berg: I can't answer that right now.

Ms. X: If you would call *Inside Edition* and verify the document, ask permission for us to use it and find out if the reporter who filmed the document is still around. I will go to the law library and research the laws on the citizenship status.

While Ms. X leaves for the law library, I called *Inside Edition*. The research took a few days into the laws that pertain to the citizenship status of a person born abroad and of a person either legally adopted or legally acknowledged by a foreign national and residing in the foreign national's country.

Ms. X makes a phone call to the person who originally called my Office.

Ms. X: Where did you say Barack Obama was born?

Caller: He was born in Kenya.

Ms. X: Do we know where in Kenya?

Caller: No, I haven't found that information yet. Supposedly, it was Mombasa, but I do not have any confirmation. What did you find?

Ms. X: Well, it may be nothing, but I found an Indonesian School Record from Jakarta and apparently, Barack Obama went to grade school in Jakarta, Indonesia under the name of Barry Soetoro, an Indonesian citizen. I have to go to the law library and research the immigration laws. I will let you know what I find.

Caller: Please call me as soon as you know something.

Ms. X: I sure will.

Ms. X to Phil: I'm still researching the laws pertaining to this particular issue. As we discussed, first we must have evidence substantiating our arguments raised. I also have to ensure I have properly researched the laws.

Phil to Ms. X: Have you researched any of these blogs?, It is all over the internet about Barack H. Obama not being a United States "natural born" citizen.

Ms. X to Phil: No, I haven't, but I will. I also want to read Obama's book, *"Dreams from My Father"*, so I will check the book out at the library.

Phil, are you aware Obama traveled to Indonesia and on to Pakistan and then to Kenya when he was twenty?

Phil to Ms. X: No, I wasn't aware of that.

Ms. X to Phil: Where in the world does a college student obtain the money to make those types of trips?

Phil: I don't know.

Ms. X: I did speak to the Director of *Inside Edition* and was given permission to use the Indonesian School Record. I was told the reporter also took live footage of the birth record located in the Registrar's Office of the Fransiskus Assisi School. Phil, can we call the reporter as a witness to testify to the accuracy and how he obtained the school record?

Phil: Yes, we can.

Ms. X: Phil, what I am finding is Obama was in fact born in Mombasa, Kenya, at a hospital named Coast General. Obama's mother was only eighteen [18] when she had Obama. Stanley Ann Dunham, Barack H. Obama's mother, met Barack H. Obama, Sr. at college in Hawaii. The two began dating and Stanley Ann Dunham became pregnant. Stanley Ann Dunham was seventeen [17] when she became pregnant and delivered Barack H. Obama, II on August 4, 1961, when she was eighteen [18]. This makes a huge difference with the immigration laws.

Apparently, Stanley Ann Dunham and Barack H. Obama, Sr. were married in Hawaii and then traveled to Kenya. Stanley Ann Dunham Obama was introduced to Barack senior's parents and family. Barack's family was from a tribe called the Luo Tribe, located in Kenya, said tribe that was the third largest community in Kenya. Stanley Ann did not care for the way Barack's family treated women and wanted to leave Kenya; however, she was too far into her pregnancy and was not allowed to board an aircraft. Stanley Ann delivered Barack, II at the Coast General Hospital. During the birth, Barack, Jr.'s grandmother, Sara Obama, was present.

Ms. X: Stanley Ann left Kenya shortly after Barack Jr's. birth and stopped at Mercer Island to see her friend from school on her way home to Hawaii.

Phil: What did you discover pertaining to the Indonesian School Record?

Ms. X: Phil, I'm just getting ready to tell you. A few years after returning to Hawaii with Barack H. Obama, Jr., Stanley Ann divorced Barack senior. Stanley Ann then met another man by the name of Lolo Soetoro at the University of Hawaii. They fell in love and eventually married. According to Obama's book, *"Dreams from My Father,"* Lolo Soetoro left Hawaii rather suddenly, from what I now have discovered was because his passport was expiring, he returned to Indonesia. Obama and his mother followed a couple of months later. Obama in his book states that upon arrival in Indonesia, his father, Lolo Soetoro introduced Stanley Ann to all of his family and introduced Obama as his son. Pursuant to our Citizenship and Immigration laws and The Hague Convention of 1930, both Obama's foreign birth and his citizenship status in Indonesia creates problems for Barack H. Obama.

I have a tape in Swahili of Sara Obama and two [2] ministers, one next to her in her home in Kenya and the other minister on the phone in Harrisburg, Pennsylvania with two [2] affidavits, one from each minister regarding the conversation whereby Sara Obama stated she was in the hospital in Kenya when Obama was born!

Obama is not "Constitutionally Eligible" to be President of the United States and the following were one hundred [100 %] percent aware of the fraud and "HOAX" that Obama was and did put forth and therefore, these individuals must be brought forth into the Criminal Justice System and be tried and when found guilty, go to prison:

Howard Dean, head of the DNC [Democratic National Committee] at the time Obama was nominated for President; top officials of the DNC; Obama's senior campaign staff and Obama's senior White House staff at the time Obama was sworn in as President; Michelle Obama; and certainly Barack Hussein Obama.

CHAPTER III
Obama's Kenyan Birth / Immigration & Citizenship Law

After Ms. X's research at the law library, she immediately contacted me at my law office.

Ms. X: Phil, I'm doing the dance.

Phil: What do you mean, what does "doing the dance" mean?

Ms. X: It's my happy dance.

Phil: Oh, okay, why, what did you find?

Ms. X: Well, with Obama being born in Kenya to only one United States citizen parent, his mother, he is not a "natural born" citizen.

Phil: What does this mean? Please explain it.

Ms. X: There appears to be no question that Obama's mother, Stanley Ann Dunham, was a U.S. citizen. It is also undisputed, however, that his father, Barack Obama, Sr., was a citizen of Kenya. Obama's parents, according to divorce records, were married on or about February 2, 1961.

The Federal Bureau of Investigation [FBI] does not perform background checks and/or verify the eligibility on our candidates to hold Office. According to the FBI, once a candidate is voted into Office of Congress, they are members of Congress and therefore, they are given a Secret Service Clearance; again, without any type of background check and/or verification processes performed.

Obama claims he was born in Honolulu, Hawaii on August 4, 1961. It is uncertain which hospital he claims to have been born. Obama's grandmother [on his father's side], his half-brother and half-sister, Maya, all claim Obama was born in Kenya... not in Hawaii. Reports reflect that Obama's mother traveled to Kenya during her pregnancy. However, she was prevented from boarding a flight from Kenya to Hawaii because of her late stage of pregnancy. This was/is a normal restriction, to avoid births during flight. By these reports, Stanley Ann

Dunham Obama gave birth to Obama in Kenya, after the birth Obama's mother returned to Hawaii by air and registered Obama's birth. There are records of a "registry of birth" for Obama, on or about August 8, 1961 in the public records office in Hawaii.

Upon further investigation into the alleged birth of Obama in Honolulu, Hawaii, Obama's birth is reported as occurring at two [2] separate hospitals, Kapiolani Hospital and Queens Hospital. Do you know anyone that was born at two [2] different hospitals?

The Rainbow Edition News Letter, November 2004 Edition, published by the Education Laboratory School did a several page article of an interview with Obama and his half-sister, Maya. The Rainbow Edition News Letter reports Obama was born August 4, 1961 at Queens Medical Center in Honolulu, Hawaii.

More interesting in February 2008, Obama's half-sister, Maya, was again interviewed in the Star Bulletin, and this time, Maya states Obama was born August 4, 1961 in Kapiolani Medical Center for Women & Children.

Obama was born in Mombasa, Kenya. His mother was not old enough and did not meet the residency requirements pursuant to The Nationality Act [INA} of 1940, (revised June 1952). Section §301(a)(7) of the INA clearly states the U.S. citizen parent, Obama's mother in this case, must have resided in the United States for ten [10] years, five [5] of which were after the age of fourteen [14] in order to give Obama "natural born" citizenship status in the United States. *See United States of America v. Cervantes-Nava*, 281 F.3d 501 (2002), *Drozd v. I.N.S.*, 155 F.3d 81, 85-88 (2d Cir.1998); *United States v. Gomez-Orozco*, 188 F.3d 422, 426-27 (7th Cir. 1999), *Scales v. Immigration and Naturalization Service*, 232 F.3d 1159 (9th Cir. 2000), *Solis-Espinoza v. Gonzales*, 401 F.3d 1090 (9th Cir. 2005).

Side bar note: *Obama's mother was only eighteen (18) in Kenya when Obama was born. Therefore, she did not meet the age or residency requirements for her child to have acquired "natural born" U.S. citizenship under the statute. Therefore, Obama could not be a "natural born" United States citizen in any event under these facts.*

The law that applies to a birth abroad is the law in effect at the time of birth, _Marquez-Marquez v. R Gonzales_, 455 F. 3d 548 (5th Cir. 2006), _Runnett v. Shultz_, 901 F.2d 782, 783 (9th Cir.1990) (holding that "the applicable law for transmitting citizenship to a child born abroad when one parent is a U.S. citizen is the statute that was in effect at the time of the child's birth"). This is law passed by the Congress of the United States.

It must be noted that if both parents, husband & wife, boyfriend & girlfriend are "both" U.S. citizens, wherever a child is born anywhere in the world, upon the child's return to the United States and going through immigration/customs, upon filing the proper paperwork, that child is considered "natural born."

Obama's Kenyan grandmother, Sara Obama, repeatedly stated that Obama was born in Kenya and she was present in the hospital during his birth. Why would granny lie? We contacted Bishop Ron McRae, who oversees the Anabaptists Churches in North America, near Harrisburg, Pennsylvania, regarding the "where" of Obama's birth. We decided to attempt to arrange an interview with Sara Obama, as the Anabaptists Church provided church services in Kenya and elsewhere throughout Africa.

I felt it was very important we speak with Sara Obama because of the critical nature and impact of the birth issue allegations. Allegations that Obama was not "Constitutionally Eligible" to be President of the United States because of his birth in Kenya. Obviously, there would be no issue if Obama was born in Hawaii, as it is part of the United States. However, it is a major issue if Obama was born in Kenya.

Sara Obama was a necessary person to interview to resolve the issue with firsthand facts. Was the grandmother lying about her grandchild's birth? If so... _Why?_ Was Obama lying about his birth? If so... _Why?_

I thought it very odd that no agency or representative of the United States government was investigating or verifying Obama's birth or interviewing Sara Obama.

So we decided to go ahead and requested Bishop Ron McRae to

try to set up an interview with Sara Obama.

Reverend Kweli Shuhubia had the opportunity in October 2008 to interview Sara Obama. Reverend Kweli Shuhubia went to Sara Obama's home in Kogello, Kenya. Reverend Kweli Shuhubia called Bishop McRae in Harrisburg, Pennsylvania from Sara Obama's home. He placed the call on speakerphone and Bishop McRae asked permission to tape the conversation. All parties, including Sara Obama, granted permission. Because Sara Obama only speaks Swahili, Reverend Kweli Shuhubia and another grandson of Ms. Obama's translated the telephone interview.

Bishop McRae asked Sara Obama, "Where Obama was born?" Sara Obama answered in Swahili, and her answer was recorded, as well as a translation of her words. She was very adamant that Obama was born in Kenya. Bishop McRae asked Sara Obama... "Were you present at the hospital during her grandson Barack Obama's birth?" Sara Obama answered, "Yes."

After the interview with Sara Obama, Reverend Kweli Shuhubia traveled to Mombasa, Kenya. Reverend Kweli Shuhubia interviewed hospital personnel where Sara Obama said Barach Obama was born in Kenya.

Reverend Kweli Shuhubia immediately had meetings with the Provincial Civil Registrar. Reverend Kweli Shuhubia learned there were records of Ann Dunham giving birth to Barack Hussein Obama, Jr. in Mombasa, Kenya on August 4, 1961. Reverend Kweli Shuhubia spoke directly with an Official, the Principal Registrar, who openly confirmed that the birthing records of Obama under the name "Barack H. Obama, Jr." and his mother were present; however, the file on Barack H. Obama, Jr. was classified. The Official explained Barack Hussein Obama, Jr.'s birth in Kenya is top secret. Why the DoubleSpeak?

Obama allowed the Daily Kos, Factcheck and his campaign website to post a Hawaiian Certification of Live Birth [COLB], purported to be Obama's on their websites. This has several problems.

Dailykos.com, factcheck.org and fightthesmears.com images were deemed, altered, and forged documents, according to document image specialists. Even if the document purported to be Obama's Certification of Live Birth was an accurate document... it still could not prove "natural born" U.S. citizenship status. The Hawaii Department of Health issues a Certification of Live Birth [COLB] to births that occurred abroad in foreign countries as well as births that occurred at home and not in a hospital. Certifications of Live Birth are issued to those born as "naturalized" U.S. citizens as well as "natural born" U.S. citizens. In fact, Obama's half-sister, Maya Soetoro, was born in Indonesia in 1970, was born a "natural" citizen of Indonesia; however, her birth was registered in Hawaii as a birth abroad and she is only a "naturalized" U.S. citizen, not "natural born"; despite this she was issued a Hawaiian Certification of Live Birth [COLB].

A Certification of Live Birth is not sufficient "legal" evidence of proof or fact of a "natural born" U.S. citizen. In fact, a Certification of Live Birth is not even proof of your Hawaiian heritage for the Department of Hawaiian Home Lands (DHHL) in order to secure a Land Lease. The Department of Hawaiian Home Lands is governed by the Hawaiian Homes Commission Act of 1920, enacted by the U.S. Congress to protect and improve the lives of native Hawaiians. The act created a Hawaiian Homes Commission to administer certain public lands, called Hawaiian Homelands, for homesteads.

As stated in the Hawaiian Home Lands manual regarding applying for Hawaiian Home Lands on page eleven [11], in order to qualify for a Hawaiian Home Land Lease, you must be fifty [50%] percent Hawaiian. In order for the DHHL to process your application, DHHL utilizes information that is found only on the original Certificate of Live Birth, which is either black or green. This is a more complete record of your birth than the Certification of Live Birth [a computer-generated printout].

Ms. X spoke with the Hawaiian Health Department on several occasions and was told the same thing. In order to register a birth abroad in Hawaii, all you need is a certified copy of the child's foreign birth certificate and proof you are a resident of Hawaii. You then fill out a registration form. At that time, the Hawaii Department of Health issues a Certification of Live Birth [COLB], which is what Obama has on the Internet.

While still researching the Indonesian laws, I reviewed what the law states and the research as far as Obama's Kenyan birth.

A very detailed article published on Alex Jones' INFOWARS.COM website:

"Evidence Obama Born in Kenya Goes Beyond 1991 Brochure by Paul Joseph Watson dated Friday, May 13, 2012 is significant and reads in part,

"Establishment media pulls a stunt in effort to diffuse 'birther' controversy. The establishment media hastily seized on yesterday's explosive story about a literary publication listing Barack Obama's birthplace as Kenya in an effort to claim that the 1991 brochure was the 'origin' of the entire 'birther' issue. In reality, evidence that Obama was born in the African country is abundant.

Side bar note: *A literary agent's promotional text for a 1991 brochure released yesterday by Breitbart.com states Obama was 'born in Kenya and raised in Indonesia and Hawaii.'*

... The literary agent, who wrote the description, Miriam Goderich, now works with Dystel & Goderich agency, which lists Obama as one of its clients. Unsurprising therefore that Goderich hastily claimed listing Obama's birthplace as Kenya was 'nothing more than a fact checking error.'

However, evidence to indicate that Obama was born in Kenya is plentiful and it goes significantly beyond the 1991 version of the brochure.

Despite claiming the passage about Obama's birthplace being Kenya was a mistake, the listing still maintained that Obama's birthplace was Kenya *until after Obama became a U.S. Senator.* 'Goderich's statement fails to explain why the 'fact checking error' persisted for sixteen years, although at least three different versions of Jane Dystel's website, and through at least four different versions of

Obama's biography,' reports Breitbart.com.

-The literary agency also updated the text in June 1998, but the part about Obama being born in Kenya was retained.

- The text was again updated in February 2005 to reflect the fact that Obama had become a Senator, but Kenya was still listed as his birthplace.

-After an April 2007 modification of the text, the passage still read Obama 'was born in Kenya.'

- As Steve Boman reveals, the Dystel & Goderich agency asks its clients to submit their own biography, meaning it's virtually impossible the listing of Obama's birthplace as Kenya could have been a 'fact checking error' on behalf of the literary company itself.

-During a speech about HIV, First Lady Michelle Obama said she and Barack Obama 'visited his home country of Kenya.'

-In 2008 Obama's, paternal step grandmother appeared to indicate publicly that Barack Obama was born in Kenya. In an interview by American Christian minister Ron McRae, Sarah Obama was asked, 'Were you present when your grandson was born in Kenya?' McRae testified in his sworn statement. 'This was asked to her in translation twice, and both times she replied, 'Yes! Yes she was! She was present when Obama was born.'

-Another source who met Sarah Obama told World Net Daily, 'I have keenly and attentively listened to the tape over and over again, and I can confirm Sarah's own confession that Barack Obama was born in Kenya in her presence.'

-A separate Kenyan government official agreed, stating, 'I have listened to the tape. The preacher asked whether Barack Obama was born in Mombasa, and the translator asked the same. When she said Mombasa, it was like a surprise, and those there thought she could not have meant to say Mombasa.'

-When New York Times bestseller author Jerome Corsi traveled to Kenya to investigate the claims, he was almost immediately kicked out of the country by Kenyan officials.

-When Kenya's National Security Intelligence Service investigated claims that Obama was born in Kenya, officials in Nairobi found 'relevant birth records may have been removed or were missing.'

... For the mainstream media to imply that the 1991 brochure is the 'source' of the claim that Obama was born in Kenya is completely inaccurate. Not only was that brochure updated many times right up until 2007, with the information about Obama's birthplace being Kenya retained, but there are numerous other factors which all indicate that Kenya could indeed be Obama's homeland."

I set forth the above article by Paul Joseph Watson to support my position and my belief that Obama was born in Kenya and is "Constitutionally Ineligible" to be President. Mr. Watson details the facts that indicate the fraud that Obama is and shows how the media grasped on anything to spin Obama's birth in Kenya as a mistake. I repeat..., how *scary* that our Free Press has not followed through on the legitimate facts that support that Obama is "Constitutionally Ineligible" to be President. Mr. Watson goes into great detail regarding Obama's literary agency, with Miriam Goderich who wrote the description, that published the truth about Obama being born in Kenya and the fact that their clients, including Obama, submit their own biography, and the statements by others including Michelle Obama, the Sara Obama interview by American Christian minister Ron McRae, who I secured to interview her, and Jerome Corsi.

And, as I have related elsewhere in **ObamaScare** this is significant but also the fact that he was adopted in Indonesia makes it completely clear that Obama is "not a natural born U.S citizen" and therefore, there is no question that he is "Constitutionally Ineligible" to be President and he has usurped that position.

This would have been resolved a long time ago if the supposed United States "Free Press" vetted Obama as they should have and also that the United States Congress, should have held Hearings when serious Constitutional questions were raised; and the issue would have been resolved a long time ago, with Obama not being President.

CHAPTER IV
Indonesian Citizenship

I thoroughly reviewed in detail, the Indonesian Laws pertaining to Immigration and Citizenship.

Obama's mother, Stanley Ann Dunham, relocated Obama in or about October 1967, when Obama was six (6) years old, when she married Lolo Soetoro, an Indonesian Citizen. At that time Indonesia did not allow dual citizenship. Obama's mother became naturalized in Indonesia and Obama, being a minor, followed his mother's nationality. *See* Nationality Act of 1940, Section 317(b).

Regardless of whether Obama was officially adopted, [which required a Court process], by his Indonesian stepfather, Lolo Soetoro, or his birth was acknowledged [which only required the signing of a governmental birth acknowledgement form], by Lolo Soetoro, one of which had to occur in order for Obama to have the name Barry Soetoro and his citizenship status listed as "Indonesian," in either and/or both cases Obama's name was required to be changed to the Indonesian father's name, and Obama became a "natural citizen" of Indonesia. This is proven by the school records in Jakarta, Indonesia showing Obama's name as "Barry Soetoro" and his citizenship as Indonesian. Again, the registration of a child in the public schools in Jakarta, Indonesia was verified with the Government Records on file with the Governmental Agencies.

Side bar note: *Indonesia Constitution, Article 2 states:* "It is stipulated that an adopted child has the same status as a natural child and that his or her relationship to the birth parents is severed by adoption.

Indonesia Constitution, Article 2 states:

"on the condition of ratification of the adoption by the District

Court: *"The law stipulates that children of mixed couples automatically assume their father's citizenship, and a divorced wife cannot take custody of her children because they have different citizenship."*

Dual citizenship in Indonesia was not allowed or permitted until the year 2006. The Indonesian citizenship law was designed to prevent apatride (stateless) or bipatride (dual citizenship). Indonesian regulations, at the time in question, did not recognize neither apatride nor bipatride citizenship. Indonesia did not allow Dual Citizenship or Dual Nationality, thus Obama is not a U.S. Citizen, as he is Indonesian. Neither Obama's place of birth or the nationality of his American parent are relevant, the Indonesian Law takes precedence under The Master Nationality Rule of Article 4 of the Hague Convention of 1930.

The United States accepts the existence of Dual Nationality only if the other country does. Hague Conventions are followed by the United States and has been in effect since before 1930. (Memorandum on Nationality, including Statelessness: Document A/CN.4/67, Prepared by Ivan S Kerno, International Law Commission, United Nations General Assembly, 6th April 1953.) Thus, Obama is not a "natural born" citizen and may not even be a "naturalized citizen" of the United States

In *"Dreams from My Father,"* Obama's memoir (autobiography), he states he had already been enrolled in an Indonesia school when he arrived. Lolo Soetoro, an Indonesian State citizen, could not have enrolled Obama in school unless Lolo Soetoro adopted Obama or signed an acknowledgement legally acknowledging Obama as his son. Such document had to be filed with the Government. Under Indonesian law, when a male acknowledges a child as his son, it deems the son an Indonesian State citizen, in this case Obama.

Constitution of Republic of Indonesia, Law No. 62 of 1958 and Indonesian Civil Code (Kitab Undang-undang Hukum Perdata) (KUHPer) (Burgerlijk Wetboek voor Indonesie) states in pertinent part:

"State citizens of Indonesia include: (viii) children who are born outside of legal marriage from foreign State citizen mother who are acknowledged by father who is Indonesian State citizen as his children and that acknowledgment is made prior to children reaching 18 years of age or prior to marriage;"

Republic of Indonesia Constitution 1945, Chapter X, Citizens and Residents, Article 26 states,

"(1) Citizens shall consist of indigenous Indonesian peoples and persons of foreign origin who have been legalized [sic] as citizens in accordance with law.

(2) Residents shall consist of Indonesian citizens and foreign nationals living in Indonesia."

Furthermore, under the Indonesian adoption law, once adopted by an Indonesian citizen, the adoption severs the child's relationship to the birth parents, and the adopted child is given the same status as a natural child, Indonesian Constitution, Article 2.

Thus, where Obama was actually born and what his mother's citizenship status at the time of his birth is irrelevant.

The laws in Indonesia at the time of Obama's arrival did not allow dual citizenship. If an Indonesian citizen married a foreigner, as in this case, Obama's mother was required to renounce her U.S. citizenship and sponsored by her Indonesian spouse. During this time, Indonesia was a Police State. The public schools did not allow foreign students, only citizens were allowed to attend as Indonesia was under strict rule and decreed a number of restrictions; therefore, in order for Obama to have attended school in Jakarta, which he did, he had to be a citizen of Indonesia, as the citizenship status of enrolled students was verified with Government records.

Obama's Indonesian school registration clearly states Obama's name as "Barry Soetoro," and lists his citizenship as "Indonesian." Obama's father is listed as Lolo Soetoro; Obama's date of birth and place of birth are listed as August 4, 1961 in Hawaii; and Obama's Religion is listed as "Islam." This document was verified by television show _Inside Edition_, whose reporter took the actual footage of the school record. At the time Obama was registered, the public

Philip J. Berg

schools obtained and verified the citizenship status and name of the student through the Indonesian Government.

All Indonesian students were required to carry government identity cards, or Karty Tanda Pendudaks, as well as family card identification called a Kartu Keluarga. The Kartu Keluarga is a family card that bears the legal names and citizenship status of all family members.

Since Obama's birth was legally acknowledged by Lolo Soetoro, (an Indonesian citizen), and/or Obama was adopted by Lolo Soetoro, (which the evidence supports), Obama became an Indonesian citizen and bears the status as an Indonesia natural child (natural-born).

For the foregoing reason, Obama would have been required to file applications with the U.S. State Department and follow the legal procedures to become a "naturalized" citizen in the United States, when he returned from Indonesia. If Obama and/or his family failed to follow these procedures, then Obama is an "illegal alien." [This was the position I took when I filed a lawsuit in the United States District Court for the District of Columbia in the case of _Berg, et al v. Obama_, Case Number 1:08-cv-01933 where I alleged Obama was an "illegal alien" and therefore, his term as a United States Senator for Illinois was fraud, as one must be at least a "naturalized" citizen]

As I stated earlier, the Indonesian citizenship law is designed to prevent apatride (stateless) or bipatride (dual citizenship). Indonesian regulations recognize neither apatride nor bipatride citizenship.

In addition, since Indonesia did not allow dual citizenship, neither did the United States. _See_ Hague Convention of 1930.

In or about 1971, Obama's mother sent Obama back to Hawaii. Obama was ten [10] years of age upon his return to Hawaii.

Because of Obama's Indonesia "natural" citizenship status, there is absolutely no way in hell, Obama could have ever regained U.S. "natural born" status, if he in fact ever held such. Obama could have only become "naturalized," if the proper paperwork was filed with the U.S. State Department, in which case, Obama would have received a Certification of Citizenship.

There has been no record located verifying that Obama was

naturalized in the United States after his return from Indonesia. Obama was ten [10] years old when he returned to Hawaii to live with his grandparents. Obama's mother did not return with him, and therefore, unable to apply for citizenship for Obama in the United States. If citizenship of Obama had ever been applied for, Obama would have a Certification of Citizenship.

Nor has there been any record located legally changing Obama's name from Barry Soetoro back to Barack H. Obama, Jr. thus, his true and legal name is still to this date, Barry Soetoro.

Now, with the above breakdown of the law and the information we have substantiating Obama's birth, we can file suit.

I asked Ms. X, can you draft the law suit?

Ms. X: Yes, when do you want to file it?

Phil: I said I want to file this case before the Democratic National Convention on August 24, 2008. So, I want to file it tomorrow.

Ms. X: Tomorrow? Are you kidding?

Phil: No, tomorrow, can you do it?

Ms. X: I will do my best Phil.

Another theory – and if you believe the following, then I am incorrect regarding Obama serving as a U.S. Senator, but AGREE with me that OBAMA is "Constitutionally Ineligible" to be President:

Attorney Albert W.L. Moore, Jr., Esquire, 221 West Lexington, Suite 114, Independence, Missouri 64050-3719 has been investigating Obama for years and he states in a letter to me dated June 26, 2014 regarding the "Constitutionally Ineligibility" of Obama from his Indonesian naturalization, a different approach than I, as he believes that Obama filed for American naturalization in 1983. I also disagree regarding the statement of Obama using the Social Security number of a deceased American citizen.

Moore states, "... It is not enough that the pretender [Obama] as a minor became a naturalized Indonesian. He must be shown to have relinquished his American citizenship when competent to do so. His

1983 American naturalization necessarily confirms that he was not an American citizen before he was naturalized. Otherwise, no naturalization would have been necessary. As you know, a naturalized citizen is not a natural born citizen, even if the party was a natural born citizen at birth. ... This is the true case for constitutional ineligibility. ... "

Further, Albert W.L. Moore, Jr., Esquire submitted a Brief of Amicus Curiae in a case before The Supreme Court of Alabama, *MCINNISH, et al v. BETH CHAPMAN, SECRETARY OF STATE, et al*, Case No. 1120465 and in part, he states:

In paragraph 3. "Obama was naturalized a citizen of Indonesia around 1968, when American Secretary of State Dean Rusk issued a certificate of loss of nationality to facilitate the Indonesian naturalization. In 1971, Obama was returned to the United States unaccompanied on his Indonesian passport. The Department of State referred him to Catholic Charities of Connecticut, under a contractual arrangement. Catholic Charities had Madelyn Lee Payne Dunham appointed guardian. In 1977, Obama started using the Social Security number of a deceased American citizen to avoid applying for one on the basis of his American citizenship. In 1979, he confirmed as an adult his relinquishment of American citizenship in favor of his underlying Indonesian naturalization by refraining from registration with the Selective Service System.

In 1981, he went to Indonesia on his Indonesian passport, obtained an American student visa from the American Embassy, and re-entered the United States on his Indonesia passport as Barry Soetoro with the American student visa. He studied at Columbia University as a foreign student. This is probably the only time in his life when he told the truth about himself. In 1983, Obama was naturalized as an American citizen, definitive confirmation that he had previously relinquished his American citizenship. A naturalized citizen is not a natural born American citizen under Article II Section I of the American Constitution. Hence, Obama is not now, never has been, and never can be President of the United States. He lost constitutional eligibility forever when he lost American citizenship. It could be argued that Obama's naturalization as an American citizen in 1983 somehow related back to the date of his birth and restored his status as a "natural born Citizen" under Article II Section I of the United States Constitution. Such an argument would be frivolous. Upon loss of American citizenship, Obama ceased to be a "natural born Citizen" because he was no longer a "Citizen" at all. As the status of "natural born Citizen" can only be acquired at birth, and Obama cannot be born again, the loss of natural born American citizenship is permanent and irreversible upon loss of American citizenship."

In paragraph 14. "The real issue of Obama's constitutional eligibility is his loss of American citizenship. The status of natural born American citizen can be acquired only at birth. However, it can be lost thereafter, by loss of American citizenship altogether. The term "natural born Citizen" subsumes the term "Citizen." Obama could not be a natural born American citizen when he ceased to be an American citizen at all, even if he was a natural born U.S. citizen on the day of his birth. By his voluntary and intentional relinquishment of American citizenship (paragraph 3 above and paragraph 15 below) Obama became constitutionally ineligible for all time."

In paragraph 15. "The State Department has noted that naturalization as a foreign citizen is a potentially expatriating act, as a conviction for treason."

"POTENTIALLY EXPATRIATING ACTS"

Section 349 of the Immigration and Nationality Act (8 U.S.C. 1481), as amended, states that U.S. citizens are subject to loss of citizenship if they perform certain specified acts voluntarily and with the intention to relinquish U.S. citizenship. Briefly stated, these acts include:

"obtaining naturalization in a foreign state [my italics]; ... "

In paragraph 16. "Appropriate discovery by the trial court will establish Obama's loss of American citizenship by voluntarily and intentional relinquishment of it as an adult, capped by his 1983 naturalization as an American citizen, which would not have been necessary if he had not previously lost American citizenship."

Mr. Moore is raising funds to further collaborate his position by investigation to secure confirming documentation.

The significance of Mr. Moore's letter to me is that he has spent years researching Obama and his in depth letter adds significant facts regarding Obama's natural born and naturalization status and especially the details he discovered regarding Obama's becoming naturalized. Mr. Moore is a determined attorney actively seeking the truth by his ongoing efforts in writing to high government officials demanding that investigations be conducted.

As I stated, the above is another theory regarding Obama's status, but AGREES with me that Obama is "not" Constitutionally Eligible to be President!

Philip J. Berg

CHAPTER V

Passports

What passport did Barry Soetoro a/k/a
Barack H. Obama use during his 1981 trip
To Indonesia, Pakistan, South India and Kenya?

Barry Soetoro a/k/a Barack H. Obama by his own admission, traveled to Indonesia; Karachi, Pakistan; Hyderabad, India; and Kenya in the 1980's. Soetoro/Obama was traveling from college in Los Angeles with his friends, Chandoo and Hamid. The obvious questions are... what Passport did he use... how and where did he secure substantial funds to travel? There have been numerous questions regarding his Passport. It should also be noted, and asked... *why did Obama travel to Indonesia?*

In 1981, his mother, Stanley Ann Dunham, was living in Hawaii with his step-sister, Maya Soetoro, as Stanley Ann had just divorced her husband, Lolo Soetoro.

Another obvious and logical question... since Indonesian passports are required to be renewed every five [5] years, did Obama travel first to Indonesia in order to renew his Indonesian passport? That would have made it very easy for Obama to enter Pakistan, South India and Kenya.

Side bar note: In response to [FOIA] Freedom of Information Act requests for Barack H. Obama's United States passport application, the State Department stated they do not have any applications on file in the name of Barack H. Obama for a United States Passport. In fact, it does not appear that Barack H. Obama obtained a United States Passport until he received his Diplomatic Passport in 2004 as a United States Senator for Illinois.

In addition, according to a travel advisory issued August 17, 1981

Philip J. Berg

by the Passport Services/Bureau of Consular Affairs Department of State in Washington, D.C. the requirements for Americans traveling to and from Pakistan and South India had changed. Pakistan was under Martial Law, opposition politicians were incarcerated, Judges sacked, media censorship enforced and anti-government strikes were underway during this time. They were at war after the Soviet invasion and Afghanistan refugees fled from their homeland to Pakistan. By the end of 1981, in excess of two [2] million refugees had fled Afghanistan. In the 1980's, the Afghan refugees' arrival in Karachi added to the turmoil sectarian and inter-ethnic frustrations deteriorating Pakistan's largest city.

In 1981 the United States increased the funding by way of Pakistan to Afghans fighting the Soviet forces. Thousands of Arab and other foreign mujahedeen fled to Pakistan and Afghanistan to connect with and join the war.

__Side bar note__: In March 1981 Pakistan International's flight PK-326 became the longest hijacking in history. At the time Obama was traveling to Pakistan it was on the list of dangerous nations banned by the State Department. How was Obama able to travel without a passport? There is much more to that story... that we want to know.

According to an Associated Press article, "On March 2, 1981, Pakistan International's flight PK-326 began as a routine domestic hop from Karachi to Peshawar. In midair three [3] heavily armed men seized the plane, diverted it to Kabul, Afghanistan, and demanded the release of ninety-two [92] "political prisoners" from the Pakistani jails. On March 7, 1981, twenty-nine [29] hostages including women, children and sick men were released in Kabul. The Boeing 720B sat in Kabul for a week, and when Pakistan's President Mohammad Zia-ul-Haq refused to give in, the hijackers shot a Pakistani diplomat, Tariq Rahim, in full view of the other passengers and dumped his body onto the tarmac." Unfortunately, it did not stop there, on March 9, 1981; the plane flew to Damascus, Syria. The ordeal did not end until March 14, 1981. By this time, in excess of one hundred [100] passengers, which had now become hostages, had been forced to endure thirteen

[13] days of horrific and fearful events. At this time, this was the longest hijacking episode in history.

During the time the passengers, or hostages, were maintained on the aircraft, the man continued threatening to blow the plane up. Fortunately, the gunmen were talked into long extensions while negotiations were continued with Pakistani and Syrian officials in the Damascus control tower via radio.

Although the gunmen stated they would settle for fifty-five [55] prisoners, they didn't do so without a horrible threat. The gunmen stated they would soon kill three [3] Americans who happened to be on board the aircraft. The gunmen stated to the towers, "be ready to pick-up the bodies." President Zia gave an Order that the prisoners were to be flown to Sanctuary in Libya, giving into the hijackers, twenty [20] minutes before the gunmen's deadline. Sarfraz Khan, Pakistan Negotiator, stated "It's over."

Unfortunately, it was not over. Some of the Pakistani prisoners did not want to leave Pakistan and Pakistani authorities stated they were unable to trace one [1] of the fifty-five [55] prisoners. The prisoners, which were being released, were placed on a PIA Boeing 707. As the PIA Boeing 707 approached Tripoli, Libya, it was announced suddenly that it had changed its mind about granting asylum to the gunmen [hijackers] and their friends. This caused the hostages lives to be placed back into danger. The gunmen finally gave up when Syria informed the gunmen that it would take the hijackers [gunmen] and the prisoners; the hijackers gave up ending the long flight. It turned out that two [2] of the three [3] Americans were wanted on criminal charges in the U.S. and Canada, for drug-related offenses. Pakistan at the time was a major source of heroin distributed in the U.S., along with fellow "golden crescent" states Iran and Afghanistan.

With all that was happening in Pakistan and the fact that Pakistan is mostly surrounded by Muslims, it would have been much easier for Obama to travel there with an Indonesian Passport as a Muslim under the name of Barry Soetoro, than it would have been for any average

American Citizen."

CHAPTER VI

The Case of <u>BERG v. OBAMA</u>, *et al*

Filed AUGUST 21, 2008

This was the 1st lawsuit in the United States Challenging Obama's Constitutional Eligibility.

Due to the seriousness of the question of "Constitutional Eligibility" of Obama/Soetoro to be President of the United States, I felt it was vital to file a federal lawsuit and serve Obama and the Democratic National Committee [DNC] prior to Obama's nomination for President at the Democratic National Convention in Denver, Colorado in 2008.

I believed Howard Dean [(Chairman of the DNC] would have to seriously confront the "Constitutional Eligibility" issue if the issue was set forth in detail to him *before the DNC.*

Therefore, I made sure that the details for consideration were set forth in a legal complaint filed prior to Obama's forthcoming nomination for President in Denver, Colorado in August 2008.

I filed a federal lawsuit in United States District Court for the Eastern District of Pennsylvania in Philadelphia, Pennsylvania on August 21, 2008. I wanted to make sure service was made to Obama and the Democratic National Committee in Denver, Colorado at the Pepsi Center, prior to the start of the Democratic National Convention in August, 2008.

Obama and the Democrat National Committee received copies of the filed Federal lawsuit on Saturday, August 22, 2008, prior to the beginning of the convention.

I did not hear from Howard Dean or any member of the Democratic National Committee or their attorneys. I was shocked! Furthermore, there was no media coverage from the Democratic National Convention, even though I had issued a Press Release to the DNC Convention.

I believed that truth, fact and due diligence would prevail over such a serious matter. I guess I should not have been shocked or surprised, but go figure!

With no initial response after proper service of the Complaint from either Obama or the Democratic National Committee, I did not hear anything until thirty [30] days later when I received a joint response from Obama and the Democratic National Committee denying all allegations set forth in the Complaint.

Aside from my Press Release, I held a Press Conference in Philadelphia, after filing the federal lawsuit in the United States District Court for the Eastern District of Pennsylvania.

The Complaint was _Philip J. Berg, Esq. v. Barack Hussein Obama a/k/a Barry Soetoro a/k/a Barry Obama a/k/a Barack Dunham a/k/a Barry Dunham; The Democratic National Committee; The Federal Election Commission; the Secretary of the Commonwealth; Pennsylvania Department of State; Pedro A. Cortes, Secretary of the Commonwealth; Dianne Feinstein, Chairman of the U.S. Senate; U.S. Senate, Commission on Rules and Administration; and Does 1-50 Inclusive_ and was assigned Case No. 2:09-04083-RBS.

The basis of the lawsuit was:

"Article II, Section I of the United States Constitution, states in particular part,

"No Person except a natural born Citizen, or a Citizen of the United States at the time of the Adoption of this Constitution, shall be eligible to the Office of President; neither shall any Person be eligible to that Office who shall not have attained to the Age of thirty five Years, and been Fourteen Years a Resident within the United States."

"The general doctrine of our Constitution is, that the executive power of the nation is vested in the President; subject only to the exceptions and qualifications, which are expressed in the instrument." 7 Works of Alexander Hamilton, J. C. Hamilton ed. (New York: 1851), 76, 80–81 (emphasis in original), U.S. Constitution, Article II (Hamilton and Madison.).

I am a life-long Democrat who had always been proud of my Party. I was a licensed attorney in good standing and had taken an oath to uphold the United States Constitution. I had donated money and billable hours to Democratic Presidential candidates, as well as to the Democratic National Committee. I had relied on the Democratic National Committee's promises to uphold our Constitution. That included the responsibility of properly vetting a Presidential Nominee and ensure our Party's Nominee was eligible to serve as President of the United States, pursuant to Article II, Section 1 of "our" United States Constitution.

I trusted the Federal Election Commission to ensure our Presidential and Congressional candidates were eligible for the positions which they were seeking and running a fair and legitimate campaign process. I had relied on the FEC, DNC and all our Elected Office Holders to uphold our Constitution and to ensure an illegal alien and/or a naturalized citizen would not be able to secure the position of President of the United States.

The Democratic National Party was supposed to represent Democratic Americans in seeking Honest Leadership, Open Government, Real Security, Energy Independence, Economic Prosperity, Educational Excellence, a Healthcare System that works for Everyone and Retirement Security. The Democratic Party is supposed to represent and protect the interests of working Americans and guaranteeing personal liberties for all. This includes securing a Democratic Nominee on the Presidential Election ballot who represents the Democratic vision and who is qualified and eligible to run for the Office of the President, pursuant to the qualifications of the United States Constitution.

Knowing full well that he was not eligible, the actions of Barack Hussein Obama have been entirely without authorization under the United States Constitution, completely ignoring the qualification and procedures created by the United States Constitution he purports to enforce. Also, remember Obama taught Constitutional Law!

I, as well as other Democratic Americans, suffered Irreparable Harm as we were deprived of our right to cast our vote for an eligible Democratic Presidential Nominee who could secure the Office of the President of the United States.

Obama and his campaign brought in donations in excess of Four

Hundred Million [$400] Dollars by fraudulent means in 2008.

There were and are - unanswered questions:

* As to where Obama was actually born, in the United States or abroad, registering his birth in Hawaii;

* Regarding Obama's United States Citizenship, if he ever held such;

* Being expatriated and his failure to regain his citizenship by taking the Oath of Allegiance once he turned eighteen [18] years of age;

*Regarding Obama's "natural" citizenship status in Indonesia;

* If in fact Obama ever took the steps necessary and filed the appropriate immigration paperwork to become a "naturalized" citizen of the United States; and

* Regarding Obama's multi-citizenships with foreign countries, which he still maintains.

To date, Obama has refused to prove he is qualified under the U.S. Constitution and his eligibility to run and be President of the United States.

I said Ms. X: Can you prepare a Motion for a Temporary Restraining Order [TRO] or Injunction and Expedited Discovery? I want to stop the Democratic National Convention from nominating Obama as he is "Constitutionally Ineligible" to be President.

Ms. X: I'm done with the Motion for a Temporary Restraining Order [TRO] and for Expedited Discovery. Here is the basis I used. Philip J. Berg, Esquire hereby Requests a Temporary Restraining Order [TRO], to enjoin Defendant Barack Hussein Obama, a/k/a Barry Obama, a/k/a Barry Soetoro, a/k/a Barack Soetoro, a/k/a Barry Dunham, a/k/a Barack Dunham [hereinafter "Obama"] from running for the Office of President of the United States; to enjoin Defendant, Democratic National Committee from Nominating Defendant Barack Hussein Obama, a/k/a Barry Obama, a/k/a Barry Soetoro, a/k/a Barack Soetoro, a/k/a Barry Dunham, a/k/a Barack Dunham's from placing Obama's name on the ballot for Presidential election; and for Expedited Discovery in this case.

My Complaint challenged Obama's "eligibility" to run for the Office of President. Obama is unqualified and "Constitutionally Ineligible" to run for the Office of President of the United States, as he is not a "natural born" citizen as required by Article II, Section I of the United States Constitution. The Democratic National Committee [hereinafter at times "DNC"] has failed to perform due diligence, and to verify the "eligibility" of Defendant Obama to run for the Office of President of the United States.

I sought focused and expedited discovery, so that I could demonstrate to the Court, as soon as possible, the full breadth of innocent people affected by Defendant Obama's fraudulent campaign.

Obama proclaimed himself a Constitutional scholar and lecturer, but apparently failed to detect his own "ineligibility" to become President.

The denial of injunctive relief would foster an overwhelming degree of disrespect and cynicism for the electoral process [already sullied in the public mind by irregularities in the last several election cycles]. It would also threaten to confirm the unfortunately widespread belief that no potential candidate has to obey the laws of this country, respect our election process, follow the Constitution, or even suffer any consequence for lying and defrauding voters to get onto the ballot, when they have no chance of lawfully serving, if they fraudulently manage to get elected.

The DNC had failed me as well as voters across the country, by its failure to perform due diligence, and to properly ascertain Obama's "eligibility" to run for the Office of the President.

I also sought Leave from the Court to begin Discovery immediately so that I could demonstrate to the Court, as part of preliminary injunction proceedings, the full extent of Obama's fraudulent schemes in a way of attempting to run and get elected as President of the United States knowing he is "Constitutionally Ineligible," as he is not a "natural born" citizen. It is crucial that I obtain certified copies of Obama's birth records, adoption records, Oath of Allegiance if it exists, passport records, and all other records which prove he is not a citizen of the United States and/or a "natural born" citizen.

The reasons furnished by me in support of my request passed all of the legal thresholds used by Federal District Courts in assessing motions to expedite discovery. Here, there was good cause for discovery to begin immediately. I believed there was a strong likelihood that, *in the absence of injunctive relief,* Obama would be formally nominated by the Democratic Party as its nominee for the Office of President of the United States, which ultimately occurred. My request also worked minimal prejudice or unfairness to Obama, himself, as [at most] all that Obama would have to do in person [although certainly he would be entitled to appear and give testimony, or submit an affidavit stating the facts] would be to execute authorizations, prepared by his attorneys or by members of his staff, for relevant birth, passport, consular (Oath of Allegiance) and other relevant documents to be obtained and certified.

My discovery request was narrowly tailored to obtain only the information needed to pursue preliminary injunctive relief prohibiting Obama from running for President, and enjoining the DNC from naming Obama as a Democratic Presidential Nominee.

I took and personally filed the Complaint and the Motion for the Temporary Restraining Order [TRO] and Expedited Discovery to the United States District Court, Eastern District of Pennsylvania. Due to the time of filing, the Court requested me to return the next morning to see Judge R. Barclay Surrick regarding my Emergency Motion for a Temporary Restraining Order [TRO] or Injunction and Expedited Discovery.

Upon my return to the office, Ms. X and I tried to find someone who could set up a Website. We found a person that creates and runs websites for other people. Ms. X and I called right away and within hours, a website was set up called "***obamacrimes.com***."

What a thought, in 2008, to have our website called "***obamacrimes.com***," as there have been so many crimes committed by Obama and his administration.

On August 22, 2008, I appeared at Federal Court and waited until Judge Surrick was able to see me. Judge Surrick asked during this hearing if all the Defendants had been served. I explained to Judge Surrick that the Complaint and the Emergency Motion for the Temporary Restraining Order [TRO] or Injunction and Expedited Discovery were faxed to each of the Defendants. However, they had not been personally served as of yet. Case No. 2:09-04083-RBS was assigned. This was the very first lawsuit filed against Barack H. Obama in the United States questioning his

"Constitutional Eligibility" to run for and serve as President of the United States. Unfortunately, no one from the mainstream media appeared at the Courthouse, an ongoing example of the non-coverage of "our" supposed "Free Press" of anything controversial about Obama from when he announced his intention to be a candidate for president to today.

Judge R. Barclay Surrick held the Hearing and told me once I had all the Defendants personally served to contact his [Judge Surrick's] chambers and inform his staff that personal service had been completed. Judge Surrick stated once that takes place, he will hear my motion.

On August 27, 2008, the Democratic National Committee announced they had nominated Barack H. Obama as the Democratic Party's Presidential Candidate.

All Defendants were served by September 4, 2008 and I immediately contacted Judge Surrick's chambers informing his staff that personal service had been completed. Judge Surrick ultimately denied my Motion for an Emergency Temporary Restraining Order [TRO] or Injunction and Expedited Discovery.

I was not giving up. Ms. X drafted another motion for expedited discovery; extensive discovery; and a request for the Court to appoint a special master over the discovery issues. My Motion was filed on September 9, 2008.

Ms. X then began working on Request for Admissions, which is a form of discovery you serve upon the Defendants. The Request for Admissions was served upon Obama on September 15, 2008. Obama had thirty [30] days to respond to my Request for Admissions.

Barack H. Obama, The DNC, The FEC, the Secretary of the Commonwealth, and all the other Defendants in the case responded to this lawsuit by filing a Motion to Dismiss on September 24, 2008. I researched the Motion to Dismiss and prepared a Response in Opposition to Obama and the other Defendants Motion to Dismiss and filed it on September 29, 2008.

Ms. X began working on the First Amended Complaint to strengthen areas in the original Complaint and a Motion to file a First Amended Complaint was filed along with the actual First Amended Complaint on

October 6, 2008.

A couple of hours later, I received notification that Obama and the other Defendants filed a Motion for a Protective Order Staying All Discovery pending the outcome of their Motion to Dismiss.

After a thorough review of Obama and the other Defendants Motion for a Protective Order, Ms. X researched the law and drafted a Response in Opposition to the Defendants Motion. My Response in Opposition to Obama and the other Defendants Motion for a Protective Order was filed with the Court on October 9, 2008.

Regardless of the pending motion, the Request for Admissions served upon Obama were not protected until the Judge ruled on his Motion, therefore the clock was still ticking and the Responses to the Request for Admissions were due on or before October 15, 2008.

Obama and The DNC filed another Motion to Dismiss my First Amended Complaint on October 20, 2008. This was followed by the FEC filing their Motion to "Dismiss my First Amended Complaint" on October 21, 2008.

Meanwhile, Obama never answered my Request for Admissions within thirty [30] days and were therefore, deemed "Admitted." To make sure the Request for Admissions were admitted in the Court Record, I decided to file a Motion Requesting the Court to Order the Request for Admissions deemed "Admitted." Ms. X immediately began working on the Motion. My Motion was filed October 21, 2008, deeming my Request for Admissions, as to Obama, "Admitted."

A few of the Request for Admissions to Obama that were "Admitted" are as follows:

Admit you were born in Kenya.

Admit you are a Kenya "natural born" citizen.

Admit your mother gave birth to you in Mombasa, Kenya.

Admit the COLB [Certification of Live Birth] posted on the "Fightthesmears.com" is a forgery.

Admit you were adopted by Lolo Soetoro, M.A., a citizen of Indonesia.

Admit you were not born in Hawaii.

Admit you are a citizen of Indonesia.

Admit you are not a "natural born" United States citizen.

Admit the United States Constitution does not allow for a person to hold the Office of President of The United States unless that person is a "natural born" United States citizen.

Admit you are ineligible pursuant to the United States Constitution to serve as President and/or Vice President of the United States.

Admit you are not a "Naturalized" United States Citizen.

Admit you were born in the Coast Province Hospital in Mombasa, Kenya.

Being that I filed a Motion for the Court to Deem the Request for Admissions served upon Barack H. Obama deemed "Admitted," Ms. X also drafted a Motion for an Expedited Ruling on my Motion for Summary Judgment, on October 22, 2008.

Side bar note: Summary Judgment was appropriate since Obama admitted everything asked; there were absolutely no triable issues of fact for the Court to rule upon.

On Friday, October 24, 2009 at approximately six [6:00] p.m., a fax came into the office from Judge Surrick, granting Obama, the DNC and the FEC's Motions to Dismiss. No hearing was granted and no mention of the pending Motions before the Court. I was deprived of my due process rights to be heard.

Judge Surrick's dismissal of my case was based on **"Standing,"** the right to bring an action. Judge Surrick made some outlandish comments claiming Obama had been properly vetted, and that was completely untrue.

Judge R. Barclay Surrick stated that I was not injured and therefore, could not bring this action or as I stated, I did not have standing and basically said that no individual in the United States has standing to sue a presidential candidate or a president. Judge Surrick further stated that perhaps in the future the United States Congress would decide who would have standing to bring such an action.

How ridiculous as I know that the U.S. Constitution begins with the words, **"WE THE PEOPLE"** and I believe that all of us, all citizens of the United States individually, have a right to bring such an action by having standing.

Needless to say, Ms. X prepared the Notice of Appeal and filed it on October 30, 2008, appealing Judge Surrick's dismissal of my case. After full discussions and reviewing the law pertaining to emergency relief, Ms. X and I decided to also file with the United States Supreme Court pursuant to the United States Supreme Court Rules ten [10] and eleven [11], a Writ of Certiorari and a Request for an Emergency Stay of the Presidential Election, before the Third Circuit Court of Appeals ruled on my Appeal.

Emergency Appeals pursuant to the United States Supreme Court Rules ten [10] and eleven [11] are not very common and the granting of a Writ of Certiorari prior to judgment from the Lower Court is even less common. Unfortunately, the United States Supreme Court denied my Writ of Certiorari and all Emergency Requests for a Stay of the Presidential Election.

Ms. X and I prepared and filed with the United States Supreme Court the following Emergency Requests for Injunctions:

*Stay of the Presidential Election of November 4, 2008;

*Stay of the Meeting of Electors on December 15, 2008 where each State issues "Certificate of Vote" based upon the Electoral College;

*Stay of the Joint Session of Congress on January 6, 2009 where the Electoral Votes are counted; and

*A Stay of the Presidential Inauguration on January 20, 2009.

All of which were denied.

My case was then pending before the Third Circuit Court of Appeals in Philadelphia, Pennsylvania. All briefs were filed and Oral Argument was granted and set for October 26, 2009. Unfortunately, on or about

October 15, 2009, the Third Circuit Court of Appeals sent a letter stating there would not be any oral argument. This is not unusual in the Circuit Courts. What this means is the Appellate Court feels that oral argument will not assist in their decision of the case, which is not always good news for the Appellant. Although, M. X and I were confident in my arguments submitted on the briefs, attorney's always like to have the opportunity to address the Court on any portion of the law which the Court may have questions.

All was not lost however; I received the Court transcript of the proceedings held in the California case of _Alan Keyes, et al v. Obama, et al_, United States District Court, Central District of California, Southern Division, Case No. 09-cv-0082. This case was filed on January 20, 2009 at approximately 3:06 p.m. pacific standard time [PST]. This case was also questioning the citizenship status and "Constitutional Eligibility" of Barry Soetoro a/k/a Barack H. Obama to serve as our President of the United States. .

In the Court proceedings of October 5, 2009, in the 9th Circuit Court of Appeals, with me being present, at the Hearing in California, some very important events took place. The Court asked very good questions. In fact, questions and answers which agreed with and supported my arguments, which went like this:

Page 12, Lines 22-25 and Page 13, Lines 1-18:

"THE COURT:

I'm going to talk about both eventually, so I've got plenty of time. Let's just start with Arnold Schwarzenegger. I'm going to suggest to you the Courts are going to have to intervene at some time in what you perceive to be a political question and stop Schwarzenegger from running for President."

"MR. WEST:

Well, I believe, your Honor, the question of whether a person is properly qualified as a candidate is a different breed of cat altogether from someone who is a sitting President whom the plaintiffs are seeking to remove from office."

"THE COURT:

Are you going to answer my question?"

"MR. WEST:

Yes. I believe that the Courts could have some jurisdiction over the question of whether a candidate is qualified to be on the ballot."

"THE COURT:

Do you agree, Counsel?"

"MR. DeJUTE:

I do agree, your Honor."

"MR. SOSKIN:

I don't believe we need to take that position at this time, but it's conceivable that there would be standing in a scenario in which such a case could be adjudicated. This exchange was extremely important to my case, as I brought my action questioning the citizenship status and "Constitutional Eligibility" of Barry Soetoro a/k/a Barack H. Obama, questioning the legal status of Obama to be on the ballot, said action timely filed while Obama was a "candidate."

Mr. West is an attorney with the United States Attorney's Office in Los Angeles, California; Mr. DeJute is an attorney with the United States Attorney's Office in Los Angeles, California and Mr. Soskin is an Attorney with the United States Department of Justice and - **all three [3] agreed, if the case was brought before the election, <u>which my case was</u>, the Court could intervene and "standing" would not be an issue.**

Thus, the Government and the Federal Court in California conceded the fact I had "standing" and the Court could intervene, as I brought my action prior to the election. The Government's position agreed with me and disagreed with Mr. Lavelle, Mr. Sandler and Mr. Bauer, Attorney's for the Democratic National Committee and Barry Soetoro a/k/a Barack H. Obama, who were each from private law firms in my case in Federal Court in the Eastern District of Pennsylvania.

The Democratic National Committee and Barry Soetoro a/k/a Barack H. Obama wanted the Court to believe that I did not have standing and our Courts did not have jurisdiction, despite the fact the case was brought before the election. I, as well as all democratic voters, was deprived of our right to vote for a valid candidate; and the United States

Government and another Federal Court conceded I had "standing."

Ms. X and I immediately worked on and filed a Request for Judicial Notice of the October 5, 2009 Transcript of the Proceedings in _Alan Keyes, et al v. Obama, et al_, United States District Court, Central District of California, Southern Division, Case No. 09-cv-0082. Ms. X was convinced that the Third Circuit Court of Appeals had made up their mind and the issue would have to go to the United States Supreme Court. I agreed, however, the important part of this was that the Request for Judicial Notice was part of the record and therefore, would follow to the United States Supreme Court, once appealed.

Philip J. Berg

CHAPTER VII

The "SEALED" Case: BERG, as Relator v. OBAMA

Obama "not" a U.S. citizen and therefore, fraud as a U.S. Senator
Conflict-of-Interest by Eric Holder, U.S. Attorney General
Filed November 7, 2008

I had "Standing" and this case would have exposed Obama

An enormous amount of research was required before arriving at the conclusion that Obama was not eligible to hold the Office of United States Senator for Illinois. I decided to file a False Claims Action or *Qui Tam* case pursuant to 31 U.S.C. Sections 3729 through 3733.

Side bar note: A False Claims Act is an action you file against a party who has obtained monies from the United States Treasury based on false claims made. In this case, in order for Obama to be paid for his position as a United States Senator for Illinois, he would have had to be legally qualified to hold the Office.

Being that Obama became an Indonesian citizen and there is absolutely no record of him ever applying for immigration to become a United States citizen or that he legally changed his name of Barry Soetoro, which means that Obama, really Barry Soetoro, is still today an Indonesian citizen and not a United States citizen at all.

Therefore, the pay and benefits Obama received as a United States Senator was based on his false statements and false claims that he was legally eligible for the Office of United States Senator for Illinois, that he was at least a "naturalized" United States Citizen.

I filed the *Qui Tam* (False Claims Action) on November 7, 2008 in the United States District Court for the District of Columbia in Washington, D.C., with the caption of the case, *PHILIP J. BERG, ESQUIRE, on his own BEHALF and on BEHALF of the GOVERNMENT of the UNITED STATES of*

AMERICA, Relator v. BARACK HUSSEIN OBAMA, JR., Defendant, and the case was assigned the Case Number 1:08-cv-01933 before the Honorable Richard W. Roberts.

The case was filed under "seal" as required pursuant to statute and served upon the United States Attorney's Office and the United States Department of Justice; both parties were served on November 10, 2008 and had until January 9, 2009 to respond.

Typically a *Qui Tam* (False Claims Action) remains under "seal" for sixty [60] days to give the Government time to decide whether they are going to prosecute the case or decline to prosecute and allow the Relator, in this case, me, to prosecute on the Government's behalf, or dismiss the case.

Under "seal" means that Court dockets are private, no publicity, no press, and no public discussion.

The basis for this False Claims Action against Obama was the fact the United States Supreme Court held in *Sprint Communications Co. L.P. v. APCC Services Inc.,* 554 U.S. __, 128 S.Ct. 2531 (2008) quoting *Vermont v. United States,* 529 U.S. 765 (2000) that a private citizen such as the Relator, in this case me, has **standing** to bring an action under the False Claims Act. Thus, there was no valid assertion whatsoever that the Relator, in this case me, did not have standing to bring the action.

Compare this to the first case I filed against Obama in the United States District Court for the Eastern District of Pennsylvania in August 2008 where Judge R. Barclay Surrick ruled that I did not have "standing" to bring the case. See *Berg v. Obama, et al.,* U.S. District Court, Eastern District of Pennsylvania, Case No. 2:09-04083-RBS.

The United States Government is the party on whose behalf the Relator also brings this action, as well as on his own behalf, as required by the False Claims Act.

My allegation was that Barack Hussein Obama, Jr. was not a citizen of the United States, but was nevertheless a United States Senator from the State of Illinois, improperly elected to that office, in November 2004.

Article I, Section 3 of the United States Constitution mandates that a

United States Senator *"shall"* be a citizen of the United States. [Emphasis added by me]

I alleged Obama was not a citizen of the United States, as indicated by the information contained in the following Exhibits which were filed with the Court:

a. Affidavit of Bishop Ron McRae, who interviewed Sara Obama, Obama's grandmother;

b. Affidavit of Bishop Kweli Shuhubia, who interviewed Sara Obama, Obama's grandmother, while sitting next to her at her home;

c. Transcript of taped interview of Sara Obama, Senator Obama's Kenyan Paternal Grandmother that was interviewed by Bishop Ron McRae and Bishop Kweli Shuhubia; and

d. Obama's Indonesian School Record.

Obama of course knew he was not a United States citizen. Nevertheless, he fraudulently filed papers with the intent and purpose of running for the federal office of United States Senator. Despite his inability to qualify for that office as required by the United States Constitution, Obama was elected to that office.

Upon his wrongful election, Obama received payment from the United States Government, specifically from the United States Department of the Treasury, of a salary and benefits as a United States Senator. This payment of a salary to Obama resulted from his submission of a false claim, within the full meaning of the False Claims Act, that he is a United States citizen entitled to a salary and benefits as a United States Senator. He was not, as he could not legally hold this federal office by virtue of his not being a United States citizen.

This ruse by Obama as a United States citizen and thus entitled to the payment of a salary and benefits for the performance of duties while in the Office of United States Senator constitutes a clear violation of 31 U.S.C. 3729, et sequitur, for which there was a certain mandatory remedy.

On my own behalf and on behalf of the United States Government, I, as the Relator, sought all remedies available to me pursuant to the remedies set forth in the False Claims Act, including a refund of all salary and benefit monies paid to Obama and other certain fiscal penalties set forth in the False Claims Act.

I, as the Relator, also requested the United States Attorney General to avail himself of all investigative tools on an expedited basis as provided under 31 U.S.C. 3733 in order that the matter be resolved expeditiously. More specifically, I asked that the Attorney General of the United States to secure the following:

a. Original certified "vault" birth certificate of the Defendant Obama purportedly held by the State of Hawaii;

b. Original certified "vault" birth certificate of the Defendant Obama from Kenya;

c. Certified copies of all change of name Court documents of Obama changing his name from Barry Soetoro;

d. Certified copy of Adoption record from Indonesia of Obama;

e. Certified copy of the Governmental Acknowledgement form signed by Lolo Soetoro, M.A., an Indonesian citizen "acknowledging" Obama as his son; and

f. Certified copy of United States Immigration form of Certificate of Citizenship issued upon the return to United States from Indonesia of Obama, all of which Defendant Obama refuses to provide to the public.

STATE OF HAWAII		CERTIFICATE OF LIVE BIRTH		DEPARTMENT OF HEALTH		
		FILE NUMBER 151		61 10641		
1a. Child's First Name (Type or print)		1b. Middle Name		1c. Last Name		
	BARACK	HUSSEIN		OBAMA, II		
2. Sex	3. This Birth	4. If Twin or Triplet, Was Child Born	5a. Birth Date	Month	Day	Year	5b. Hour
Male	Single ☒ Twin ☐ Triplet ☐	1st ☐ 2nd ☐ 3rd ☐		August	4, 1961	7:24 P.M.
6a. Place of Birth: City, Town or Rural Location				6b. Island		
	Honolulu				Oahu	
6c. Name of Hospital or Institution (If not in hospital or institution, give street address)			6d. Is Place of Birth Inside City or Town Limits? If no, give judicial district		6e. Island	
Kapiolani Maternity & Gynecological Hospital			Yes ☒ No ☐			
7a. Usual Residence of Mother: City, Town or Rural Location		7b. Island		7c. County and State or Foreign Country		
	Honolulu	Oahu		Honolulu, Hawaii		
7d. Street Address			7e. Is Residence Inside City or Town Limits? If no, give judicial district			
6085 Kalanianaole Highway			Yes ☒ No ☐			
7f. Mother's Mailing Address			7g. Is Residence on a Farm or Plantation?			
			Yes ☐ No ☒			
8. Full Name of Father			9. Race of Father			
BARACK	HUSSEIN	OBAMA	African			
10. Age of Father	11. Birthplace (Island, State or Foreign Country)	12a. Usual Occupation	12b. Kind of Business or Industry			
25	Kenya, East Africa	Student	University			
13. Full Maiden Name of Mother			14. Race of Mother			
STANLEY	ANN	DUNHAM	Caucasian			
15. Age of Mother	16. Birthplace (Island, State or Foreign Country)	17a. Type of Occupation Outside Home During Pregnancy	17b. Date Last Worked			
18	Wichita, Kansas	None				
I certify that the above stated information is true and correct to the best of my knowledge.	18a. Signature of Parent or Other Informant		Parent ☒ Other ☐	18b. Date of Signature 8-7-61		
I hereby certify that this child was born alive on the date and hour stated above.	19a. Signature of Attendant		M.D. ☒ D.O. ☐ Midwife ☐ Other ☐	19b. Date of Signature 8-8-61		
20. Date Accepted by Local Reg. AUG -8 1961	21. Signature of Local Registrar		22. Date Accepted by Reg. General AUG -8 1961			
23. Evidence for Delayed Filing or Alteration						

I CERTIFY THIS IS A TRUE COPY OR ABSTRACT OF THE RECORD ON FILE IN THE HAWAII STATE DEPARTMENT OF HEALTH

APR 2 5 2011

Alvin T. Onaka, Ph.D.
STATE REGISTRAR

I have enclosed a copy of the **"Certificate of Live Birth"** and the **"Certification of Live Birth."** As I indicated the **"Certificate"** is the "original from Hawaii. However, this can be... and in my opinion... was issued when Hawaii was presented with Obama's Birth Certificate from Kenya. The **"Certification"** is a computer generated printout from the Hawaii records.

The most significant fact to indicate that the documents are fraudulent is Obama's Father's race that is listed as "AFRICAN." In 1961, No one was called **"African."** Documents in 1961 stated **"Colored"** or **"Negro."**

The following is a copy of the fraudulent Certificate of Live Birth of Obama with on Line 9 is Obama's Race of Father = "African."

No one was called "African" in 1961. One was either "Colored" or Negro."

CERTIFICATION OF LIVE BIRTH

STATE OF HAWAII
HONOLULU

DEPARTMENT OF HEALTH
HAWAII U.S.A.

CERTIFICATE NO. ████████

CHILD'S NAME
BARACK   HUSSEIN   OBAMA II

DATE OF BIRTH	HOUR OF BIRTH	SEX
August 4, 1961	7:24 PM	MALE

CITY, TOWN OR LOCATION OF BIRTH	ISLAND OF BIRTH	COUNTY OF BIRTH
HONOLULU	OAHU	HONOLULU

MOTHER'S MAIDEN NAME
STANLEY   ANN   DUNHAM

MOTHER'S RACE
CAUCASIAN

FATHER'S NAME
BARACK   HUSSEIN   OBAMA

FATHER'S RACE
AFRICAN

DATE FILED BY REGISTRAR
August 8, 1961

OHSM 1-1 (Rev. 11/01) LASER   This copy serves as prima facie evidence of the fact of birth in any court proceeding. [HRS 338-13(b), 338-19]

ANY ALTERATIONS INVALIDATE THIS CERTIFICATE

The following is an authentic "Certificate of Live Birth" from Hawaii with the name blocked out, but a date of birth of June 9, 1961, two [2] months **before** the birth of Obama. *Please note that on "Line 9 it indicates the Race of Father as "Colored" and crossed-out and says "Negro." That says it all.*

Philip J. Berg

Ms. X prepared a Motion and Brief requesting the Court to "unseal" the False Claims Action as a result of the United States Attorney's Office and the United States Department of Justice's failure to intervene, decline intervention or request an extension of time. These documents were filed in Court on January 31, 2009.

Please note that my request was proper and I felt should have been granted as the U.S. Attorney's Office and the U.S. Department of Justice had until January 9, 2009 to respond and I did not rush to Court, but waited twenty-two [22] days to file.

Judge Roberts issued an Order on February 4, 2009 instructing the Government to Show Cause by February 17, 2009 in writing Why its Silence Should Not be Deemed to Allow the Relator, which was me, to Prosecute the Case.

Of course, the United States Attorney General's Office and the United States Department of Justice responded to my Motion on February 17, 2009 stating in one breath they were not served and then in another breath that they did a search and finally located the Complaint. The government asked that the sixty [60] day period of time be extended to give the Government time to review my *Qui Tam* case (False Claims Action).

Judge Roberts questioned the Government's statements that they had not been served, however, did Grant their Request for an Extension of Time while "Denying my Request" to "unseal" the Case. I felt that this was unjust, but again, it was up to the Judge. It made me wonder again as to the pressures against me, as I was challenging the now president of the United States, who, at the time of my filing, was president-elect.

On or about March 30, 2009, the government moved to "Dismiss my Relator's False Claims Action." In other words, instead of declining intervention, and allowing me to prosecute the case, the United States Attorney's Office and the United States Department of Justice wanted to "Dismiss the Entire Action." Ms. X researched the issues raised in the government's Motion to Dismiss and found they must meet the "rational relation" standard that is the substantive due process analyses requirement, which they had not done. The Government had a duty to investigate the allegations outlined in my False Claims Act action.

Exactly what investigation had the Government done in the case? Ms. X began working on my Response in Opposition to the Government's Motion to Dismiss my False Claims action. I reviewed the Response in Opposition to the Government's Motion to Dismiss and filed the document on or about April 20, 2009.

In my argument, I point out that unlike the False Claim Act provisions relating to settlements, which are found in Section 3730(c)(2)(B), there were absolutely no guidelines for the Court contained in 31 U.S.C. § 3730(c)(2)(A) to consider if the Government makes a Motion to Dismiss.

The Government failed to inform the Court of a Standard of Review for Dismissal of a *Qui Tam* Case by the Government under Section 3730(c)(2)(A). In *United States ex rel. Sequoia Orange County v. Sunland Packing Company*, 912 F. Supp. 1325, 1340 (E.D. Cal. 1995) aff'd, 151 F.3d 1139 (9th Cir. 1998), a case of first impression, it was held that the Government's right to dismiss *Qui Tam* actions was subject to judicial review. The *Sequoia* case established what is called the "Sequoia Test" which had been adopted by the Federal District of Columbia Courts and although giving substantial deference to the government's discretion to dismiss a declined case, the Court did not hold that the government has an absolute right to dismiss such cases. See *Swift v. United States*, 318 F.3d 250 (D.C. Cir. 2003).

Under *Sequoia*, the Ninth Circuit upheld the use of a two-step analysis applied by the District Court. The Court held that the standard of review that applies to a Government's Motion to Dismiss under Section 3730(c)(2)(A) is the "rational relation" standard, the standard that applies to substantive due process analyses. The Court **shall** [Emphasis added by me] consider: (1) whether the government has identified a valid government purpose for the dismissal; and (2) whether there is "a rational relation between dismissal and accomplishment of the purpose," *Sequoia*, 151 F.3d 1139, 1145.

The Government had not given any basis for their requested dismissal except they claimed the Relator's allegations lacked merit and concluded they should not be pursued on behalf of the United States. The Government went on further and listed other cases the Relator was involved in to simply prejudice the Relator, as they did not have any bearing to the case at hand. I, the Relator, was involved with other litigation that was still active in the Court's; said other litigation had nothing to do with the false claims presented by Barry Soetoro a/k/a Barack H. Obama while sitting as United States Senator for Illinois. The Government's Motion clearly lacked a valid government purpose for the dismissal; and there was no rational relation between dismissal and accomplishment of the purpose. In fact, the Government had done nothing more than attempt to prejudice the Relator; they did not offer any reasons for dismissal that are rationally related to a legitimate government interest in order to justify the Court to dismiss the *Qui Tam* action. *Sequoia*, 151 F.3d 1139, 1147.

I pointed out many serious questions as to the citizenship status of Barack H. Obama. Based on the evidence presented to the Court and to the Government by me, Barack H. Obama was still an Indonesian Citizen. His legal name was and is Barry Soetoro. Thus, he was never qualified to serve as a United States Senator for Illinois; he usurped said office and obtained money from the United States based on false claims.

I feared that the United States Attorney General's Office and the United States Department of Justice, may have been biased as to the within action. It appeared they had a "Conflict-of-Interest" with any action brought against Barack H. Obama wherein they are a party as Barack H. Obama had been elected and was currently the president of the United States and directly supervises these agencies, the United States Attorney General's Office and the United States Department of Justice. After all, the Constitution entrusts the Executive with duty to take care that the Laws be faithfully executed.

More importantly, I had clearly shown a substantial threshold entitling me to discovery relating to the Government's prosecutorial decision to seek dismissal of my False Claim Action, of which I was entitled. *See* <u>*Swift v. United States*</u>, 318 F.3d 250, 254 (D.C. Cir. 2003). I had supplied the Government with numerous documents as to how Obama had defrauded the Government for salary and benefits as a U.S. Senator for Illinois, of which he did not qualify to hold.

Information filed or gathered by the Government relating to its decision whether to intervene has been held non-exempt from disclosure. In <u>*United States ex rel. Mikes v. Strauss*</u>, 846 F.Supp. 21 (S.D.N.Y. 1994) the Court denied the Government's Motion to retain the documents filed in relation to the Government's investigation of a *Qui Tam* Complaint under "seal."

Judge Roberts set a Hearing on June 9, 2009 on the matter. I was present for the Hearing in the United States District Court in Washington, DC and since the case was filed under "seal," as soon as everyone arrived that was allowed to be present, counsel and no press, the doors were locked and the windows covered.

I argued the problems with the Government's attempt to have the case dismissed instead of just declining intervention and allowing me, as the Relator, to prosecute the matter on behalf of the United States Government. After I presented my argument and then the government, Judge Roberts stated he would not inquire as the District of Columbia District Court had decided they would not have any input in *Qui Tam* cases. I immediately questioned Judge Roberts as to the purpose of a Hearing if the Judges have no input and advised the Court that the Federal Courts in the 9th Circuit [15 Judicial Districts in Western United States] have the Judges having input in *Qui Tam* cases. Judge Roberts stated he would not ask questions or have any input.

Judge Roberts then asked the two [2] government agencies, the Department of Justice and the U.S. Attorney General's Office their position and both departments stated they wanted my *Qui Tam* case Dismissed. Judge Roberts, without any other comment stated, "Case Dismissed, Case Unsealed."

Despite my valid efforts, Judge Roberts dismissed my *Qui Tam* case (False Claims Action).

Upon return to the Office, I asked Ms. X to research the issues so I could determine if there were grounds to seek reconsideration. Ms. X complied and did find problems which needed to be addressed and that granted me the right to seek reconsideration of the Court's dismissal.

Based on the findings, a Motion for Reconsideration was drafted which involved the United States Attorney General, Eric Holder, his office and his staff's "Conflict-of-Interest" pertaining to this particular case. My argument was that this *Qui Tam* based on the False Claims Act [FCA] action was a unique case with unique circumstances because of the nature of the False Claims.

The reason was due to the allegations of fraud were against now, sitting president Barack Hussein Obama regarding his fraudulently holding the Office of United States Senator from Illinois and the fact that review of these proceedings to decide to prosecute rests with the United States Attorney General Eric Holder, who reports directly to the alleged violator; gives opinions and legal advice to the alleged violator; was senior legal advisor to Barack H. Obama's Presidential campaign; served as one [1] of three [3] members on Obama's Vice-Presidential Selection Committee that selected Joseph Biden as Vice-President; and who was selected by Obama to be Attorney General of the United States and was confirmed by Congress; and thus a major "Conflict-of-Interest" exists.

There are four [4] Federal Statutory prohibitions and related regulations addressing "Conflicts-of-Interest" on the part of present officers or employees of the Federal [and in some instances of the District of Columbia] government. None of the statutory prohibitions are limited in application solely to lawyers. The conflicts dealt with by the several provisions are, in each instance, conflicts between public responsibilities and private interests. All of the statutory provisions are found in Chapter 11 [Bribery, Graft and Conflicts of Interest] of Title 18 of the United States Code, the Federal Criminal Code.

There are statutory restrictions on Conflicts-of-Interest during

Government Service. Although there are four [4] statutory provisions regarding conflicts between governmental responsibilities and private interests of government employees, all of which apply to employees of the District of Columbia as well as the Federal Government, only two [2] apply in this case and are as follows:

• A prohibition on certain representational activities relating to claims against and other matters affecting the government, 18 USC § 205.

• A prohibition on certain acts by government employees affecting a personal financial interest - applying, inter alia, to negotiations for post-government employment, 18 USC § 208.

Pursuant to the Code of Federal Regulations, 5 CFR § 2635.101:

"(a) Public service is a public trust." Each employee has a responsibility to the United States Government and its citizens to place loyalty to the Constitution, laws and ethical principles above private gain. To ensure that every citizen can have complete confidence in the integrity of the Federal Government, each employee shall respect and adhere to the principles of ethical conduct set forth in this section, as well as the implementing standards contained in this part and in supplemental agency regulations.

(b) General principles. The following general principles apply to every employee and may form the basis for the standards contained in this part. Where a situation is not covered by the standards set forth in this part, employees shall apply the principles set forth in this section in determining whether their conduct is proper.

(1) Public service is a public trust, requiring employees to place loyalty to the Constitution, the laws and ethical principles above private gain.

(5) Employees shall put forth honest effort in the performance of their duties.

(6) Employees shall not knowingly make unauthorized commitments or promises of any kind purporting to bind the Government.

(14) Employees shall endeavor to avoid any actions creating the appearance that they are violating the law or the ethical standards set forth in this part. Whether particular circumstances create an appearance that the law or these standards have been violated shall be determined from the perspective of a reasonable person with knowledge of the relevant facts.

(c) Related statutes. In addition to the standards of ethical conduct set forth in this part, there are "Conflict-of-Interest" statutes that prohibit certain conduct. Criminal "Conflict of Interest" statutes of general applicability to all employees, 18 U.S.C. §§ 201, 203, 205, 208, and 209, are summarized in the appropriate subparts of this part and must be taken into consideration in determining whether conduct is proper. Citations to other generally applicable statutes relating to employee conduct are set forth in subpart one [I] and employees are further cautioned that additional statutory and regulatory restrictions may apply generally or as employees of their specific agencies. Because an employee is considered to be on notice of the requirements of any statute, an employee should not rely upon any description or synopsis of a statutory restriction, but should refer to the statute itself and obtain the advice of an agency ethics official as needed.

As to the restrictions on "Conflicts-of-Interest" during government service, only section 208 is illuminated by formal regulations, which are found in the Code of Federal Regulations [CFR]. 5 CFR § 2635 and in 5 CFR Part 2640, which involves: statutory prohibition; particular matter; personal and substantial participation; and direct and predictable effect.

I argued that Eric Holder joined president Obama's presidential campaign as senior legal advisor and also served as one [1] of three [3] members on Obama's Vice-Presidential Selection Committee who selected Joseph R. Biden. In December 2008, then President-elect Obama asked Eric Holder to serve in his Cabinet as the U.S. Attorney General.

Mr. Holder was appointed by president Obama and now serves as the United States Attorney General; is the head of the United States Department of Justice and United States Attorney General's Office. Eric Holder is paid by the United States Government and reports directly to president Obama. Eric Holder has a direct financial interest in that he draws a salary based on his position as United States Attorney General.

Furthermore, the conflict goes beyond financial. The United States Attorney General is the Chief Law enforcement officer of the Federal Government, represents the United States in legal matters, and gives advice and opinions to the President of the United States.

My *Qui Tam* action was against our now president based on the salary and expenses drawn when he served as the United States Senator from Illinois by false and fraudulent means. If I would have been allowed to litigate this case, there was a great potential that it would affect Obama's Presidential position.

If the U.S. Attorney General, his staff and Office, including the United States Department of Justice are not conflicted out, then justice will never be served. If Mr. Holder had allowed the action to go forward, he was at great risk of losing his position, which is a financial interest, as he would lose his government pay. U.S. Attorney General Holder is aware of this and for this reason will never allow a *Qui Tam* action which bears the name Barack Hussein Obama to go forward. Any involvement by U.S. Attorney General Eric Holder and/or any of his staff, which he over-sees in this *Qui Tam* case, are clear violations of the Code of Federal Regulations and the United States Codes.

Despite my hard work and valid arguments, Judge Roberts denied my Motion for Reconsideration. At that juncture, I was deciding whether or not it would be beneficial to appeal this case.

At that time, I had two [2] other cases pending. See *Berg v. Obama, et al.*, U.S. District Court, Eastern District of Pennsylvania, Case No. 2:09-04083-RBS was assigned to Judge R. Barclay Surrick and *Hollister v. Soetoro, et al.*, U.S. District Court, District of Columbia, Case No. 08-cv-02254 and assigned to Judge James Robertson.

This case would have exposed or cleared Obama:

This case, but for the obvious Conflict-of-Interest, would have been the deciding factor in resolving the "natural born," "naturalized" or "illegal alien" issue regarding Obama/Soetoro because of two [2] things:

1. I had "Standing," or the right to bring this type case, *Qui Tam*, as the United States Supreme Court ruled that the person bringing the lawsuit, the *Relator*, in this case, me, has "Standing"; and

2. The information filed or gathered by the Government relating to its decision whether to intervene has been held non-exempt from disclosure. In *United States ex rel. Mikes v. Strauss*, 846 F.Supp. 21 (S.D.N.Y. 1994) the Court denied the Government's Motion to retain the documents filed in relation to the Government's investigation of a *Qui Tam* Complaint under "seal."

However, because of the Conflict-of-Interest and the Judge's decision not to have any input in the decision of the case, the government did not produce any of the documents which were gathered by the government relating to its decision whether to intervene. The entire handling by the United States Attorney General's Office and the United States Department of Justice was unjust.

The Judge, even if he was not going to have input, he should have required the government by these two departments, U.S. Attorney General's Office and the U.S. Department of Justice, to produce the documents which they gathered relating to their decision.

Because of the Conflict-of-Interest by Attorney General Eric Holder I feel that the order came down from him not to seek any of the documents which were required to be gathered and reviewed to be presented to the Court.

Think about it, if there was no input which must have occurred from Eric Holder or one of his top assistants, then the two [2] agencies would have reviewed the documents I presented and did some research on their own and then they would have had to produce these documents to say why they were not proceeding in this case. The Conflict-of-Interest prevented the gathering of appropriate documents because if they were, then this issue would have been resolved whether Obama was "natural born" or "naturalized" or as I believe, an "illegal alien."

What a tragedy that our government with an opportunity to resolve this issue one way or the other, did not do so to protect president Obama.

What a disgrace!

This matter should be reviewed by appropriate government individuals in our government and our Free Press to resolve this issue once and for all.

CHAPTER VIII

The Case of HOLLISTER V. SOETORO, et al

Military Colonel subject to "lifetime recall" by the President
Wanted to know if Obama "Constitutionally Eligible"
Filed December 31, 2008

A decision was made by Ms. X, another attorney and me to file an action on behalf of Col. Gregory S. Hollister, a retired Military Colonel who was subject to "lifetime recall" by the President of the United States. Mr. Hollister is referred to as the Plaintiff.

It was decided to file an Interpleader action asking the Court to find Barry Soetoro a/k/a Barack H. Obama "Constitutionally Eligible" to serve as the United States President or find him "Constitutionally Ineligible" to serve as the President of the United States.

Mr. Hollister was in a particular position, he was young and therefore, at risk of being recalled into the military by the President of the United States and he was unsure if Barack H. Obama's Orders will be legal Orders he was sworn to uphold or illegal Orders he was sworn to disregard. Without having the correct legal answers to the "Constitutional Eligibility" of Barack H. Obama to serve as the President, Mr. Hollister was at grave risk of multiple lawsuits; losing his Military retirement pension; and being Court Martialed and jailed for making the wrong decision on how to treat any Order issued by Barry Soetoro a/k/a Barack H. Obama.

We came up with the pleadings and idea to file Interpleader and worked extremely hard on drafting the lawsuit. The suit was filed December 31, 2008 before the Inauguration of Barack H. Obama as our sitting and acting president. In addition, neither the other attorney nor I were admitted in the United States District Court, District of

Columbia to practice law and therefore, we needed an attorney admitted to the United District Court for the District of Columbia to sponsor us *Pro Hac Vice*. *Pro Hac Vice* is when you have an out-of-state attorney wishing to appear in a case in another jurisdiction in which they are not licensed. The attorney must have another attorney licensed in the jurisdiction in which they are asking to appear and be admitted to sponsor them. A motion is then made to the Court requesting permission, called *Pro Hac Vice*, for the out-of-state attorney to practice before the Court.

Attorney John D. Hemenway agreed to sponsor both attorney's in the Hollister Case. At the time of the filing of the Complaint a Motion to Appear *Pro Hac Vice* was filed. The problems began with the initial filing of the Complaint. The United States District Court for the District of Columbia Clerk demanded that a Motion for Leave to File an Interpleader action be filed with the Complaint. This is not a normal request when filing a complaint. Ms. X spoke to the Clerk and disagreed with the requirement of a Motion for Leave.

In an attempt to resolve the issue, John D. Hemenway, Esquire, local Counsel sponsoring the other out-of-state attorney and I for Mr. Hollister went to the Court and asked to see the Judge who would be assigned to Mr. Hollister's Complaint. In fact, the Clerk not only refused Mr. Hemenway access to the Judge, she refused to state who the Judge assigned would be.

Counsel for Mr. Hollister complied with the Clerk's demands in order to protect Mr. Hollister's rights.

Ms. X drafted a Motion which all three [3] attorneys reviewed and agreed upon. The requested Motion for Leave was filed and Mr. Hollister's Complaint was accepted. The case was given Case No. 08-cv-02254 and assigned to Judge James Robertson.

Counsel for Mr. Hollister also filed a Motion Requesting an Order Shortening Time for Barry Soetoro a/k/a Barack H. Obama and the other Defendants to Respond to Mr. Hollister's Complaint and the Motion for counsel to appear *Pro Hac Vice*. The Court issued the Summons to Barry Soetoro and Joseph R. Biden.

Defendants, Barry Soetoro a/k/a Barack H. Obama and Joseph R. Biden were served with Mr. Hollister's Interpleader Complaint and all Motions on January 6, 2009. The Proof of Service was filed with the Court on January 14, 2009.

On January 26, 2009, Robert Felix Bauer, Esquire of Perkins and Coie, Entered his Appearance representing both Barry Soetoro a/k/a Barack H. Obama and Joseph R. Biden. On this same date, Mr. Bauer also filed a Motion to Dismiss.

Ms. X was skeptical as she had stated before the filing of the Interpleader Complaint that she felt another cause of action should be added; that being a *Bivens* action. The *Bivens* case was similar to state actions under 42 U.S.C. §§1983, 1985 and 1986 claims which are civil rights claims against State Governmental entities and employees.

Bivens is the same theory except the causes of action are against Federal Governmental entities and employees.

Interpleader shifts the burden of proof upon the Defendants in a case. Interpleader is where there is potential damage that could subject the Plaintiff to multiple suits. Mr. Hollister to be subject to Presidential Recall was in that situation. If Barry Soetoro a/k/a Barack H. Obama recalled Mr. Hollister to military duty, he was unsure whether to treat the Order as lawful or unlawful. If Mr. Hollister made the wrong choice he could be subjected to Court Martial; loss of pension; loss of respect; multiple lawsuits; etc. Thus, he wanted the Court to decide whether or not any Orders issued by Barry Soetoro a/k/a Barack H. Obama were legitimate and lawful Orders or illegitimate and unlawful Orders.

Remember, military personnel's oath is to the U.S. Constitution.

On February 4, 2009, the Court entered an Order denying Mr. Hollister's Motion to File an Interpleader Complaint and Deposit Funds with the Court. This Court found said Motion to be frivolous. Again, this is the Motion this Court's Clerk made Plaintiff's counsel file in order to file Plaintiff's Complaint. Also, the Court Denied as Moot Mr.

Hollister's Motion to Shorten Time for the Defendants to Respond to the Complaint and held the two [2] pending Motions for Philip J. Berg, Esquire and Lawrence J. Joyce, Esquire to be entered *Pro Hac Vice* in abeyance until the Court has had the opportunity, in open Court, to examine their credentials, their competence, their good faith and the factual and legal bases of the Complaint they have signed. **_Note:_** At that time, I had been admitted *Pro Hac Vice* in other jurisdictions and never was my Motion for *Pro Hac Vice* held in abeyance, nor had any Hearing taken place.

Pursuant to the Federal Rules of Civil Procedure, Rule 15, a party may amend their complaint once as a matter of right before any type of responsive pleading is filed. In other words, if no one has answered the Complaint, then the Plaintiff, in this case, Mr. Hollister, can amend his complaint without leave of Court or permission from any of the Defendants. A Motion to Dismiss is not a responsive pleading. For this reason, Ms. X drafted a First Amended Complaint adding the _Bivens_ claim; all attorneys' reviewed the First Amended Complaint, made the appropriate changes and filed the First Amended Complaint on February 9, 2009. The filing of Mr. Hollister's First Amended Complaint, by law, made Barry Soetoro a/k/a Barack H. Obama and Joseph R. Biden's "Motion to Dismiss" moot. Unfortunately, the Court did not see things that way.

Two [2] days after the filing of Mr. Hollister's First Amended Complaint, on February 11, 2009, Judge James Robertson entered a very prejudicial Order that Defendants, Barry Soetoro a/k/a Barack H. Obama and Joseph R. Biden, did not need to respond to Mr. Hollister's First Amended Complaint.

Judge Robertson further Ordered Mr. Hollister to Respond to Barry Soetoro a/k/a Barack H. Obama and Joseph R. Biden's Motion to Dismiss by February 13, 2009. Judge Robertson was aware that the other out-of-state Attorney and I were not on the ECF filing system, as we had not been granted *Pro Hac Vice*. Despite this, Judge Robertson mailed the Order to Mr. Hollister's attorney's knowing they would never receive this Order in time to comply with it. Again, very prejudicial acts by this Judge. Despite this, individuals who agreed with my theories that Barack H. Obama was not "Constitutionally Eligible" to serve as the President of the United States were kind enough to raise the issue of Judge Robertson's February 11, 2009 Order.

Numerous Emails were received from individuals informing of Judge Robertson's Order on February 12, 2009. Ms. X immediately notified the other attorneys and me, of the Order and immediately began responding to Judge Robertson's Order. The issues raised in Mr. Hollister's Opposition to Barry Soetoro a/k/a Barack H. Obama and Joseph R. Biden's Motion to Dismiss included the facts that Mr. Hollister plead in his Complaint:

That he is a retired Military Officer subject to Presidential Recall; and Mr. Hollister had taken an Oath to uphold the United States Constitution and defend against all enemies, both foreign and domestic; and Mr. Hollister had a sufficient basis to question Barry Soetoro a/k/a Barach H. Obama's citizenship status, as plead in his Complaint.

Defendants filed their Motion to Dismiss on or about January 26, 2009.

Mr. Hollister filed a First Amended Complaint on February 9, 2009. Mr. Hollister's First Amended Complaint added new information pertaining to the Hawaii Department of Home Lands as well as a new Cause of Action under *Bivens*.

The Honorable Court issued an Order February 11, 2009, which Plaintiff's counsel did not receive from the Court, and did not even receive by any means at all until the evening of February 12, 2009, since counsel have been refused an ECF log-in until they were entered *Pro Hac Vice*. Thus, when documents are electronically filed, Counsel does not receive them electronically. This Court Ordered that "Plaintiff's Amended Complaint [#11] adds nothing to the original Complaint except rhetoric and legal theory and creates no obligation upon the Defendants to respond to it. Nor is the Amended Complaint responsive to Defendants' Motion to Dismiss [#9], opposition to which was due on 2/09/09. Unless points and authorities in opposition to the

Motion to Dismiss are filed by 2/13/09, the Motion will be treated as conceded and granted." Again, Mr. Hollister's counsel did not receive this Court's Order until the evening of February 12, 2009.

In Defendants Motion to Dismiss Counsel for the Defendants state the following on Page 2, footnote 1:

"president Obama has publicly produced a certified copy of a birth certificate showing that he was born on August 4, 1961, in Honolulu, Hawaii." See, e.g., Factcheck.org, "Born in the U.S.A.-The truth about Obama's birth certificate," available at:

http://www.factcheck.org/elections-2008/born_in_the_usa.html [concluding that the birth certificate is genuine, and noting a contemporaneous birth announcement published in a Honolulu newspaper). Hawaii officials have publicly verified that they have president Obama's "original birth certificate on record in accordance with state policies and procedures." See "Certified," Honolulu Star Bulletin, Oct. 31, 2008. This Court can take judicial notice of these public news reports. See *The Washington Post v. Robinson*, 935 F.2d 282, 291 (D.C. Cir. 1991); *Agee v. Muskie*, 629 F.2d 80, 81 n.1, 90 (D.C. Cir. 1980)."

Defendants footnote is not completely accurate. In response to requests from the general public for Soetoro/Obama to produce proof of his citizenship, Soetoro/Obama allowed the Daily Kos to post on their website an image of a Certification of Live Birth with Obama's name on it purporting to be Obama's birth certificate at www.dailykos.com. This same image was also placed on Obama's website, http://fightthesmears.com and on another website located at http://factcheck.org. Obama's website "*fightthesmears.com*" states:

"*Smears claiming Barack Obama doesn't have a birth certificate aren't actually about that piece of paper — they're about manipulating people into thinking Barack is not an American citizen. The truth is Barack Obama was born in the state of Hawaii in 1961, a native citizen of the United States of America.*"

"Next time someone talks about Barack's birth certificate, make sure they see this page."

The website then claims to present "Barack Obama's Official Birth Certificate." This so-called "Official Birth Certificate" is dated 11/01 at the bottom left hand side and the certification number has been blacked out. Further, factcheck.org misleadingly states the "director of Hawaii's Department of Health confirmed Oct. 31 that Obama was born in Honolulu." This is not the case. Dr. Chiyome Fukino's statement that she has "personally seen and verified that the Hawaii State Department of Health has Obama's original birth certificate on record in accordance with state policies and procedures" does not confirm Obama's birth in Hawaii.

Further, the image placed on these websites is of a Hawaiian Certification of Live Birth [COLB] which is provided for children's births in Hawaii as "natural born," as well as births abroad, which have been registered in Hawaii, whether the citizenship status was "natural born" or "naturalized." It should be noted that Maya Soetoro-Ng, Soetoro/Obama's half-sister, was born in Indonesia in 1970. She was born a "natural" citizen of Indonesia. However, her birth was registered in Hawaii as a birth abroad and she is only a "naturalized citizen, not "natural born"; despite this she was issued a Hawaiian Certification of Live Birth [COLB]. Thus, the posting of Obama's purported birth certificate did not prove Obama was a "natural born" citizen.

A Certification of Live Birth is not sufficient evidence to prove one is a "natural born" U.S. citizen. In fact, a Certification of Live birth is not even sufficient evidence of Hawaiian heritage for the Department of Hawaiian Home Lands [DHHL] to secure a land lease for someone.

The other Attorneys and I drafted and agreed to arguments pertaining to our Client's First Amended Complaint. Defendants Soetoro/Obama and Biden filed their Motion to Dismiss Plaintiff's Complaint on January 26, 2009. Plaintiff filed a First Amended Complaint, which Plaintiff was entitled to do. From the time of the filing of Plaintiff's First Amended Complaint, Defendants' pending Motion to Dismiss is deemed moot. *See*: *McAlister v. Potter* (J. Collyer),

570 F.Supp.2d 24, fn.3 (D.D.C., 2008); *Amos v. The District of Columbia* (J. Collyer), Not Reported in F.Supp.2d, 2008 WL 5227177, (D.D.C., 2008); *Catholic Cemeteries of Archdiocese of Washington, Inc. v. Nordlinger Inv. Corp.* (J. Collyer), Not Reported in F.Supp.2d, 2005 WL 525415, fn.#2, (D.D.C., 2005.).

Federal Rules of Civil Procedure, Rule 15(a)(1) states in pertinent part:

Rule 15. Amended and Supplemental Pleadings:

(a) Amendments before trial.

(1) Amending as a matter of course.

A party may amend its pleading once as a matter of course:

(A) Before being served with a responsive pleading; or

(B) Within 20 days after serving the pleading if a responsive pleading is not allowed and the action is not yet on the trial calendar.

According to the District of Columbia Circuit Court of Appeals, Rule 15(a) "guarantee[s] a plaintiff an absolute right" to amend the complaint once at any time so long as the defendant has not served a responsive pleading and the court has not decided a motion to dismiss. *See*: *James V. Hurson Assocs., Inc. v. Glickman*, 229 F.3d 277, 282-283 (D.C. Cir. 2000).

This Court has also recognized that Rule 15(a) guarantees "a plaintiff a right to amend a complaint once at any time before the defendant has filed a responsive pleading." *See*: *Evans v. Chase Manhattan Mortg. Corp.* (J. Collyer), Not Reported in F.Supp.2d, 2005 WL 555411, pg. 2, (D.D.C., 2005.)

The motion filed by Defendants does not constitute a responsive pleading. As the District of Columbia Circuit Court of Appeals has stated, "We have repeatedly clarified that a motion to dismiss is not a responsive pleading for the purposes of Rule 15." *James V. Hurson Associates, Inc. v. Glickman*, 229 F.3d 277, 283, (C.A.D.C., 2000). *See* also: *Confederate Memorial Assn., Inc. v. Hines*, 995 F.2d 295, 296, (C.A.D.C., 1993) ("As a motion to dismiss is not ordinarily considered a "responsive pleading" under Rule 15(a), (citation omitted), appellants could have amended their complaint as of right prior to the court's decision on the motions."). This Court has reached the same conclusion. *See*: _Davis v. U.S.,_ (J. Collyer), Not Reported in F.Supp.2d, 2006 WL 2687018, fn. #1, (D.D.C., 2006). Thus, Plaintiff was entitled under Rule 15(a) to file his First Amended Complaint as a matter of right and therefore, the pending Motion to Dismiss should have been deemed moot.

In _Pure Country, Inc. v. Sigma Chi Fraternity_, 312 F.3d 952 (8th Cir. 2002), the Eighth Circuit decided a case similar to Plaintiff's filing of a First Amended Complaint herein. In that case, Sigma Chi moved to dismiss Pure Country's Complaint and then, while that motion still was pending, Pure Country moved to amend its complaint. The District Court granted the motion to dismiss, and held that the motion to amend thereby was rendered moot. The Court of Appeals disagreed and held, "[t]hat approach, as a procedural matter, was plainly erroneous," id. at 956, and stated that, "[i]f anything, Pure Country's motion to amend the complaint rendered moot Sigma Chi's motion to dismiss the original complaint." Id. Plaintiff herein was entitled to file a First Amended Complaint as Defendants had not answered his Complaint; the filing of Plaintiff's First Amended Complaint was a matter of course. However, just as in Pure Country, the filing of Plaintiff's Amended Complaint herein rendered the Defendants' "Motion to Dismiss" moot.

Regarding the "Standing" issue raised by Barry Soetoro a/k/a Barack H. Obama and Joseph R. Biden, the Defendants, Plaintiffs' Attorneys argued:

Defendants state that the allegations of the Complaint are too speculative for this Court to have jurisdiction. They state that supposedly, Plaintiff Hollister must show: 1.) injury in fact; and 2.) a causal connection between the injury in fact and the conduct complained of; and 3.) a substantial likelihood that the requested relief will be redressed by a favorable decision. Ibid. Such statements demonstrate a lack of knowledge of the fundamentals of Interpleader, however.

In Interpleader, a Plaintiff need not show harm or an immediate threat of harm. As we pointed out in the Complaint, Courts have recognized that all that need be shown is a real, reasonable, bona fide fear of exposure to multiple claims or the hazards and vexation of conflicting claims. *See American Fidelity Fire Insurance Co. v. Construcciones Werl, Inc.,* 407 F. Supp. 164 (D. Virgin Islands 1975). *See* also, *Underwriters at Lloyd's v. Nichols*, 363 F.2d 357 Nichols, 363 F.2d 357 (8th Cir. 1966) (in such circumstances, the court has a duty to allow Interpleader). The Fifth Circuit has even gone so far as to say that no specific demand need have been made on the plaintiff by the defendants for the property in question. [Complaint at ¶ 37]. *See Dunbar v. United States*, 502 F.2d 506 (5th Cir. 1974).

Defendants simply fail to appreciate the fact that Interpleader is for those cases in which the threat of harm is speculative as well as for those cases in which the threat of harm is immediate. This addresses both point one [1] and point two [2] of Defendants' three-part test, since if injury or an immediate threat of injury need not be shown, it would be irrational to require Plaintiff Hollister to establish a causal connection between an injury and the Defendants' conduct.

As for the third part of the Defendants' test, in Interpleader, relief consists of the Court's dispelling of the fear of multiple claims, and of the potential hazards and vexations thereof. Given the fact that the relief we have requested will do precisely that if granted as plead (Complaint at Prayer for Relief A-J, pp. 19-21), there is a substantial likelihood that the requested relief will be redressed by a favorable decision.

Defendants also fail to appreciate the point raised in the Complaint about the significance of *United States ex rel. New v. Perry*, 919 F. Supp. 491 (D.D.C. 1996); aff'd sub nom. *New v. Cohen*, 129 F.3d 639 (D.C. Cir. 1997), cert. den., 523 U.S. 1048, 118 S.Ct. 1364, 140 L.Ed.2d 513. Any argument about Plaintiff Hollister's Complaint alleging things that are too speculative must be considered in light of the fact that by Act of Congress [as construed in *New v. Perry*], if Hollister is recalled to active duty, from that moment on, the Article III

Courts are closed to him under the precedent of this very Court and of the District of Columbia Circuit. Accordingly, this is the only chance which Plaintiff Hollister has to prevent a potentially catastrophic confrontation between himself and his superiors as to what may or may not be an illegal order that he is obligated to disobey, or a legal order which he must obey; and right now, before his reactivation, is the only window of time available to him to straighten this potential conflict out before such a confrontation can happen, with potentially devastating consequences for him and for others. Plaintiff Hollister, we ask the Court to keep in mind, has a present-tense status, right now, of being someone who is subject to a recall order. Thus, the Act of Congress which bars active duty members of the Armed Forces from having access to this Court right now hangs like a Sword of Damocles over Plaintiff Hollister's head. And that is not speculative.

Defendants also cite multiple other cases in support of their Motion to Dismiss, and we asked this Court to consider each of those cases carefully in context in reaching its decision concerning that Motion. For instance, Defendants cite _Rann v. Chao_ for the proposition that a Court is not required to accept inferences unsupported by the facts or legal conclusions that are cast as factual allegations. _Rann_, however, was a case in which the plaintiff continually failed to submit the affidavit that was requested by the Court. _Rann_, 154 F.Supp. 2d 61, 64 (D.D.C. 2001). When and if a situation should arise in the instant case in which Plaintiff Hollister were to be guilty of similar misconduct, perhaps _Rann_ would then apply, but not a moment sooner.

Defendants also rely on _Bell Atlantic Corp. v. Twombly_. (Mot. at 4.) _Twombly_, however, was a case brought under the Sherman Anti-Trust Act, which has its own requirements for the sufficiency of a complaint. _Twombly_, 127 S.Ct. 1955, 1964 (2007). Furthermore, Defendants went so far as to quote _Twombly_ for the proposition that a plaintiff must provide "more than labels and conclusions" and they quoted _Twombly_ for the proposition that the allegations in the Complaint "... must be enough to raise a right to relief above the speculative level." [Mot. at 4.] If, however, the Defendants were to have continued their quotations of the paragraph in _Twombly_ from which they got those two quotes, this Court would have seen that the Supreme Court also said, in that exact same paragraph, the following:

"('Rule 12(b)(6) does not countenance... dismissals based on a judge's disbelief of a complaint's factual allegations'; (a well-pleaded complaint may proceed even if it appears 'that a recovery is very remote and unlikely')." _Twombly_, 127 S.Ct. at 1965 (citations omitted).

Defendants also cite _Shirk v. Garrow_, apparently for the proposition that there is a precedent from this Court (which supposedly might have application to this case) in following _Twombly_. But in _Shirk_ the party who brought a third-party complaint simply alleged the conclusion that a real estate broker was liable to the third-party plaintiff without stating any basis at all for that conclusion, nor was there any basis in the original complaint which the Court could look to in order to find any such basis, either. _Shirk v. Garrow_, 505 F.Supp. 169, 173 (D.D.C. 2007).

In similar manner, Defendants refer this Court to _Smith v. Shimizu_, 544 F.Supp. 2d 15 (D.D.C. 2008); but in _Smith_ this Court said that the plaintiffs' allegations were in fact similar to those of another case which the exact same plaintiffs had filed in this Court, a case in which the allegations had eventually been found by the District of Columbia Circuit to be "fantastic or delusional." _Smith_, 544 F Supp. at 17.

Defendants also ask this Court to look to _Kowal v. MCI Communications Corp_. That was a case in which the District of Columbia Circuit said that a court need not accept inferences in a complaint if the inferences are unsupported by the facts set out in the complaint, and need not accept legal conclusions cast in the form of factual allegations. [Mot. at 4.] But _Kowal_ was a case in securities fraud, and the Court based its dismissal on the grounds that the complaint did not allege the basis of fraud with the particularity required by Federal Rule of Civil Procedure 9(b). _Kowal_, 16 F.3d 1271, 1277-1278 (D.C. Cir. 1994).

Defendants also refer this Court to _Papasan v. Allain_. But in that case, in the very same paragraph to which the Defendants apparently refer, the Supreme Court also noted that the plaintiffs had provided no facts upon which anyone could conclude that the defendants had denied the plaintiffs "a minimally adequate education," which supposedly formed the very foundation of their complaint. _Papasan_, 478 U.S. 265, 286, 106 S.Ct. 2932, 2944, 92 L.Ed.2d 209, 232 (1986).

Now the last issue raised by Barry Soetoro a/k/a Barack H. Obama and Joseph R. Biden, the Defendants, in their Motion to Dismiss was the Plaintiff Failed to State "A Claim Upon Which Relief could be Granted." Standing and failure to state a claim which relief can be granted are typical of Motions to Dismiss in any federal lawsuit. However, I and the other two [2] attorneys properly responded. Our argument included:

In deciding a Motion to Dismiss pursuant to Federal Rules of Civil Procedure 12(b)(6), the Court accepts the factual allegations of the Complaint as true and draws all reasonable inferences therefore in favor of the Plaintiff. _Armstrong Surgical Center, Inc. v. Armstrong County Memorial Hospital_, 185 F.3d 154, 155 (3d Cir. 1999), _Morse v. Lower Merion School District_, 132 F.3d 902, 906 (4d Cir. 1997). In making a determination, the Court must construe the pleading in the light most favorable to the non-moving party. _Budinsky v. Pennsylvania Dept. of Environmental Resources_, 819 F.2d 418, 421 (3d Cir. 1987).

Defendants do more than just insinuate that Plaintiff Hollister's Complaint is nothing more than me, as Counsel, is my own lawsuit in a different form; they actually come right out and say it. Aside from the impropriety of attempting to prejudice Plaintiff Hollister's rights by ascribing to him the efforts of me as a party himself in other suits, Defendants do not even give this Court citation to authority which, in context, supports their contention that Hollister's Complaint states no claim upon which relief can be granted. They first cite an Interpleader case, _Mallinckrodt Medical v. Sonus Pharmaceuticals_. But in _Mallinckrodt_, the plaintiffs actually tried to get this Court either to order the defendants to institute an interference proceeding alleging patent infringement before the U.S. Patent and Trademark Office, or to order the defendants to pursue such a claim in this Court. *Mallinckrodt*, 989 F.Supp. 265, 270 (D.D.C. 1998). The Defendants in the instant case point to no portion of Plaintiff Hollister's Complaint that is similar in that respect, nor could they, for there is no portion of Hollister's Complaint that is so similar.

Defendants next cite to another Interpleader case, *Bierman v. Marcus*, for the proposition that a plaintiff must not be allowed to misuse Interpleader on a mere pretense of adverse claims in order to obtain adjudication of controversies other than entitlement to the fund in question. [Mot. at 7.] But Bierman was a case in which an interpleaded defendant had claimed that he was owed a completely different type of relief [in fact, an antithetical type of relief] than that which was supposedly the basis of the Interpleader claim; the defendant did not claim that he was owed any money, but rather that he had been defrauded, and that the whole agreement between him and the plaintiffs should be voided, rather than be affirmed by the Court's granting him a sum of money pursuant to the agreement. *Bierman*, 246 F.2d 200, 201-202 (3rd Cir. 1957). The Third Circuit also went on to say in *Bierman*,

"In this case it is clear that the plaintiffs did not believe or assert in good faith that there was any danger of Milmar, Inc., claiming the unpaid purchase money. We say this because of a fact not heretofore mentioned in this opinion. At the time Miller and Bierman filed their complaint expressing fear that Milmar, Inc., might claim the purchase price of the shares, they were the sole stockholders of Milmar, Inc., and in complete control of that corporation. ... Thus, when they impleaded Milmar, Inc., they knew that corporation had no claim on them for the purchase price and could not even assert a fictitious claim without their consent." *Bierman*, 246 F.2d at 203 (3rd Cir. 1957).

Aside from the fact that neither Plaintiff Hollister nor his counsel have engaged in such scandalous behavior, once again the Defendants in the instant case, in their Motion to Dismiss, point to nothing in Plaintiff Hollister's Complaint which could support such a comparison, nor could they.

Defendants go on to cite another Interpleader case, _Truck-A-Tune, Inc. v. Re_; this case, however, has substantive similarities to _Bierman_. In _Truck-A-Tune_, before filing suit, the plaintiff had first refused to obey the Order of a Court of the State of New York to turn over to the administrator of an estate a certain Mercedes-Benz automobile. _Truck-A-Tune_, 23 F.3d 60, 61 (2nd Cir. 1994). While the proceedings were still underway in the New York Court, Plaintiff Truck-A-Tune filed an affidavit with the Tax Assessor of the Town of Greenwich, Connecticut, stating that Truck-A-Tune had possession of the vehicle and that the owner was deceased. Because the deceased owner had failed to pay personal property taxes on the vehicle for many years, the Assessor filed a petition with the Connecticut Probate Court asking the Court to prevent the car from leaving Connecticut. Ibid. Having thus created that conflict, Truck-A-Tune sought to use Interpleader to obtain an order of a federal court against the defendants from their seeking an injunction in any court against Truck-A-Tune for its failure to deliver the Mercedes pursuant to the Court Order at the earlier date. Ibid. Thus, in _Truck-A-Tune_, as in _Bierman_, the plaintiff had sought to create a conflict where none had otherwise existed in order to avoid the consequences of the law to which the Plaintiff would otherwise be answerable.

And so yet again, in the instant case we see no allegation in Defendants' Motion to Dismiss alleging any basis for thinking that Plaintiff Hollister's Complaint points to similar conduct here, except of course for whatever implications may be present in their own attempt to prejudice Plaintiff Hollister's rights with their reference to me, as counsel, my efforts on my own behalf in another case.

Of course, the above arguments in opposition to Barry Soetoro a/k/a Obama and Mr. Biden's Motion to Dismiss were filed timely which appeared to upset Judge Robertson. Although Counsel for Mr. Hollister were not afforded a sign in and password for the electronic filing system (ECF), they were able to Email their pleadings to the ECF Division of the Court for filing.

Judge James Robertson next issued an Order that Counsel for Mr.

Hollister must Show Cause Why the Defendants, Barry Soetoro a/k/a Barack H. Obama and Joseph R. Biden's Motion to Dismiss should not be granted. Judge Robertson stated Mr. Hollister's Response in Opposition to Barry Soetoro a/k/a Barack H. Obama and Joseph R. Biden's "Motion to Dismiss" could not be read; that it appeared to be blank pages with botanical drawings. Judge Robertson stated either it was a joke which he didn't get or there was an error in its filing. This Order was issued February 25, 2009 and Mr. Hollister was only given until February 26, 2009, one day, to correct it. Again, these Orders were not being emailed to Mr. Hollister's Counsel, but Ms. X luckily learned of this Order on the Internet.

Ms. X immediately went onto Pacer and was able to pull the documents with no problems; and then contacted the Electronic Filing Division of the Court and explained the problem to them. The Clerks in the Electronic Filing Division of the Court did not have any problems accessing the documents. They then transferred Ms. X to the Judge's secretary. Judge Robertson's secretary was not pleasant at all and continued stating she could not pull the filings. Ms. X again contacted the Electronic Filing Division of the Court and they themselves contacted the Judge's Secretary. Judge Robertson finally discharged his Order to Show Cause, however, made the statement that the document was too large for filing and of course, blamed counsel for Mr. Hollister. The Judge, we guess, was unaware of the fact his own Court filed the documents on behalf of Mr. Hollister, the Plaintiff.

It did not matter what argument Mr. Hollister's counsel and Ms. X came up with to show why Mr. Hollister's case should go forward. The Court did not like this case and was determined to get rid of it. The more Mr. Hollister's legal team fought, the angrier the Judge became and he made it known in his ruling granting Barry Soetoro a/k/a Barack H. Obama and Joseph R. Biden's Motion to Dismiss on March 5, 2009.

In Judge James Robertson's ruling he called me and the other out-of-state Attorney **"Agent Provocateurs"**; Judge Robertson made the very prejudicial statement that Barry Soetoro a/k/a Barack H. Obama's candidacy had been tweeted and he, Barry Soetoro a/k/a Barack H. Obama had been fully vetted, which was completely false; that I in essence was using my client, Mr. Hollister, to carry on my own lawsuit; which was completely absurd and among other nasty statements and comments; Judge Robertson even went on the attack of Ms. X. Judge Robertson also issued an Order to Show Cause Why the local Attorney, John D. Hemingway, Esquire, Should Not be Sanctioned. Of course, Counsel for Mr. Hollister appealed Judge Robertson's ruling.

Ms. X, the out-of-state Attorney and I immediately began drafting a response to Judge Robertson's Order to Show Cause on behalf of Mr. Hemenway. Ms. X discovered that the law did not allow a Judge to issue sanctions sua sponte or, on its own initiative, for attorney fees. In other words, the party seeking attorney fees must file their own motion; a Judge on his/her own cannot issue them in the way of sanctions. A couple of the main points being made was Mr. Hollister's Interpleader Complaint was by no means frivolous; Judge James Robertson's ruling was extremely prejudicial and biased; and Judge Robertson was not within the power to issue Sanctions to be paid as Attorney Fees on his own initiative. The argument included:

Under Rule 11(c), a court may impose sanctions either by motion, *See* Rule 11(c)(1)(A), or, on its own initiative, *See* Rule 11(c)(1)(B). Rule 11(c), however, also limits the types of sanctions that may be imposed for violation of the rule as follows:

A sanction imposed for violation of this rule shall be limited to what is sufficient to deter repetition of such conduct or comparable conduct by others similarly situated. ... [T]he sanction may consist of, or include, directives of a nonmonetary nature, an order to pay a penalty into court, or, if imposed on motion and warranted for effective deterrence, an order directing payment to the movant of some or all of the reasonable attorneys' fees and other expenses incurred as a direct result of the violation. Fed. R. Civ. P. 11(c)(2).

As the language indicates, a court may award attorneys' fees under Rule 11 only "if imposed on motion" under Rule 11(c)(1)(A). *See Thornton v. General Motors Corp.,* 136 F.3d 450, 455 (5th Cir. 1998) (per curium). By its terms, the rule thus precludes a court from awarding attorneys' fees on its own initiative. *See* Fed. R. Civ. P. 11 advisory committee's note to 1993 amendments (The revision [to subsection (c] provides that a monetary sanction imposed after a court-initiated show cause order be limited to a penalty payable to the court."); *See* also *Thornton*, 136 F.2d at 455 ("[W]here sanctions are imposed under Rule 11(c)(1)(B) by a district court on its own initiative, ... the award of attorney's fees ... [does not] constitute a valid sanction."); *Johnson v. Waddell & Reed, Inc.,* 74 F.3d 147, 152 n.3 (7th Cir. 1995) (per curium) ("[W]here sanctions are imposed under Rule 11(c)(1)(B) by the district judge on his own initiative, Rule 11(c)(2) provides that payment of sanctions may be directed only to the court as a penalty.")

Although Judge James Robertson did reprimand John D. Hemingway, Esquire, which was under appeal, the Judge did acknowledge that he was unable to sanction an Attorney as Attorney Fees, on his own initiative, without a Motion by the Defendants before him.

When you file an appeal on a case, typically within thirty [30] days, the Court issues a scheduling Order. This is when all your appellate forms are due; you present your questions on appeal; it gives the dates in which the briefs on the merits are due, etc. Unfortunately, since Mr. Hemenway was the local attorney sponsoring me and the other out-of-state attorney to appear *Pro Hac Vice*, the scheduling Order went to John D. Hemenway, Esquire. For whatever reason, Mr. Hemenway did not learn of the scheduling Order until two [2] days before the deadline date for the Appellant, Mr. Hollister, to file his opening Brief on the merits. This was discovered by Ms. X when she went onto Pacer to check the case. She immediately talked to me and the other out-of-state attorney and we all agreed it was best to file a Motion Requesting an Extension of Time to file Mr. Hollister's Opening Brief on the basis that the local attorney never received the Order. All attorneys' discussed the issue and Mr. Joyce, the other out-of-state attorney, spoke directly with Mr. Hemingway regarding the Motion for an Extension of Time. It just is not smart to attempt to file an Opening Brief in an Appeal of this importance within two [2] days. All parties ultimately agreed.

Ms. X prepared a quick Motion and sent it to Mr. Joyce and me for review and approval. The entire time Mr. Joyce was communicating with Mr. Hemenway for his approval through the process. The Motion was then sent to the printer in Washington, D.C. which I had been using for all of my cases. At the last second, Mr. Hemenway decided he wanted his Affidavit changed. This of course was after the printing company had finalized the printing. Mr. Hemenway picked up the copies, made his changes and filed it with the Appellate Court.

The next thing that happened and to all of our surprise, Mr. Hemenway filed an Opening Brief, which was not properly filed, as a joint Brief with Mr. Hollister. It was a bit more complicated as there were two [2] Appeals which had been consolidated: Mr. Hollister's Appeal on the issue of his case dismissal; and Mr. Hemingway's Appeal on the issue of his reprimand. This was a huge concern, when Ms. X found out, she immediately informed Mr. Joyce and me she did not agree and she feared it would not only deem the Motion for an Extension of Time moot, it would muddy the issues.

Mr. Hemenway did not stop there. Mr. Joyce became admitted in the United States Court of Appeal for the District of Columbia. Mr. Hollister, who had come to me first, signed an attorney retainer agreement that Mr. Joyce would be his exclusive attorney until I became admitted in the Court of Appeals for the District of Columbia, at which time Mr. Joyce and I would be his exclusive attorneys. Mr. Hollister agreed and signed the retainer agreement.

Mr. Hemenway acknowledged the fact that Mr. Joyce was Mr. Hollister's exclusive attorney in writing, however, not a few hours later, filed a Motion Requesting Judicial Notice of a Forged Kenyan Birth Certificate and other garbage which had been filed in several of Orly Taitz, Esquire's cases. These documents completely discredited Mr. Hollister's Appeal. Despite this, Mr. Hemenway filed it on behalf of himself and on behalf of Mr. Hollister. The only way Mr. Hemenway could have obtained the word files of Ms. Taitz's garbage, was from Ms. Taitz. Not to mention the fact, the PDF file that Mr. Hemenway had was authored by Ms. Taitz's legal team.

Ms. X immediately told me and contacted Mr. Joyce and informed him of this new filing. Mr. Joyce and I were extremely upset. However, a decision was made to file a simple Motion Setting Aside the Filing from Mr. Hollister. On October 20, 2009, the Appellate Court ruled upon Mr. Hollister's Request for an Extension of Time, granting the extension and resetting the Briefing schedule. This was fantastic news as it allowed us to properly file Mr. Hollister's Opening Brief and protect him regarding his rights if forced to go to the United States Supreme Court.

The case proceeded without me and ultimately, on March 22, 2010 a three [3] Judge panel for the United States Court of Appeals for the District of Columbia Rejected Hollister's Appeal and Affirmed the District Court.

CHAPTER IX

Jealousy Versus Attention

The DRAMA caused by Orly Taitz, Esquire

During all the time spent by Ms. X and I researching the laws and drafting Briefs and Responses in the pending Court cases; radio interviews; newspaper interviews; and media coverage; to learn the truth about our now sitting president Barack H. Obama came the drama involving a supporter of mine and Orly Taitz.

Orly Taitz had become a public figure and made the effort to learn of our president Barack H. Obama's citizenship status and legal constitutional eligibility to serve as President of the United States and Commander-in-Chief of our Military, look like a foolish joke.

It began with Orly Taitz surfacing in or about November 2008. Orly Taitz was calling my office continually seeking for me to return her calls. Meanwhile, Orly Taitz was filing a case in California and was plagiarizing my work and Ms. X's. This case was called the "*Lightfoot*" case, *See Lightfoot v. Bowen*, California Supreme Court Docket No. S16869.

After being denied by the Courts in California, Orly Taitz said she filed an Appeal to the United State Supreme Court; however, the only documents which ever appeared on the United States Supreme Court Docket at that time was Ms. Taitz Request for an Emergency Stay. Ms. Taitz Request for an "Emergency Stay" was denied by a Justice so she made a new application with another United States Supreme Court Justice.

Pursuant to the Rules of the United States Supreme Court, it is typical when you make an emergency request for any type of stay and it is declined by the first Justice, any time you make a second application, it is set for conference. The reason for this is so the United States Supreme Court Justices are not bogged down by being continually papered with filings for the same case. This gives the United States Supreme Court the ability to have all the Justices at one time, deny the application or agree to hear the application. Ms. Taitz obviously did not understand this.

Ms. Taitz put out a press release stating Justice Roberts agreed to hear her "*Lightfoot*" case. This was completely untrue, or as I have expressed regarding Obama, a blatant lie. Justice Roberts set Ms. Taitz second filing for the emergency stay for conference which is normal action of the United States Supreme Court.

Orly Taitz, Esquire went on further, stating and quoting Supreme Court Chief Justice Roberts as saying:

"Hold on, not so fast, there is value in this case, read it. Hawaiian statue 338 allows Foreign Born children of Hawaiian Residents to obtain Hawaiian Birth Certificates; it allows one to get Hawaiian Certification of Life birth based on a statement of one relative only, without any corroborating evidence. If only one Congressman or one Senator presents a written objection, then there has to be a formal investigation by the joint session of Congress and Senate. During this investigation original birth certificate from Hawaii will be subpoenaed. All other pertinent documents will be subpoenaed: Obama's immigration records, any and all passports from Indonesia, Kenya and Great Britain; University enrollment records, showing if he was enrolled in US schools and universities and received financial aid as a foreign exchange student from Indonesia or Kenya. All of it can be subpoenaed and obtained within a day or two."

"Each and every member of US Congress and Senate owes it to 320 million American citizens to do his due diligence and demand all necessary records. When American servicemen are told to risk their lives defending Constitution of this country against all enemies, foreign and domestic, each and every Congressman and each and every Senator can spend a day or two of their time defending this

Constitution, reviewing necessary documents, in order to see if Barack Hussein Obama is a Natural Born Citizen, if he is a citizen at all."

The problem with the above statements you ask?   Justice Roberts never made any of the above statements.

In fact, Justice Roberts did set her Request for an Emergency Stay for Conference, but the request was ultimately denied by all the Justices of the United States Supreme Court during said conference.

Ms. Taitz was also screaming that, "Obama and his thugs" had removed her United States Supreme Court *Lightfoot* Case from the Docket; accusing a United States Supreme Court Clerk of tampering with her cases; illegally taking bribes in the tobacco cases; and also "hacking" her website and *PayPal* accounts.

And Ms. Taitz was literally chasing down two [2] United States Supreme Court Justices, Justice Roberts and Justice Scalia, throwing brief cases full of documents at them and then again claiming they, Justice Scalia and Justice Roberts, had agreed to hear her case. An important factor at that time was missing however, that being Ms. Taitz had never filed a case before the United States Supreme Court or appealed to the United States Supreme Court, she only filed for an Emergency Stay, which is far different and was of course denied.

Meanwhile, Ms. Taitz was taking in large amounts of *PayPal* donations, she then began accusing "Obama and his thugs" of "hacking" her dental website [Ms. Taitz is a dentist and an attorney]; which was a false accusation as it was discovered by Ms. Taitz's own webmaster that Orly Taitz herself had taken down her own dental website; Ms. Taitz response, "I was installing a traffic analyzer."

Ms. Taitz did not stop there. Ms. Taitz made posts and Emailed people all over the World Wide Web asking for Ms. X to call her. When this failed, Ms. Taitz spread all over the World Wide Web derogatory remarks about Ms. X and me.

Meanwhile, at the same time, another person was very busy; seeking attention during a time Ms. X and I were extremely busy with the *Hollister* case and attempting to meet all deadlines affixed upon them; she began calling members of my website blog, accusing them of "hacking" my website; and contacting the Moderators and Webmasters of my website accusing Ms. X of being a liar; deleting my phone messages and Emails that she didn't want me to see; falsely accusing Ms. X of having a long criminal history, etc. She did not do this just telephonically, but done by mass Emailing; she even posted nasty comments about Ms. X and me on my website. Well, she received the attention she was seeking; on or about March 6, 2009, she was completely banned from my website and Ms. X and I cut all ties with her. This did not stop her; she then sent mass Emailing continuing her unacceptable behaviors.

She even went as far as calling me accusing Ms. X of stealing Twelve Thousand [$12,000.00] Dollars a month from me [I wish I had raised that amount of money] to pay a supposed restitution. She told me that Ms. X had been sending out nasty Emails attacking her. However, this too back fired. I went on the radio publicly and made it known, no one had stolen any monies from me. I then told her to send me all the "supposed" Emails Ms. X had sent and I requested Ms. X to do the same regarding the Emails being sent by her. I received over thirty-eight [38] pages from Ms. X and received nothing from this person. What I and Ms. X did not know at the time was that this person had teamed up with Orly Taitz in January 2009.

When Ms. Taitz efforts pertaining to Ms. X and me failed, Orly Taitz, Esquire threatened to take me down and to do so she was going to destroy Ms. X.

This individual and Ms. Taitz's behaviors did not stop. Now, Ms. X was being falsely accused by Orly Taitz and this individual of having a long lengthy criminal record; stealing Twenty-One Thousand [$21,000.00] Dollars monthly from me [again, as I stated above, I wish I had raised that amount of money] to pay her restitution; murdering her sister; having open criminal cases; illegally fundraising and accepting donations for me in violation of her probation; having ties to Barack Obama and his wife, Michelle Obama; having multiple Social

Security numbers; falsely accused Ms. X's husband of being on parole and having credit card accounts set up on my website deterring donations; accusing Ms. X and her husband of "hacking" her website and *PayPal* account; etc. - the list goes on. Ms. Taitz then published Ms. X's full Social Security number, mother's maiden name, place of birth, date of birth, and other private confidential information all over the WWW [world wide web] and sent it out to over one hundred and forty thousand [140,000] individuals and businesses, including internationally. Ms. Taitz even filed false law enforcement reports with the Federal Bureau of Investigation [FBI] in Los Angeles, California and the Orange County Sheriff's Department in California that Ms. X was the same person as her past webmaster and was stealing her *PayPal* donations. Ms. Taitz even falsified a story to law enforcement that she and I fundraised together.

Unfortunately, during this same time, Ms. Taitz was also accusing her past webmaster, a radio show host and other individuals of also "hacking" her website and "hacking" *PayPal* accounts.

Ms. X, other Plaintiffs' and I finally filed a lawsuit against Orly Taitz, this individual and other Defendants for their illegal and unacceptable behaviors which had caused damages to the parties. As a result, Ms. Taitz began accusing Ms. X of tampering with her car; threatening her and her family; murdering (killing) her own sister; and other untrue horrible things.

Ms. Taitz then began "attacking" other attorney's and other individuals. She continued claiming her websites, Email, accounts, etc. had been "hacked" and was being "hacked." Ms. Taitz was calling the mainstream media "brown shirts"; Nazi's; stating they need to be tried for "treason" and "aiding and abetting"; but you know what they say, no bad deed goes unpunished.

Ms. Taitz continued on her destructive behaviors and now was going after Judges. Orly Taitz was posting on her website that the Judges that did not agree with her should be tried for treason, they were being controlled by Obama and his administration, and even went as far as accusing one Judge, Judge Land, Judge in the United

States District Court for the Middle District of Georgia of having investments with Microsoft and Comcast and therefore, had a financial interest in the outcome of her case.

The reality was Judge Land dismissed her first case, _Cook v. Obama, et al_, because the Military withdrew Mr. Cook's deployment orders; and dismissed Orly Taitz's second case, _Rhodes v. McDonald, et al_, because of separation of powers. An Article III Court does not have the jurisdiction or power to interfere with military orders. Judge Land found Orly Taitz's arguments nothing more than speculation and her lawsuits that had been filed in his Court frivolous. Judge Land Ordered that Orly Taitz was to refrain from any further filing of frivolous lawsuits. Instead of listening, Orly Taitz immediately filed a Motion for Reconsideration and a Motion for an Immediate Stay Pending her Appeal. Judge Land did not take kindly to this: Dismissed Ms. Taitz Motions and Ordered Ms. Taitz to Show Cause within fourteen [14] days, which was by October 2, 2009, why she Should Not be Sanctioned Ten Thousand [$10,000.00] Dollars for her filing of frivolous actions.

Orly Taitz never did respond to Judge Land's Order to Show Cause Why she Should Not be Sanctioned. Instead, Orly Taitz filed a Motion to Recuse Judge Land and didn't accuse him of treason this time, but instead accused him of being a Judge, Jury and Prosecuting Attorney regarding the Sanction Issue and falsely claiming Judge Land had conflicts-of-interest because of his investments with Microsoft and Comcast and that he had a financial interest in the case involving her client, Dr. Rhodes. Orly Taitz did not stop there; she then filed another Motion Seeking an Enlargement of Time until the Motion to Recuse Judge Land was heard or until he was able to state how he was able to be the Judge, Jury and Prosecuting Attorney on the issues of Sanctions pursuant to the Federal Rules of Civil Procedure, Rule 11.

Judge Land didn't take this kindly. On or about October 13, 2009 Judge Land Denied Ms. Taitz's Motion to Recuse Him; Denied Ms. Taitz's Request for an Enlargement of Time; and Sanctioned Attorney Orly Taitz Twenty Thousand [$20,000] Dollars and Ordered the Clerk of his Court to forward this Sanction Order and Opinion to the State Bar of California. The State Bar of California mandates all attorneys licensed by them to report sanctions issued upon the attorney over certain dollar amounts.

Meanwhile, Ms. Taitz filed her famous *"Dossier Number Six"* which was nothing more than slanderous statements about Obama, Ms. X and her husband and other individuals. This Dossier is also the document where Ms. Taitz publicized Ms. X's full Social Security number and other private personal identifying information, with the United States District Court, Central District of California, Southern Division in the case of *Barnett, et al v. Obama, et al*, which was assigned to Judge Carter.

I immediately sent a letter to Judge Carter regarding this "Dossier Number Six" which contained all kinds of personal information about Ms. X including her Social Security number. I informed Judge Carter there was a pending civil suit against Orly Taitz for the distribution of Ms. X's Social Security number, mother's maiden name, date of birth, place of birth and other private information. I requested Judge Carter to "seal" the information, as it did not have anything to do with the case before him and Orly Taitz had simply used his Court to further her publication of Ms. X's private confidential information. Judge Carter did more than that. Judge Carter made it clear he normally did not entertain letters from third parties; however, in this case he was going to... based on the confidential private information pertaining to Ms. X and her husband. Judge Carter issued an Order "sealing" Ms. Taitz's filing and Ordered Ms. Taitz to retract all Social Security numbers, dates of births and other personal identifying information. Judge Carter further ordered Orly Taitz to refile the redacted documents on or before October 2, 2009. Ms. Taitz did comply and ironically didn't bother refiling her "Dossier Number Six" as it never pertained to the case before Judge Carter.

On October 5, 2009, Orly Taitz had a Hearing before Judge Carter in the *Barnett, et al v. Obama, et al* case. Pending before the Court was Obama and the other Defendants Motion to Dismiss; another

Attorney's Motion for Severance from Orly Taitz; and Discovery. Judge Carter made it clear he was concerned he did not have subject matter jurisdiction and he was not convinced the Plaintiffs in the case had standing.

Orly Taitz had a crowd of spectators in Judge Carter's Courtroom. Judge Carter made it clear in Court that Orly Taitz had her supporters calling his chambers, which created forty [40] to one hundred [100] calls per day his chambers was receiving. Judge Carter made it known to Orly Taitz that her supporters calling him was not going to sway his decisions in the case. Judge Carter stated this is America and I am American, in our Courts we listen to both sides and rule on the merits. Judge Carter then asked Orly Taitz to stop having her supporters call him. Judge Carter then looked at the audience and stated to the audience that their cheering and clapping was not going to sway his decision on the case either.

Judge Carter took the matters under submission and ultimately ruled dismissing the case.

The one good thing that did come out of Ms. Taitz and Mr. Kreep's California case is the reasoning of Judge Carter. In particular, the Judge posed a hypothetical event wherein Arnold Schwarzenegger was on the ballot. It is well known that Arnold Schwarzenegger is not a natural born United States citizen and therefore, ineligible to run for or serve as President of the United States. The Government and Judge Carter all agreed that had a case been brought before the election and/or inauguration that the person would have "standing" and the Court could intervene. This was critical to the case of _Berg v. Obama, et al_, United States District Court, Eastern District of Pennsylvania, Case No. 08-cv-04083 which was currently before the Third Circuit Court of Appeals. This was the entire argument presented by me in my filings of August 21, 2008, before the Court of Appeals, that eventually Affirmed the District Court, meaning they agreed with the Lower Court.

With all of Ms. Taitz's propaganda, it caused the general public, unaware of the issues surrounding the citizenship issue of Barry

Soetoro a/k/a Barack H. Obama and his eligibility, or lack thereof, to serve as President of the United States, to consider this a laughing joke instead of a true legal question.

Meanwhile, Orly Taitz has had a lot of media coverage and has become the laughing stock. In so doing, she has single handedly destroyed, what the media calls the "Birther Movement" and has labeled all parties seeking to learn the truth about Barack H. Obama and his Constitutional Eligibility to serve as President of the United States and Commander-in-Chief of the Military, as nuts. If this is what Orly Taitz has been contracted and paid to do, discredit the questions into Barack H. Obama's Constitutional Eligibility and citizenship status, she has done a magnificent job.

If Orly Taitz truly believes she is doing a good job, then psychiatric therapy might be in order for her.

I discuss Orly Taitz further in the next chapter titled: "Orly Taitz, Esquire, Involved to Ruin Efforts to Expose Obama"

Philip J. Berg

CHAPTER X

Orly Taitz, Esquire

Involved to Ruin Efforts to Expose Obama

In my opinion, one of the biggest problems exposing Obama for the last five and three-quarter [5 ¾] years has been and is Orly Taitz, Esquire.I first met Orly Taitz on December 8, 2008 at the National Press Club in Washington, DC where we both spoke about Obama. Robert Schulz of "We the People Foundation" sponsored the event.

Shelli Baker, the host of AM radio's Morning Song, spoke about her theory that tied Obama to Arab sheiks and world government. She said, "I would be willing to testify that, indeed, the media has been corrupted by foreign oil money."

I said, "This is the largest hoax in 200 years. Obama knows where he was born. He knows he was adopted in Indonesia. Obama places our Constitution in a crisis situation, and Obama is in a situation where he can be blackmailed by leaders around the world who know he is not qualified."

I criticized the press… "You guys have been traveling with him for two years!" [and as the press noted, Berg said, 'white knuckles gripping the podium'] "You guys have access. Someone could stand up and say where is your birth certificate? What's your status in Indonesia?'

Ms. Taitz contacted my office immediately and asked me to sponsor her for admission to the United States Supreme Court. I turned her down because one of the requirements is that you know an individual for at least one [1] year; a factor that I could not confirm.

From the time I refused to sponsor her, Orly Taitz, Esquire, decided to "take me down." She decided to do it by going after Ms. X from that day forward. Orly Taitz to this day continues her revenge against Ms. X, me and several other people.

Question: Why take me down?

The only reason would be because I was untouchable and believable.

Everyone says it was and is... a right wing conspiracy against Obama. Well, I blow that theory out the door because I have been and still am a lifelong Democrat.

Next, the question comes up is why would a Democrat sue a Democrat?

The reason is that I believe and stand by the fact that the U.S. Constitution is more important than any political party.

I have been on more than 2,000 radio appearances; it invariably comes up that I must be a racist. No... I am far from racist.

"I am white, Jewish, and a paid-up Life Member of the NAACP." Therefore, I state, "I am the best individual to proceed against Obama."

So, again... why *take me down?*

I believe that Orly Taitz has been... and is on someone's Obama support payroll or benefit list. It could even be Obama himself, George Soros, or some other individual.

It takes only a quick review of all the cases Orly Taitz, Esquire has been involved with, to ascertain that she maintains only one overriding position. And that is... Orly Taitz has done everything in her power to negate, diffuse, refute all efforts to expose and fully disclose Obama.

Orly Taitz, Esquire of course would publicly deny this and say otherwise. Nevertheless, case-by-case she has said and done many unconscionable things to the detriment of her clients and to the movement to expose Obama.

Orly Taitz, Esquire has filed documents improperly, including documents with incorrect information; argued positions that have irritated judges; received sanctions against her; and issued press releases with misinformation.

Additionally, Orly Taitz, Esquire tracked down and attended two [2] separate functions where two [2] U.S. Supreme Court Justices spoke and specifically, asked them questions which were "ex-parte" and therefore, if one of her cases ever appeared before the U.S. Supreme Court, these Justices, who could be favorable, would have to recuse themselves because of the prior "ex-parte" contact by Orly Taitz, Esquire.

March 9, 2009: Taitz confronted and raised questions about Obama in Los Angeles, California to U.S. Supreme Court Justice Antonin Scalia; and March 14, 2009: Taitz confronted and raised questions about Obama at the University of Idaho to U.S. Supreme Court Chief Justice John Roberts.

During this exchange, Taitz criticized U.S. Supreme Court Clerk Danny Bickle and said her case was taken off the Dockets; both statements unsubstantiated.

I could list case after case to substantiate my statements.

One such case was *Rhodes v. MacDonald*, Middle District of Georgia, No. 4:09-cv-106, where the United States Supreme Court on or about August 16, 2010 allowed to stand a ruling where Orly Taitz, Esquire was fined Twenty Thousand [$20,000] Dollars on October 13, 2009 in a case that questioned Obama's U.S. citizenship.

Federal Judge Clay Land of the Middle District of Georgia heard the case of Capt. Connie Rhodes, an Army physician from Columbus, Georgia who protested her pending deployment to Iraq. Orly Taitz, Esquire had argued in Court the deployment was illegal because Obama had no authority to act as commander-in-chief since he was unconstitutionally serving as president.

[When I first heard about this case, I knew that Orly Taitz had given wrong information to Capt. Connie Rhodes, as Obama had no direct connection to the Orders to Capt. Rhodes. By contrast, I had filed a case in federal court in the United States District Court for the District of Columbia, Washington, DC, *Col. Gregory S. Hollister v. Barry Soetoro a/k/a Barack H. Obama and Joseph R. Biden*, Case No. 08-cv-02254, where a retired officer was on Presidential recall that could have ordered him back to duty by the President of the United States.]

A Motion for a Restraining Order was ultimately rejected by Judge Land. Orly Taitz, Esquire then filed for a Rehearing and publicly labeled the ruling an "act of treason." Capt. Rhodes later said the second motion that also was rejected was filed without her consent. Judge Land then ruled the lawyer [Taitz] had filed "frivolous" litigation, had abused the civil judicial process and fined her. Judge Land wrote about Orly Taitz, Esquire:

"Counsel's pattern of conduct conclusively establishes she did not mistakenly violate a provision of law. She knowingly violated Rule 11 [of the Federal Rules of Civil Procedure]. Her response to the court's show cause order is breathtaking in its arrogance and borders on delusional."

Judge Land issued a Rule to Show Cause to Orly Taitz, Esquire to Respond Why he Should Not Impose a Fine of Ten Thousand [$10,000] Dollars to her. Orly Taitz, Esquire's Response was such an insult to Judge Land that he increased the fine to Twenty Thousand [$20,000] Dollars. Taitz appealed to the Eleventh Circuit Court of Appeals who affirmed and ultimately, the U.S. Supreme Court rejected her appeal. This was the type of case/action that Orly Taitz, Esquire continually has done to hinder the true purpose to expose Obama.

The facts are clear... Orly Taitz, Esquire's primary goal was to raise money for herself and make a mockery of all efforts to expose Obama for the fraud he is.

Why was Orly Taitz, Esquire always on radio and TV?

Easy answer: Orly Taitz, Esquire made such a fool of herself, which in turn undermined the legitimate efforts to expose Obama; the left media wanted her on.

One example was her appearance on MSNBC in August 2009. Orly Taitz, Esquire made a complete fool of herself. David Shuster and Tamron Hall [the talk show hosts] recorded the interview. It is available on the internet. Alex Koppelman in an article called "Birther leader Orly Taitz loses it, live on MSNBC" on salon.com on 08/03/2009, "..., but even I'm more than willing to admit that on my best day I can never be as, um, entertaining as Taitz was." And Koppelman continued:

"The segment was, from the very beginning, a train wreck. It started with Taitz asking how much time she'd be given to respond - not exactly the kind of question anchors likes to get, as it means you're eating in to the time scheduled for your segment – and spiraled swiftly downward from there, with Taitz calling host David Shuster a "Brownshirt"…" and Koppelman continued:

"…I think this interview served a purpose, as Taitz did a fair amount of damage to her cause all by herself. Anyone who was on the fence and watched the interview could not possibly come away from it thinking she's credible."

And Jason Linkins of Huffington Post on 08/03/2009 in an article titled "Orly Taitz Melts Down On MSNBC" said in part regarding the same appearance,

"…Taitz came on, speaking as if in a panic, presaging her answers with complaints about CNN, referring to David Shuster as a 'brownshirt,' and making oddball claims about how 85% of Americans think Barack Obama was not properly vetted."

"Anyway, this is like Shuster and Hall attempting to interview an angry Fraggle."

Another article about an Orly Taitz appearance on TV: Lawrence O'Donnell and Birther Orly Taitz Have Wild Shout fest About Obama (VIDEO) The Huffington Post | By Jack Mirkinson
Posted: 04/28/2011 7:18 am EDT Updated: 06/28/2011 5:12 am EDT

"Lawrence O'Donnell had a wild, high-decibel, nearly incomprehensible interview on his Wednesday program with so-called "birther queen" Orly Taitz, at whom he grew so enraged that he cut the interview short halfway through.

O'Donnell had brought Taitz on in the wake of president Obama's release of his long form birth certificate.

O'Donnell wanted to see if Taitz would finally admit that her doubts about Obama's citizenship were false. Taitz, however, had other plans, and began holding up what she said was a copy of Obama's Selective Service papers and accusing him of committing Social Security fraud.

In response, O'Donnell began shouting over and over again, "will you talk about his birth certificate?!" Taitz, no stranger to television hosts shouting at her, continued implacably, not letting O'Donnell's fury interrupt her. Finally, O'Donnell simply ended the interview. "All right, that's it," he shouted. "Get her out of here. Get her off this show!"

Turning to the camera, he addressed the viewers. "Look, she's crazy," he said. "I invited a crazy person on this show to see if the crazy person... could say something responsive, something human, to the document that was released today... and she wants to play with all of her other kid's toys."

There are so many other appearances by Orly Taitz that has undermined the efforts of others and yes, my efforts to expose the real fraud of Soetoro/Obama.

CHAPTER XI
Benghazi & ObamaCare

The Issues that will Bring Obama Down

Obama should never have been elected President of the United States. Numerous facts and documentation prove he is not "Constitutionally Eligible" to be President. I believe he is not even a U.S. citizen and therefore, his term as United States Senator from Illinois was illegal as a requirement for that office is that you are a citizen of the United States. However, Obama was elected two [2] times to be president.

BENGHAZI:

Benghazi, Libya should have been the issue to bring Obama down. Benghazi is to Obama what Watergate was to President Nixon. Watergate was a break-in and Nixon eventually resigned because of the cover-up. **Benghazi is a major "Cover-up."**

Benghazi, that occurred on 09/11/2012, is one thousand [1000] times worse than Watergate. No one died in Watergate. Benghazi resulted killing "our" U.S. Ambassador Chris Stevens and three [3] other U.S. citizens: Information Specialist Sean Smith, and Former Navy SEALs Ty Woods and Glen Doherty. It is now known that president Obama knew that it was a terrorist attack within several hours of the attack/murders that took place in Benghazi.

Secretary of State Hillary Rodham Clinton spoke with president Obama on the evening of 09/11/2012.

Also, by way of an article on Personal Liberty Digest dated April 29, 2014 titled: "Email Shows Blaming Benghazi Attack In 'The Video' Was Obama Administration's Idea" by Ben Bullard states in part;

"... A top Obama administration official strongly urged Susan Rice, National Security Advisor at the time of the Benghazi, Libya terror attack on Sept. 11, 2012, to go before the press and blame the strike on grass-roots Islamist backlash against "The Innocence of Muslims," a satirical YouTube video. ... "

According to a White House Email obtained by Judicial Watch, White House Deputy National Security Advisor Ben Rhodes specifically fingered the video on Sept. 14, 2012 as a talking point Rice should focus on when making the obligatory TV news junket following the attack. Oh, and the Email unswervingly calls what happened "protests," not a terror attack, or even, simply an "attack."

United States Ambassador to the United Nations Susan Rice was sent out the following Sunday, September 16, 2012, to five [5] major TV networks to spin that the attacks were because of an internet video.

HOWEVER, more significant is the fact that Obama himself, on two [2] occasions blamed Benghazi on the internet video.

Seven days after September 11, 2012, on September 18, 2012, Obama is on the Late Show with David Letterman, and 26:31 minutes in his interview with Letterman states the attack was from the video released about the Prophet Muhammad and the extremists and terrorists use it as an excuse to attack. **This is a "cover-up" and "lie";** and Fourteen [14] days after the attack, yes, **fourteen [14] days after the attack, on September 25, 2012, Obama addresses the United Nations** in New York City and five [5] times, yes, **five [5] times, in his speech, Obama blames the attack on the internet video. This is a massive "cover-up" and lie.**

If Benghazi is not a "cover-up" then the word "cover-up" shall be removed from all dictionaries, law books, crimes, etc.

And Secretary of State Hillary Clinton on 05/08/2013 testifying before the U.S. Senate Foreign Relations Committee in the Hart Office Building on the Benghazi Consulate Attack stated in the following exchange with Wisconsin Senator Ron Johnson,

"**Johnson:** No, again, we were misled that there were supposedly protests and that something sprang out of that – an assault sprang out of that – and that was easily ascertained that... that was not the fact, and the American people could have known that within days and they didn't know that.

Clinton: With all due respect, the fact is we had four dead Americans. Was it because of a protest or was it because of guys out for a walk one night who decided that they'd they go kill some Americans. ***What difference at this point does it make?***..." [Emphasis added by me].

Obama and *Hillary* Clinton are confused... they work for us, we don't work for them!

An outrageous statement by Clinton, as their families need to know as well as the American public. We are concerned with the death of Americans who were serving our country.

Another significant statement was put forth on May 30, 2013 by:

Colonel Phil "Hands" Handley, USAF (Ret.) In an article titled: ***"Betrayal in Benghazi"*** who said in part, "The combat code of the US military is that we don't abandon our dead or wounded on the battlefield. In US Air Force lingo, fighter pilots don't run off and leave their wingmen. If one of our own is shot down, still alive and not yet in enemy captivity, we will either come to get him or die trying. Among America's fighting forces, the calm, sure knowledge that such an irrevocable bond exists is priceless. Along with individual faith and personal grit, it is a sacred trust that has often sustained hope in the face of terribly long odds.

The disgraceful abandonment of our Ambassador and those brave ex-SEAL's who fought to their death to save others in that compound is nothing short of dereliction-of-duty. Additionally, the patently absurd cover-up scenario that was fabricated in the aftermath was an outright lie in an attempt to shield the President and the Secretary of State from responsibility.

It is two [2] years since the attack on our compound in Benghazi. The White House strategy, with the aid of a "lap dog" press has been to run out the clock before the truth is forthcoming.

The recent testimonies of the three "whistle blowers" have reopened the subject and hopefully will lead to exposure and disgrace of those responsible for this embarrassing debacle. It would appear that the most recent firewall which the Administration is counting on is the contention "that there were simply no military assets that could be brought to bear in time to make a difference" mainly due to the unavailability of tanker support for fighter aircraft.

This is simply Bull Shit, regardless how many supposed "experts" the Administration trot out to make such an assertion. The bottom line is that even if the closest asset capable of response was half-way around the world, you don't just sit on your penguin ass and do nothing.

The fact is that the closest asset was not half-way around the world, but as near as Aviano Air Base, Italy where two squadrons of F-16Cs are based.

It is time our "leadership" gets its priorities straight and put America's interests first. The end result would be that our U.S. Ambassador Chris Stevens and three [3] others would be alive. Dozens in the attacking rabble would be rendezvousing with "72 virgins" and a clear message would have been sent to the next worthless P.O.S. terrorist contemplating an attack on Americans that it is not really a good idea to "tug" on Superman's cape.

Of course all this depends upon a Commander-In-Chief more concerned with saving the lives of those he put in harm's way than getting his crew rested for a campaign fund raising event in Las Vegas the next day. It also depends upon a Secretary of State who actually understood "What difference did it make?," and a Secretary of Defense who was watching the feed from the drone and understood what the attack consisted of instead of making an immediate response that, "One of the military tenants is that you don't commit assets until you fully understand the tactical situation." YGBSM! [You Gotta Be Shittin' Me]

Ultimately it comes down to the question of those of who gave that order to stand down. Whoever that coward turns out to be should be exposed, removed from office, and face criminal charges for dereliction of duty. The combat forces of the United States of America deserve leadership that really does "have their back" when the chips are down."

...

Thank you, Stephen Al

In God We Trust.

I included the above article by Colonel Phil "Hands" Handley, USAF (Ret.) as his military knowledge and experience gives great weight to his remarks about Benghazi. He reinforces my remarks that Benghazi is a major cover-up for which we must get to the bottom of and those responsible and as Colonel Handley said, "...that coward [who gave the stand down order] ... be exposed, removed from office, and face criminal charges of dereliction of duty. ..."

In an article in "Newsmax" [www.newsmax.com] dated June 3, 2014: by Drew MacKenzie, titled: *"Poll: Most Americans Outraged by VA Scandal; Many Blame Obama"* says in part: **"... The survey also explored the attacks on the U.S. mission in Benghazi**, Libya. [Emphasis added by me]

Democratic leaders have claimed that the special select committee impaneled by the GOP-controlled House to investigate the tragedy was purely a political ploy to damage Obama in the midterm elections and to hurt potential Democratic presidential front-runner Hillary Clinton in 2016.

But the public does not appear to agree with the Democrats, according to the survey, which showed that 51 percent of Americans "support an additional congressional investigation," as opposed to 42 percent who think there's been enough oversight into the attacks that killed four Americans.

And the results were just as bad for Clinton, who was the secretary of state at the time of the Benghazi attacks. Fifty percent of

Americans disapprove of her handling of the siege and its aftermath, while only 37 percent approved.... "

This article by Drew MacKenzie highlights the fact that our U.S. citizens believe we have to look further at what occurred at Benghazi, a position that reinforces what I call for.

And now, over two [2] years later, we still do not know all the facts. WHY? It is a massive **cover-up!** Does that *scare* you?

ObamaCare:

This will be the downfall of Obama, if not causing him to resign, one of the major issues that will cause him to be the worst president in the history of the United States. ObamaCare is a complete disaster; it cannot and will not work and it is time that Obama admits it. Obama's statements on June 15, 2009 at the annual meeting of the American Medical Association that "If you like your doctor, you will be able to keep your doctor. Period." and "If you like your health care plan, you will be able to keep your health care plan. Period." were and are obvious lies.

And how can we forget, the amazing statement from Obama's close confidant, Nancy Pelosi (D – CA), regarding the Affordable Care Act [ObamaCare] that, "... we have to pass the bill so that you can find out what is in it, away from the fog of the controversy. ... "

Obama realizes there are great pitfalls with ObamaCare and what does he do, he keeps making changes; over forty [40+]. Laws are written and established by Congress and Congress has the only authority to change the law and not a president and specifically, in this case, not president Obama.

Yes, we need improvements in our medical delivery services in this country. However, ObamaCare is not the answer; it does not solve the existing problems. Yes, there are several good features, but overall it fails. There are two [2] major problems, one being forty [40] million people who do not have insurance and the other, one of the significant reasons for high medical costs is the fact that more people go to emergency rooms and emergency room costs have skyrocketed.

ObamaCare is the disaster that Obama has created with people losing their healthcare coverage; new policies being issued with high premiums; and the fact that it did not resolve the issue of covering the forty [40] million people that did not have insurance. So it is time that ObamaCare be withdrawn and/or major changes and a concerted effort must come forth to rectify the medical delivery system in our country.

VA:

Major Issue – The VA [Veterans Administration] Scandal that has been uncovered! Think about it – if the VA system does not work, and it doesn't, how can ObamaCare work? It cannot!

Breitbart On 09/26/2014 posted an article titled: **Report: Busted Obamacare Website Cost $2.1 Billion--Twice What White House Claimed** by Wynton Hall.

New data compiled by Bloomberg Government reveal that Obamacare has already cost taxpayers $73 billion, including $2.1 billion on its busted Obamacare website--a figure more than double what the Obama administration originally claimed.

Healthcare.gov Is More Than Double HHS Estimates

Cumulative dollars in millions

■ Estimates ■ Differences between BGOV and OIG estimates

BGOV estimate	Timing differences	Inclusion of paper backup	Inclusion of IRS and other agencies	Records open to interpretation	HHS OIG estimate	Burwell estimate
$2,142	$255	$300	$387	$400	$800	$834

Notes: The chart focuses on differences between the estimates by BGOV and the HHS OIG, which lists the contract records it includes in its count thus allowing for a closer comparison. The BGOV total is based on contracts data through Aug. 20. To avoid overstating the difference between estimates, projected full-fiscal-year 2014 numbers are not used here as they are elsewhere in BGOV's analysis. Sources: Burwell's written response to Senate committee questions (May 8), HHS OIG (Aug. 26), Bloomberg Government proprietary contracts database

"As Bloomberg notes, its "analysis shows that costs for both healthcare.gov and the broader reform effort are far greater than anything publicly discussed" and are "substantially greater than what the Congressional Budget Office (CBO) initially estimated health reform would cost by this point."

The $73 billion figure, however, is a drop in the bucket compared to Obamacare's 10-year spending total. According to the Senate GOP Budget Committee, Obamacare will costs U.S. taxpayers $2.6 trillion over the decade.

Nationally, Obamacare remains unpopular. The Real Clear Politics average of polls finds that "just 41% of Americans support Obama's signature legislative achievement."

This is unbelievable, really not, as Obama has lied about everything regarding ObamaCare. I attribute the enormous expenditure for the website of $2.1 Billion Dollars to incompetence and an initial benefit to Michelle Obama's college classmate, Toni Townes-Whitley as reported in **The Daily Caller** on 10/25/2013, titled, "Michelle Obama's Princeton classmate is executive at company that built Obamacare website."

By Patrick Howley, Political Reporter, an investigative reporter for The Daily Caller, that reads in part:

"First Lady Michelle Obama's Princeton classmate is a top executive at the company that earned the contract to build the failed Obamacare website.

Toni Townes-Whitley, Princeton class of '85, is senior vice president at CGI Federal, which earned the no-bid contract to build the $678 million Obamacare enrollment website at Healthcare.gov. CGI Federal is the U.S. arm of a Canadian company. ... ."

This article by Wynton Hall is explosive as it details the enormous amount of money expended for a failed website and failed program that the Obama Administration has hidden from the American public and Obama continues to promote ObamaCare, a failed program.

After spending the initial $678 million, the website did "not" work and therefore the continued wasting of "our" money to fix the website on a healthcare program, ObamaCare that is not and will not work is unbelievable! As stated above, we have now been advised that the cost was $2.1 Billion Dollars.

Philip J. Berg

CHAPTER XII
Lies – DoubleSpeak

Obama's Entire Life is a Lie

Wow! It is amazing that so many people are now calling Obama a liar about facts that he has related regarding ObamaCare. Yes, it is significant that he lied about the fact that "If you like your doctor, you will be able to keep your doctor. Period." and "If you like your health care plan, you will be able to keep your health care plan. Period." were and are obvious lies.

It should be no surprise that Obama lied about ObamaCare because his entire life is a lie from his birth to the present day. A trail of... lie after lie.

Question: If Obama has nothing to hide, why then are his records sealed?

Obama's records are obviously "sealed" because he is hiding most things about his life and the reason someone hides something is because they are not being truthful. As I stated in 2008 and today, I stand by this statement regarding Obama:

"Obama is a fraud, phony and an imposter and has put forth the greatest 'HOAX' against the United States of America in over two hundred and thirty years."

Obama has told so many lies that I'm not sure where to start and think about it, with so many lies, does Obama know what he is saying because of his "DoubleSpeak."

Obviously, the first lie is where he was born and he continues to relate that he was born in Hawaii when he knows from information given to him that he was born in Mombasa, Kenya, Africa.

More significant is the fact that he was adopted in Indonesia, as evidenced by the books he wrote. His name when he was adopted became Barry Soetoro and I really believe that he has never legally changed his name since then. People remember calling him "Barry" when he attended Occidental College in California. Therefore, his legal name is Barry Soetoro and his nationality is Indonesia. This is confirmed by the school record we have from ***Inside Edition*** that indicates his name is "Barry Soetoro," his nationality is "Indonesia" and his religion is "Islam" that is "Muslim." Obama presented fraud information that he was a United States citizen to become a candidate and thereafter, elected as a United States Senator from Illinois.

Significant are Obama's lies about drugs and sex. I personally spoke with Larry Sinclair at length about his allegations of drugs and sex with Illinois State Senator Barack Obama, yes, our current president. Larry Sinclair has made various statements and appeared at the National Press Club in Washington, DC where he gave a statement and answered questions thereafter. My conversations with Larry Sinclair were on the telephone and recently, on July 4, 2014, I personally met and spoke with Larry. Larry confirmed that he was with State Senator Barack Obama on November 6 and November 7, 1999 during which time Obama purchased for him an eight ball of cocaine with $250 that Larry gave to him; and watched Obama smoke crack cocaine and while doing so Larry did fellatio on Obama on November 6 and again on November 7, 1999 at Larry's hotel when Obama came to Larry's room and knocked on the door.

Can you imagine if a Republican admitted to the use of drugs and having allegations of gay sex? That person would have been destroyed by the press, but Obama was given ongoing free rides, the first when he was never "vetted" before or during his campaign and, as a matter of fact, during his 1st and now 2nd term as president.

In my opinion, the biggest lie with Obama is Benghazi that occurred on 9/11/2012. As I have stated elsewhere in the book, Benghazi was and is one thousand [1000] times worse than Watergate and the resignation of President Nixon, caused by the cover-up. Well, if we don't have a massive "cover-up" of Benghazi, the word "cover-up" should be removed from all law books, crimes codes and dictionaries.

However, it appears that the biggest lie that will live forever attributed to Obama is the lies about ObamaCare. Obama received the award for the biggest lie of 2013 by PolitiFact's 2013 Lie Of The Year regarding his statement that if "you want to keep your doctors you can keep them." His other lie had to be a close second: if "you want to keep your health care plan, you can." ObamaCare will be the end of Obama in many ways: the biggest: "his legacy."

The only legacy that Obama will receive from ObamaCare is the disaster that he has created with people losing their healthcare coverage; new policies being issued with high premiums; and the fact that it did not resolve the issue of covering the forty [40] million people that did not have insurance. As I stated earlier, it is time that ObamaCare be withdrawn and a concerted effort must come forth to rectify the medical delivery system in our country.

At this time I will make a list of various lies from Obama:

In an article in BizPac Review dated December 18, 2013 by John R. Smith titled: "our" U.S. Ambassador Chris Stevens and three [3] other *"Pinocchio Obama's Top presidential lies"*

John R. Smith states: "President Barack Obama seems to be setting a record among U.S. presidents. But it's a record he'd rather keep secret. In this era of ubiquitous cameras capturing everything, Obama may have set a new record for presidential lies.

Turns out that Obama is a man of empty pledges and unkept promises. Yet mainstream media sympathizers or accomplices, with their *'nothing to report here'* have largely let him get away with lies and broken promises by diverting attention to other events, or whitewashing them with soft-ball reporting. What happened to hard-ball reporting?

Let's take a stroll down Obama's liar Lane and see what we find:

'We will close the detention camp in Guantanamo Bay.' Still open.

Philip J. Berg

'If we have not gotten our troops out [of Iraq] by the time I am president, it is the first thing I will do.' *Didn't happen.*

'Today I'm pledging to cut the deficit in half by the end of my first term in office.' Instead, the national debt increased $5 trillion on his watch.

'We've got shovel-ready projects all across the country.' Later, Obama admitted his own lie, saying, 'There's no such thing as shovel-ready projects.'

'We reject the use of national security ... to spy on citizens who are not suspected of a crime.'

We 'will ensure that federal contracts over $25,000 are competitively bid.'

We 'will eliminate all income taxation of seniors making less than $50,000 per year.'

'We are going to work with you to lower your [health care] premiums by $2,500,' and we'll 'do it by the end of my first term as president.'

'I don't take a dime of their [lobbyists'] money, and when I am president, they won't find a job in my White House.' In fact, Obama granted waivers at will, and more than a dozen lobbyists got jobs in the Obama administration.'

'I pledge to preserve, protect and defend the Constitution.' But Obama has ignored the constitutional amendment granting powers not enumerated in the Constitution to the states.

'If you've got a business – you didn't build that. Somebody else made that happen.'

'The sequester is not something that I've proposed. It is something that Congress has proposed.' The truth is that the White House proposed an 'automatic sequester' on July 12, 2011.

'I didn't set a red line [in Syria].' And yet, at a prior news conference, using unscripted language in a statement, he said, 'a red line for us is we start seeing a whole bunch of chemical weapons moving around.'

'It's here that companies like Solyndra are leading the way

towards a brighter and more prosperous future.' After Obama's administration gave the company $535 million, Solyndra and its solar panels went belly up.

To Israel, 'We have not only made sure that they [Iran] have to stop adding additional centrifuges, we've also said that they've got to roll back their 20 percent advanced enrichment ... down to zero.' In fact, the deal allows Iran uranium enrichment of 5 percent.

'Eighty percent of Americans support including higher taxes as part of the [debt ceiling] deal.' However, that same week, a poll by Rasmussen showed only 34 percent supported a tax hike as part of the deal.

'In 2006, America has a debt problem and a failure of leadership. Americans deserve better. I, therefore, intend to oppose the effort to increase America's debt limit.' But as president, Obama has led the charge each year to increase America's debt.

'And let's not forget PolitiFact's 2013 Lie Of The Year: 'If you like your health care plan, you'll be able to keep your health care plan, period. No one will take it away, no matter what ... You can keep your family doctor.'

Love Obama or detest him, the evidence mounts that millions of Americans don't know the man who is their president."

There are many more lies by Obama and the most disturbing fact is that Obama DoubleSpeak's in that he says one thing and does something else. Obama is a total disgrace and embarrassment and Obama really needs help!

Philip J. Berg

CHAPTER XIII

Oprah Winfrey

Philip J. Berg Letters to Oprah Winfrey

What does Oprah Winfrey have to do with my cases? I believed Oprah Winfrey could/would be more concerned about America than party line or race and convince Obama to withdraw as a candidate once she knew the truth and facts. In 2008 I thought she had the respect around the world and would do just that.

So, I wrote two [2] letters to Oprah Winfrey explaining in detail the supporting fact and documentation of my position that Barack Obama was not "Constitutionally Eligible" to be President of the United States. I sent the letters by certified mail so I know they were received. Surprisingly, I received no response from my first letter sent on October 31, 2008

So, I sent a second letter on January 15, 2009 and enclosed a copy of my first letter. That letter contained even *more* facts and details why Barack Obama was not "Constitutionally Eligible." I suggested she should do everything in her power to have Obama withdraw for the benefit of "our" United States of America.

Boy was I wrong! It turned out that Oprah Winfrey was and still is one of the greatest supporters of Obama.

Now fast-forward to 2013, Oprah says; "Obama is being hampered because of racism." *Wow – so wrong!* Obama was elected president for two [2] terms; blacks compromise about thirteen [13%] percent of the United States; so where is racism Oprah? The race card was played because it created a great sound bite and divide to sway the mindset of the undecided or emotional voter base. Sometimes the truth is *scary*.

On November 15, 2013 during an interview with BBC about the

film, *The Butler*, Oprah Winfrey was asked by Will Gompertz, "If president Obama weren't an African-American would he be treated differently?" Oprah responded, "Just the level of disrespect. When the senator yelled out, 'You're a liar.' Remember that? Yeah, I think there is a level of disrespect for the office that occurs in some cases, and maybe even many cases, because he's African-American."

Oprah recanted Republican U.S. Congressman from South Carolina Joe Wilson yelling "liar" while Obama was delivering a speech to Congress in 2009. The fact is... he has proven to be very good at it.

Wilson's remark had nothing to do with Obama as an African-American! What does lying having to do with skin color... nothing! And for people like Oprah, Al Sharpton and Jessie Jackson to play the race bait card is just a cover-up for the incompetent way Obama has governed. Most Americans are smarter than that.

Oprah's words were said with the intent to create a "divisive" racist conflict in order to diffuse the fact that Obama was/is "Constitutionally Ineligible" and to cover-up for his failure of leadership as president.

I have been thinking of drafting another letter to Oprah that raises the question that she was and is involved in the cover-up of Obama and a legal case should proceed against her.

I set forth hereinafter the two [2] letters which I sent to Oprah Winfrey and I look forward to your comments regarding my letters.

Shown below: Letter to Oprah dated November 7, 2008 and Letter to Oprah dated January 19, 2009

ObamaScare

The United States Constitution Requires

that our President be a natural born

citizen of the United States

h

01/19/09: PRESS RELEASE - Berg sends 2nd letter to Oprah, stressing that she is one that can have Obama withdraw his name to avoid damage to racial relations in the U.S. for years to come because when the truth comes out that Obama does "not" meet the "qualifications" for President as Obama is "not" "natural born" we are headed for a 'Constitutional Crisis' by having an 'ineligible' President

(Contact information and PDF at end)

(Lafayette Hill, PA – 01/19/09) - Philip J. Berg, Esquire, the Attorney who filed suit against Barack H. Obama challenging Senator Obama's lack of "qualifications" to serve as President of the United States and his case, Berg vs. Obama, in the U.S. Supreme Court is still pending as well as two [2] other cases, announced today that he wrote a 2nd letter to Oprah requesting her to speak with Obama to withdraw his name before our country is in a Constitutional Crisis as Obama's lack of 'constitutional qualifications' for President. 1st letter was dated November 7, 2008 and the 2nd today, January 19, 2009. [A copy of the two [2] letters are at the end of this Release]

Berg said, "I wrote to Oprah on November 7, 2008 hoping that she would peacefully resolve the issue of Obama's lack of 'qualifications' and thereafter, Obama should withdraw his name before our country enters into a Constitutional Crisis."

"I hoped that Oprah, because of her closeness to Obama and her significant role as a national leader, would review the facts I sent to her, and speak with Obama and then come to a resolution for the best interest of our great nation. I had hoped and still hope that Obama, because he knows he is 'not constitutionally qualified,' should hold a Press Conference and Obama should state that I, as a black African American, received more votes than anyone else on November 4, 2008 for President and on January 8, 2009 the Joint Session of Congress counted the Electoral College votes and announced that I am President-elect, but because of things in my background, I cannot be sworn in as President.

However, apparently Obama is not man enough to state the above!

Accordingly, I told Oprah that I am committed to keeping our efforts going to continue litigation until the truth of Obama being 'not qualified' for President comes out.

The Obama candidacy is the biggest 'HOAX' ever put forth to the citizens of the United States in 230 years.

There is nothing more important than 'our' U.S. Constitution and we will fight on!"

The letters I, Philip J. Berg, Esquire, sent to Oprah follows:

January 19, 2009

Oprah Winfrey
Harpo Studios, Inc.
1058 West Washington Blvd.
Chicago, Illinois 60607

Philip J. Berg

Page   Page 2 of 4

Re: Obama

Dear Oprah:
It is unfortunate that you did not take my suggestion set forth in my letter that I sent to you on November 7, 2008 by FedEx and received on 11/11/08 by J. Craft, Jr. I have enclosed a copy thereof.

I hoped that you would review the issue of Obama's lack of 'constitutional qualifications' with Obama and thereafter, have Obama withdraw his name before our country enters into a Constitutional Crisis. Also, I believe racial relations will be damaged for years to come when the truth of Obama is discovered, that being that Obama is not constitutionally qualified to be President.

I hoped that you, Oprah, because of your closeness to Obama and your significant role as a national leader, would review the information I sent to you, and speak with Obama and then come to a resolution for the best interest of our great nation. I had hoped that Obama, because he knows he is 'not constitutionally qualified.' that he should hold a Press Conference and Obama should state that I, as a black African American, received more votes than anyone else on November 4, 2008 for President and on January 8, 2009 the Joint Session of Congress counted the Electoral College votes and announced that I am President-elect, but because of things in my background, I cannot be sworn in as President.

Accordingly, Oprah, I am committed to keeping our efforts going to continue litigation until the truth of Obama being 'not qualified' for President comes out. The Obama candidacy is the biggest 'HOAX' ever put forth to the citizens of the United States in 230 years.

There is nothing more important than 'our' U.S. Constitution and we will fight on!

Thank you.

Respectfully,

Phil

November 7, 2008

Oprah Winfrey
Harpo Studios, Inc.
1058 West Washington Blvd.
Chicago, Illinois 60607

Personal & Confidential

Re: Obama

Dear Oprah:

URGENT -

I observed how excited you were with the election of Obama.

I am writing to you as an intermediary in hope that a resolution of the following can be accomplished with the least possible negative impact on Obama and our great nation. Many are concerned that we are headed for riots in the streets with injury and death. I hope not.

I am a proud citizen of the U.S.A., an attorney, a Democrat, white, Jewish and a Life Member of the NAACP with no axe to grind.

To me, there is nothing more important than our U.S. Constitution!

Governor Arnold Schwarzenegger has been approached about running for President and he responds, "Amend the Constitution."

I am in litigation against Obama and it is my 100% belief that Obama does "not" satisfy the "qualifications" for President. And the longer the litigation goes forth, the uglier it is going to get.

174

ObamaScare

That is why I am requesting you to step in and resolve this matter, one way or another. I am either right or wrong and Obama either satisfies the "qualifications" or not.

One of my cases is now pending in the United States Supreme Court [Docket # 08-570 with Defendant Obama's response due by December 1, 2008]; another in the U.S. District Court for the District of Columbia; and other attorneys have filed lawsuits elsewhere with many others about to be filed.

The issue: Is Obama a "natural born" citizen? This is one of the three [3] "qualifications" for President: 1) be 35 years of age - Obama is; 2) live in the United States for 14 years - Obama has; and 3) be a "natural born" citizen - Obama is not [for several reasons].

This issue has been discussed for over a year. In an attempt to resolve the issue, in June of 2008 Obama's Campaign Web Site posted a COLB [Certification of Live Birth] indicating that Obama was born in Hawaii. This document had been altered as determined by several experts [and at the bottom it says if there is any alteration, the document is invalid] and described as a forgery.

Please note that Obama has never produced his "birth certificate."

Our investigation has determined that Obama was born in Kenya and then brought to Hawaii where his birth was "registered." If so, Obama would only be "naturalized" and not "natural born."

When one parent is from the United States and one not, one must look at the law in effect at that time. Obama's Mom was from Kansas and Dad was from Kenya. The law says the U.S. citizen must have lived in U.S. for ten [10] years and she did, but five [5] of these years must have been "after" the age of fourteen [14]. Fourteen [14] and five [5] equals nineteen [19], but Obama's Mom was only eighteen [18] - therefore, Obama only "naturalized."

Even if Obama was born in Hawaii, thereafter, he lost his U.S. Citizenship. His parents divorced and Obama's Mom remarried in the United States to Lolo Soetoro from Indonesia. In his book, Obama states that my step-father returned to Indonesia before my Mom and I. When I went to Indonesia, I immediately began school. Indonesia was in turmoil in the 1960's and the only children who could go to school were "natural" children of Indonesia. Obama's step-father either "adopted" Obama or "acknowledged" Obama and he became "natural" of Indonesia. His school record supports this - it is on my web site: obamacrimes.com - it states: Name: Barry Soetoro; Nationality: Indonesia; and Religion: Islum.

Obama attended school from age six [6] to ten [10]. At age ten [10] Obama's Mom sent him to Hawaii to live with her parents. Next set of problems. Did Obama go through U.S. Immigration or just return to Hawaii on the passport he used to go to Indonesia?

If Obama went through U.S. Immigration, he would have been given a "Certificate of Citizenship" that would indicate he was "naturalized" since he had been a citizen of Indonesia. If Obama did not go through U.S. Immigration, then, believe it or not, he would be an "illegal alien" and not eligible to be President or a U.S. Senator from Illinois. Of course, this could have changed if he at some time thereafter gone through immigration, but he would not have status of "natural born."

Another problem, if the above wasn't enough. At age twenty [20] Obama traveled to Pakistan on an Indonesia passport. This was an "overt act" against the United States and would affect his U.S. citizenship, as Pakistan was a restricted nation in 1961 to U.S. citizens.

Based on the above, Obama is "not qualified" to be President.

Another issue, if Obama did not "legally" change his name after leaving Indonesia, his "legal" name today would be "Barry Soetoro."

Hopefully, you will review with Obama and contact me to resolve this before it gets ugly and hopefully, we can prevent riots in the streets.

Philip J. Berg

Phil

For copies of all Court Pleadings, go to obamacrimes.com

For Further Information Contact:

Philip J. Berg, Esquire

555 Andorra Glen Court, Suite 12
Lafayette Hill, PA 19444-2531
(610) 825-3134
(800) 993-PHIL [7445]
Fax (610) 834-7659
Cell (610) 662-3005

philjberg@obamacrimes.com

# # #

Attachments:

File	File size
01/19/09; PRESS RELEASE - Berg sends 2nd letter to Oprah, stressing that she is one that can have Obama withdraw his name to avoid damage to racial relations in the U.S. for years to come because when the truth comes out that Obama does "not" meet the "qualifications" for President as Obama is "not" "natural born" we are headed for a 'Constitutional Crisis' by having an 'ineligible' President	94 Kb

CHAPTER XIV
Glenn Beck

Phil Berg's Picture on Beck's "Blackboard"
Beck called Berg a "Provocateur"

I made Glenn Beck's "Blackboard" for several days, several years ago. I was so significant that Beck even went so far as to call me a "Provocateur." I am a star!

Actually, Beck placing me on his "Blackboard" was condemning me for going after Obama. Beck's goal was to promote issues, to gain viewership that ultimately allowed him to leave Cable TV to go to his own 'For Pay' TV that resulted in Beck making a fortune.

Glenn Beck, on February 17, 2010 included me when he called "birthers," "idiots," and "members of the fringe elements." He called all of us, "the crazy people that don't really like America."

I question Beck's remarks and the reasons for his statements because I said, "I love America and my purpose for pursuing Obama/Soetoro is he is 'Constitutionally Ineligible' to be President and he has and is destroying the United States of America that I love."

I don't know what I did to deserve this recognition, but it shows that I was and still am a major factor in the efforts to expose Obama/Soetoro.

An article in **POLITICO** Titled, *"Glenn Beck recalls 'awful lot of mistakes'"* By TAL KOPAN on 1/22/14, states:

"TV and radio personality Glenn Beck says he regrets some of his time at Fox News, saying he helped "tear the country apart." "I remember it as an awful lot of fun and that I made an awful lot of mistakes," Beck told Megyn Kelly on Fox News on Tuesday. "I think I played a role, unfortunately, in helping tear the country apart."

When asked to reflect on his time at the network by Kelly, Beck said he would be more "uniting" if he could do it all over again. "I wish I could go back and be more uniting in my language," Beck said. "I didn't realize how really fragile the people were. I thought we were kind of a little more in it together.

And now I look back and I realize if we could have talked about the uniting principles a little bit more, instead of just the problems, I think I would look back on it a little more fondly."

Beck had a show on Fox News from 2009 to 2011, when he left the network and launched his Internet-based radio and TV program, what is now The Blaze TV. Beck's time at the network was notable for both the attention and ratings he brought in and the controversy he caused with sometimes inflammatory rhetoric.

All sides said his split from the network in 2011 was relatively amicable. As for his regrets at the network, Beck added that he wasn't making generalizations about Fox. "That's only my role," he said.

Read more: http://www.politico.com/story/2014/01/glenn-beck-fox-news-102464.html#ixzz3E3ZzqiSx"

Perhaps I was part of his mistakes.

CHAPTER XV

Obama Taking Away "our" 1st and 2nd Amendments

Freedom of Speech and Right to Bear Arms

1st Amendment

First Amendment to the United States Constitution

Congress shall make no law respecting an establishment of religion, or prohibiting the free exercise thereof; or abridging the freedom of speech, or of the press; or the right of the people peaceably to assemble, and to petition the Government for a redress of grievances.

Obama has been in the forefront of curtailing the 1st Amendment rights guaranteed by our U.S. Constitution and Bill of Rights.

The NSA spying and the IRS targeting of opposition are two [2] examples of Obama's efforts, as I explained elsewhere in my book and I restate in this chapter.

Further, U.S. Senate Majority Leader Harry Reid's [D-NV] attempts to change our 1st Amendment to the detriment of our citizens.

And recently an effort to force Rush Limbaugh off the air, to curtail his free speech that I will discuss in this chapter.

It is amazing what Obama tries to do and does to the detriment of "our" United States of America. Obama is a disgrace.

NSA spying – The warrantless wiretapping and data-mining of

American citizens ... constitute a direct violation of the Fourth Amendment, and has a distinct chilling effect upon the First Amendment right of free speech.

IRS targeting the opposition – The President has used the IRS ... to directly harass and impede the First Amendment protected rights of free speech, religious liberty and political activity of conservative and libertarian American citizens, in an attempt to silence dissent and opposition.... could be construed as violations of a person's Fourth Amendment right against unreasonable search and seizure and Fifth Amendment right of due process and self-incrimination.

Obama's efforts to change "our" 1st Amendment by U.S. Senate Majority Leader Harry Reid. Wake up America!
Harry Reid showing Americans what he thinks of them.

Opinion: Wall Street Journal [WSJ]
titled: Harry Reid Rewrites the First Amendment

When politicians seek to restrict speech, they are invariably trying to protect their own incumbency.

By
Theodore B. Olson

Sept. 7, 2014

"Liberals often deplore efforts to amend the Constitution, particularly the Bill of Rights and especially when the outcome would narrow individual liberties. Well, now we know they don't really mean it.

Forty-six Senate Democrats have concluded that the First Amendment is an impediment to re-election that a little tinkering can cure. They are proposing a constitutional amendment that would give Congress and state legislatures the authority to regulate the degree to which citizens can devote their resources to advocating the election or defeat of candidates. Voters, whatever their political views, should rise up against politicians who want to dilute the Bill of Rights to perpetuate their tenure in office.

Led by Majority Leader Harry Reid, these Senate Democrats claim that they are merely interested in good government to "restore democracy to the American people" by reducing the amount of money in politics. Do not believe it. When politicians seek to restrict political speech, it is invariably to protect their own incumbency and avoid having to defend their policies in the marketplace of ideas.

This scheme is doomed to fail when it comes to a vote in the Senate, perhaps as soon as Monday. The Constitution's Framers had the wisdom to make amending the Constitution difficult, and Mr. Reid's gambit won't survive a filibuster. But Senate Democrats know their proposal is a loser. They merely want another excuse to rail against "money in politics" and Supreme Court justices they don't like.

The rhetoric of these would-be constitutional reformers is focused on two Supreme Court decisions: Citizens United v. FEC (2010) and McCutcheon v. FEC (2014). In Citizens United, the court struck down a law prohibiting unions and corporations from using their resources to speak for or against a candidate within a certain time period before an election.

The Obama administration conceded during oral argument that the law would permit the government to ban the publication of political books or pamphlets. Pamphlets and books ignited the revolution that created this country and the Bill of Rights. In pushing to overturn the court's decision, Mr. Reid and his Democratic colleagues apparently wish they had the power to stop books, pamphlets—as well as broadcasting—that threaten their hold on their government jobs.

Incidentally, president Obama's complaint in his 2010 State of the Union address that Citizens United "reversed a century of law" was false. The court preserved the architecture of the campaign-finance laws but overturned an anomalous 1990 decision in <u>Austin v. Michigan Chamber of Commerce</u> (and its progeny) that would have permitted statutory limits on corporate speech to help level, or equalize, the playing field in election campaigns. Even the Obama administration was unwilling to defend Austin's rationale in briefs to the court, presumably because it would warrant all manner of government thumbs on the scale regarding election rhetoric, possibly even imposing handicaps to balance the advantage of incumbency.

It is also a canard that Citizens United permits organizations, as Mr. Reid claimed in May, to "dump unseemly amounts of money into a shadowy political organization." The court explicitly left untouched the federal ban on direct contributions from corporations or unions to candidate campaigns or political parties. Citizens United also upheld disclosure requirements, the very opposite of shadowy.

McCutcheon struck down the aggregate limits on the amount an individual may contribute during a two-year period to all federal candidates, parties and political-action committees combined. Mr. Reid's denunciation of McCutcheon in April because "all it does is take away people's rights" is preposterous. People's rights to participate broadly in the political process are enhanced, not taken away, by the court's ruling. McCutcheon did not overturn the limits on how much individuals can give to a particular politician's campaign, which remains at $2,600 per federal election.

The critics also ignore that Citizens United and McCutcheon make it easier for the unions on which the Democrats rely to spend money on elections. Unions outspent businesses by more than 2 to 1 in 2013. If *money corrupts, then one would expect Mr. Reid and his colleagues to condemn the "corrupt" influence of unions in politics. And these Democrats presumably would brand liberal billionaire Tom Steyer's pledge to commit his political-action committee to spend $100 million to defeat Republicans in 2014 as especially corrupting—but Mr. Reid has instead welcomed the support.*

Democrats claim that the Supreme Court has made politicians and political parties less accountable by encouraging donations involving outside interest groups. Outside of what? Democrat fundraising circles? Their actual fear is that less traditional candidates—including outsiders—will have the funding necessary to challenge incumbents in primaries without the blessing of party elders.

It hardly enhances democracy to pine for the days when candidates were chosen by party bosses in secret, rather than by voters presented with candidates expressing a range of political viewpoints. If Democrats are concerned about the vitality of political parties when contending with outside groups, then Democrats should embrace McCutcheon, which enables citizens to increase contributions to parties.

"In the entire history of the Constitution," the late Ted Kennedy once stated on the Senate floor, "we have never amended the Bill of Rights, and now is not the time to start. It would be wrong to carve an exception in the First Amendment. Campaign finance reform is a serious problem, but it does not require that we twist the meaning of the Constitution."

Let's all pay attention to Kennedy's words and drop this foolishness.

Mr. Olson, a former U.S. solicitor general, is a partner at Gibson, Dunn & Crutcher and successfully argued the Citizens United case in the Supreme Court.

Theodore B. Olson article is a must read. He describes in detail the attempt by president Obama through U.S. Senator Harry Reid to curtail citizens' rights by amending "our" 1st Amendment. Mr. Olson highlights the statement by the late U.S. Senator Ted Kennedy that we never amended the Bill of Rights and now is not the time to start. As I have discussed throughout, Obama believes he is above the law, doing and attempting to do whatever he wants, to the detriment of the citizens of "our" great nation. Obama must be stopped!

Rush Limbaugh

Recently, in September of 2014, an attempt was made to have Rush Limbaugh taken off the airwaves. Another attempt to curtail Free Speech by Obama and the Democrats. Obama and other Democrats, if you cannot stand the heat, get out of the office of president, that you illegally serve and have been totally incompetent, and Democrats that are a part of the do nothing Congress that has attempted to take away 1st and 2nd Amendment rights, you too should leave office.

SEPTEMBER 22, 2014 10:27 AM "MEDIA BIAS
"Democrats Launch Campaign to Get 'Rush Limbaugh' Off the Air"
http://www.breitbart.com/Big-Journalism/2014/09/22/Democrats-petition-rush-off-air

Petition comes straight from the Democratic Congressional Campaign Committee... (Breitbart) – *"During the Bush administration, national Democrat leaders threatened to kill the ABC network's broadcast license if a miniseries unfavorable to the Clinton administration wasn't censored to satisfy Democrats. ABC complied. Earlier this year, Democrats started a push for a Constitutional Amendment to gut (literally) the First Amendment. Over the weekend, Democrats launched a campaign to get — in their own words — "Rush Limbaugh off the air."*
The petition to get Limbaugh off the air comes straight from the Democratic Congressional Campaign Committee (DCCC) in the form of a fundraising/petition email. The idea is to use the muscle of the

petition to in turn muscle Limbaugh's advertisers to drop him. The phony outrage is manifested from a toxic stew of lies crafted by the DCCC and (naturally) Sandra Fluke that take Limbaugh's recent comments about sexual assault way, way, way out of context.

Using the subject header, "PETITION: Rush Limbaugh off the air," the hysterical email reads:

300,000 Signatures Needed: Demand Rush Limbaugh's sponsors pull their ads after his sexual assault comments -

Sandra Fluke has been the target of disgusting, sexist comments from Rush Limbaugh before. So his latest abhorrent rant is no surprise to her.

Stand with Sandra and help us hit 300,000 signatures today to put real pressure on Rush's advertisers to drop him once and for all:

Yes, the very same Democrats who joined President Bill Clinton's crusade to personally destroy every woman who accused him of harassment, assault, and rape (Kathleen Willey, Paula Jones [who Clinton settled out of court with], and Juanita Broderick), are accusing Limbaugh of being a rape apologist.

The truth is that Limbaugh was talking about a proposed policy at Ohio State that would require explicit permission between students before engaging in any kind of sexual activity. Here's what Limbaugh said in full. He starts by quoting the proposal:

"Consent must be freely given, can be withdrawn at any time, and the absence of 'no' does not mean 'yes.'"

How many of you guys, in your own experience with women, have learned that "no" means "yes" if you know how to spot it? Let me tell you something. In this modern world, that is simply not tolerated. People aren't even gonna try to understand that one. I mean, it used to be said it was a cliché. It used to be part of the advice young boys were given. See, that's what we gotta change. We have got to reprogram the way we raise men. Why do you think permission every step of the way, clearly spelling out "why"... are all of these not lawsuits just waiting to happen if even one of these steps is not taken?

The campaigns the Left and their allies in the media have waged to *so silence conservatives like the Koch brothers and Limbaugh have been both big and small. Earlier this year the Left pushed to remove Limbaugh from consideration in a children's book contest that he went on to win. There is also the organized "shadow campaign" against Limbaugh that involves a small group of leftists pretending to look vast as they intimidate Limbaugh's advertisers.*

Late last year, within the context of the Senate Democrats' decision to weaken the filibuster, Limbaugh illustrated the importance of minority rights using the crime of rape. The phony outrage machines at the Huffington Post and Media Matter immediately hit warp ten: How dare Limbaugh use "rape" to make a political point!

Today Democrats and Sandra Fluke are using rape, not only to fundraise and make a political point, but as a fascist weapon to silence political speech.

http://www.breitbart.com/Big-Journalism/2014/09/22/Democrats-petition-rush-off-air

See more at: *http://www.teaparty.org/democrats-launch-campaign-get-rush-limbaugh-air-56817/#sthash.LizxUcVs.dpuf"*

In my research about Rush Limbaugh, I came across an article from March 12, 2012 regarding how three [3] individuals wanted Rush taken off the airwaves. What drew my attention was the fact that one [1] of these individuals was traitor, yes traitor, JANE FONDA a/k/a HANOI JANE! How disgusting! Of anyone to be critical, JANE FONDA! Give me a break. A traitor from the days of the Vietnam War.

The following are a few excerpts from that article. Obviously, their attempt did not succeed, as Rush is still on the air.

The beauty of "our" United States of America has been, and hopefully will continue, to have "Free speech" as guaranteed by "our" U.S. Constitution and specifically the 1st Amendment that guarantees "Free Speech."

FCC should clear Limbaugh from airwaves

By **Jane Fonda, Robin Morgan and Gloria Steinem**, Special to CNN
updated 10:05 AM EDT, Mon March 12, 2012

"Limbaugh has long history of hate speech. FCC should ask: Are stations carrying him are acting "in public interest," writers say.

STORY HIGHLIGHTS

- Fonda, Morgan, Steinem: Limbaugh long made racist, sexist, homophobic remarks
- His most recent incident drew strong rebuke, some advertisers have dropped him
- They say Clear Channel should dump him; if not FCC should evaluate station licenses
- Writers: Airwaves scarce government resource; his show not "in public interest"

Editor's note: Jane Fonda, Robin Morgan, and Gloria Steinem are the Co-Founders of the Women's Media Center... "

Jane Fonda

" . . . :Opinion: It's un-American to silence Limbaugh

That makes this a fitting time to inquire of his syndicator, Clear Channel Communications, whether it intends to continue supporting someone who addicts his audience to regular doses of hate speech. Clear Channel's Premiere Radio Networks Inc., which hosts Limbaugh's program, has defended his recent comments. . . . "

These articles highlight the extent the Democrats [some Democrats, as I am still a frustrated Democrat as I cannot believe the actions of our current Democratic leadership] will go to curtail free speech, or really speech by those that do not agree with them.

We must look carefully at Democratic Senate Majority Leader Harry Reid [D-NV] as he is a total embarrassment to the Democratic

Party. He is a total mouthpiece for president Obama, no matter what. He has been withholding a number of bills from votes and many of his comments are outrageous, a joke. It is time for Harry Reid to go.

What Obama, his administration and other Democrats in office are doing is unconstitutional, illegal and basically disgusting. As I said, Wake Up America; Wake Up "our" Free Press; and Wake Up Members of Congress – Stop following Party Lines – Be Open Minded – Save "our" United States of America!

2nd Amendment

Second Amendment to the United States Constitution

A well-regulated Militia, being necessary to the security of a free State, the right of the people to keep and bear Arms, shall not be infringed."

Obama has been after the taking away of 2nd Amendment rights during his entire term in office. Obama's largest effort was an attempt to join in the United Nations efforts that would have bound the United States. Fortunately, the United Nations Small Arms Treaty was DEFEATED in "our" United States Senate, BUT look at the 46 Democrats who voted to take away your guns. ... they must be defeated at their next election!

United Nations Gun Grab: Obama championed the United Nations Small Arms Treaty that would have taken away rights granted to United States citizens by "our" U.S. Constitution's Second Amendment. U.N. Resolution 2117 lists 21 points dealing with firearms control and point number "11" states,
"Calls for Member States To Support Weapons Collection and Disarmament"

In a 53-46 vote, the U.S. Senate on or about 04/14/2014 passed a measure that "stops" the United States from entering into the United Nations Arms Trade Treaty.

How appalling are these efforts! It makes me question why I am a Democrat. But I remain a Democrat determined to open the minds of other Democrats about what Obama, his administration and other Democrats in office are doing that are unconstitutional, illegal and basically disgusting. The 46 Democratic U.S. Senators who voted for this must be voted out-of-office!

George Washington said, "When any nation mistrusts its citizens with guns, it is sending a clear message. It no longer trusts its citizens because such a government has evil plans." www.NationalGunRights.org

As I said, Wake Up America; Wake Up "our" Free Press; and Wake Up Members of Congress – Stop following Party Lines – Be Open Minded – Save "our" United States of America!

Philip J. Berg

CHAPTER XVI
Scandal after Scandal and Other Violations

Media & Congress Ignore

During the 2008 campaign Obama claimed his administration would be the most "open and transparent" administration in the history of our country. That was just another feel-good sound bite he feed to the blind followers... *the same way Hitler did*. But it got the votes he wanted.

Not only has the Obama administration not been an open and transparent administration... but history will show that he has the largest number of significant scandals in the history of any president, over two [2] dozen and counting.

Should we start with: NSA, Benghazi, IRS, Associated Press, Fast & Furious, ObamaCare; Fort Hood, Texas; Abuse of Executive Orders; Obama's alleged connivance with Then-Judge Sotomayor; other Obama Violations; Debt & Foreign Policy, including Bowing to Saudi Arabian King Abdullah and Japanese Emperor; our Rules of Engagement in Combat Zones; the Delay in the Keystone Pipeline; the VA; and ISSI.

NSA: Illegal spying on Americans: If it wasn't for Edward Snowden, who knows when all of us would find out that "our" government has been spying on us. All the while pushing DoubleSpeak sound bites that it is required to protect our country from terrorists. Terrorists like the generals he released at GITMO.

Benghazi: I have set forth the details on Benghazi in Chapter XI. Remember that Obama has classified the attack as a *"spontaneous protest"* in response to an internet video. Both Hillary and Obama got away with feeding DoubleSpeak to the American people instead of truth and fact.

IRS: Wow! Obama "DoubleSpeak"... *again*. The abuses of

patriotic citizens. When the allegations of the IRS came forth regarding the IRS targeting conservative groups and the Tea Party, Obama said he will get to bottom of the IRS situation. Then, what occurs, Obama later, on or about 02/02/2014 in an interview with Fox News Bill O'Reilly comes out and says regarding the IRS targeting scandal "Not even mass corruption - *not even a smidgen of corruption.*" This is unbelievable!

Then, as of June 2014, it is disclosed thousands of "missing" Emails from Lois Lerner and six [6] other IRS officials. They say Lerner's computer crashed in 2011 and Emails were lost. And, the hard drives have been destroyed. What a lie! This issue calls for a Special Prosecutor.

Emails can be recovered from broken hard drives. In addition, it is automatic and mandated procedure that all data be backed up, copied and stored in another location, continually throughout each day. Therefore, the Emails have always been available. A Special Prosecutor is in order because there is definite indication of a cover-up.

How about Lois Lerner in her May 10, 2013, remarks in which she first revealed that she conceded that the requests for donor names was "not appropriate, not usual." Additional documents obtained by Judicial Watch show that 75% of the groups from whom the lists were solicited were apparently conservative, with only 5% being liberal. Was that by coincidence or design?

But, we really shouldn't be surprised, should we? This is an administration whose chief executive has repeatedly acted as if he is above the law. All he needs to govern, he claims, is "a pen and a phone." His IRS agency, it turns out, has put both to extensive use in harassing and hamstringing conservative organizations - and, perhaps, even individuals it thought might have had a negative impact on the president's efforts to retain office in 2012.

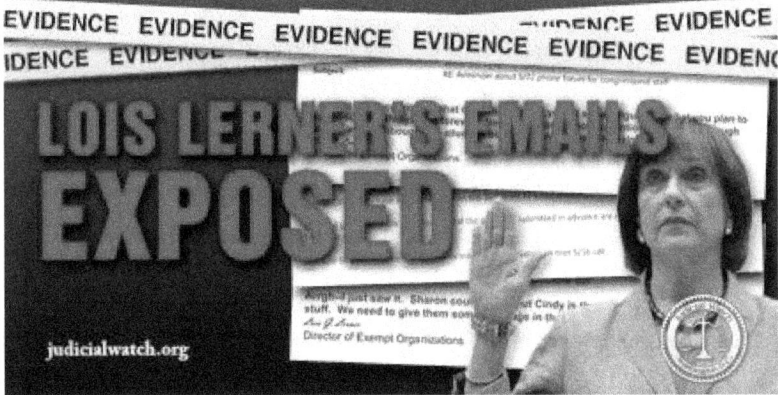

EVIDENCE EVIDENCE EVIDENCE EVIDENCE EVIDENCE EVIDENCE
IDENCE EVIDENCE
LOIS LERNER'S EMAILS EXPOSED
judicialwatch.org

AP: The Justice Department illegally wiretapping reporters, the press. We, "our" country are supposed to have a "Free Press." Well, Eric Holder, Obama's Attorney General investigating AP sure puts a damper on "our" "Free Press."

Fast & Furious: Another scandal pushed under the rug by Obama. Gun running and the lack of an in depth investigation. Obama abused Executive Privilege. And where did the investigation go – yes, to Attorney General Eric Holder – result – "no real investigation." What are they hiding?

Cover-up: Please note that U.S. Attorney General Eric Holder was held in Contempt by "our" U.S. House of Representatives on June 28, 2012. An article in: POLITICO

Attorney General Eric Holder held in contempt of Congress The vote was 255-67. | AP Photo

By JOHN BRESNAHAN and SEUNG MIN KIM | 6/28/12 4:43 PM EDT
Updated: 6/28/12 5:47 PM EDT

Stated in part: "The House has voted to hold Attorney General Eric Holder in contempt of Congress over his failure to turn over documents related to the Fast and Furious scandal, **the first time Congress has taken such a dramatic move against a sitting Cabinet official**. [**bold** added by me]

The vote was 255-67, with 17 Democrats voting in support of a criminal contempt resolution, which authorizes Republicans leaders to seek criminal charges against Holder. This Democratic support came despite a round of behind-the-scenes lobbying by senior White House and Justice Officials - as well as pressure from party leaders - to support Holder. ..."

More:
http://www.politico.com/news/stories/0612/77988.html#ixzz3ERgBj5RI

The article at Politico by John Bresnahan and Seung Min Kim is so significant, as it is a liberal leaning paper, and it highlights the vote of Contempt of Congress, the 1st time Congress has voted this way in history to a sitting Cabinet official, Attorney General Eric Holder. This article reinforces my allegations that the Obama Administration is determined to undermine "our" United States of America. We have been and are at a dangerous crossroad. WE THE PEOPLE must stop Obama now.

ObamaCare: The fraudulent implementation; the lies; the waivers and changing of the law, not by Congress, but by Obama, over forty [40+] times; needed U.S. Supreme Court to make it a "tax" because there is no Constitutional authority; the loss of medical coverage by millions; and the rising costs of medical insurance premiums. **ObamaCare** must be repealed or significant major changes must occur.

Domestic Terrorists: Fort Hood, Texas: Let us not forget the thirteen [13] murders and twenty-nine [29] wounded at Fort Hood, Texas five [5] years ago on November 5, 2009 when Nidal Hasan opened fire while screaming "Allahu Akbar." Obama, not wanting to call anything "terrorism" has classified the shootings as "Work Place Violence" thus denying the families of the dead and the survivors of benefits they should have received if a proper classification of "terrorism" had been designated to this mass shooting.

U.S. Senator Harry Reid re: Bundy Ranch: On April 17, 2014, another shocking political development. U.S. Senator Harry Reid calls the Nevada Bundy rancher's supporters, where zero [0] deaths, zero [0] injured and zero [0] shots fired, "confrontation" with the BLM [Bureau of Land Management] over his cattle, calls them "Domestic Terrorists," which now brings in Homeland Security. What a joke! Compare this to Fort Hood, Texas and what about the Wall Street Occupiers that had plenty of violence and unlawful trespass.

Domestic Terrorist in New Jersey: On June 25, 2014, the murder of 19-year-old Brendan Tevlin from Livingston, New Jersey occurred. It was definitely "Domestic Terror" as Ali Muhammad Brown was arrested and stated it was a "just kill" for Muslim deaths. And "not" a word from president Obama! Why? Because Obama consistently wants to avoid any mention of "terrorism" as he is in a false sense that terrorism does not exist! What a disgrace!

An article titled:_*"Homegrown jihadist shoots N.J. teen 8 times,* *calling it a 'just kill": report* By Jessica Chasmar - *The Washington Times* - Thursday, September 18, 2014 stated: A brutally murdered 19-year-old New Jersey man was allegedly targeted by a self-proclaimed homegrown jihadist who called it a "just kill," Fox News has revealed.

Brendan Tevlin, of Livingston, was stopped at a red light driving home from a friend's house on June 25 when Ali Muhammad Brown allegedly walked up to his car and fired 10 rounds, striking him eight times.

Mr. Brown then drove the car, with Tevlin's lifeless body still in it, to a parking lot in West Orange and left him there, Fox News reported.

Police initially announced the arrest of three suspects in Tevlin's murder, calling it a robbery gone wrong, but as the investigation continued it was discovered that Mr. Brown had undergone extensive Jihad training in California and that he's suspected of additional murders throughout the country, a local Fox affiliate reported.

Mr. Brown allegedly called Tevlin's death "a just kill" for Muslim deaths at the hands of Americans in Iraq, Syria and Afghanistan. *"All these lives are taken every single day by America, by this government. So a life for a life," he said, according to court documents."* Read more: http://www.washingtontimes.com/news/2014/sep/18/slain-nj-teen-was-shot-8-times-alleged-jihadist-wh/#!#ixzz3E4yYPeTr
Follow us: @washtimes on Twitter

Domestic Terrorist in Oklahoma:

Alton Alexander Nolen's mugshot from a previous arrest Photo: Oklahoma Department of Corrections.

A disgruntled, fired factory worker — who had tried to convert his colleagues to Islam — used a 10-inch work knife to stab and behead a female employee, law enforcement sources told The Post on Friday.

The FBI is investigating Thursday, September 25, 2014's, brutal murder at Vaughan Foods in the Oklahoma town of Moore due to the nature of the attack, which comes on the heels of recently released ISIS beheading videos.

Alton Nolen, 30, had been fired from the food distribution company early Thursday and drove back to the plant around 4 p.m., according to sources.

He barged in and attacked the first person he saw — 54-year-old Colleen Hufford — stabbing her in the back and cutting her head off with a knife he had used while working at the plant.

Numerous statements from co-workers pointed to a religious motive behind the attack — citing Nolen's background in Islam and numerous attempts to get employees to convert, sources said.

KWTV Channel 9's Robin Marsh tweeted that Nolen had been shouting Islamic phrases during his vicious attack, but that could not be immediately confirmed.

He then directed his rage toward a 43-year-old co-worker, Traci Johnson, whom he repeatedly stabbed with the same bloody blade he used to saw off Hufford's head, according to sources.

He was finally shot by Oklahoma County reserve deputy and former Vaughan Foods CEO Mark Vaughan, who used a rifle to bring down the menace.

The FBI is probing Nolen's Islamic ties and attempts to convert colleagues. Homeland Security has warned this week of "lone wolf" terrorist attacks on US soil while American forces conduct airstrikes against ISIS forces in Syria."

These two [2] incidents highlight that terrorist actions are here in the United States. Steps must be taken to increase our watch throughout the country of individuals that are ISIS sympathizers and we must seal our borders.

And not one word from Obama because Obama refuses to relate the facts about terrorists.

Abuse of Executive Orders: Obama issued twenty-three [23] Executive

Orders on gun control, Infringement of the 2nd Amendment; Bypassing Congress on Immigration; Order #13524 that gave INTERPOL jurisdiction on American soil beyond law enforcement agencies, including the FBI; and Order #13603 NDRP – government can seize anything.

Obama's alleged connivance with Then-Judge Sotomayor: As set forth by Dr. Richard Cordero, Esquire on 04/23/2014 in an article titled: ***"Doing Your Part To president Obama On Legal Grounds for Wrongdoing in Coordination With Officers of the Other Branches and Bring About Substantial Reform of Government Through 'The People's' Sunrise Civic Movement"***... that states in part:

"… 3. president Obama has done wrong by conniving with another public officer, namely, his first nominee to the Supreme Court, Then-Judge, Now-Justice Sotomayor. She was suspected of concealing assets by three top-rated, national, and even so-called liberal Democrat-leaning papers, that is, The New York Times, The Washington Post, and Politico (jur:65fn107a). He knew from the FBI vetting report on her and, had he proceeded with due diligence (65fn107c), would have known, about her concealment of assets. But he condoned it because he wanted to cater to those petitioning that he nominate another woman and the first Latina to the Supreme Court. …"

Wow! Another scandal that most Americans are not aware of. I thank Dr. Richard Cordero, Esquire for bringing this scandal to my attention so I could relate it to my readers. I am not surprised because Obama disregards our Constitution and rules and regulations to accomplish anything he wants to do, and our Free Press and Congress do not challenge him. What a disgrace!

Debt & Foreign Policy: In an article in Personal Liberty Digest on April 16, 2014 titled: *"Barack Obama Made America A Sick, Old Nation"* by John Myers, who said in part:

"… Obama promised to reduce the debt. Instead, he added $7 trillion in new debt … So prolific at spending is Obama that America has accumulated as much additional debt under his leadership as it did during

the Nation's first 227 years.

Obama has a record number of Americans hooked on food stamps. He has played the victim card with skin color. And he has made millions of American blacks feel like they, too, are victims.

... And as bad as things are domestically, they are worse internationally. And the reason is that we are being led by the most destructive President in American history: Obama. In March, an article in American Thinker stated: 'When you have a foreign policy of "leading from behind" you lose the political momentum to advance values.

With Obama, it began with his apology tour to Muslim nations in 2009 which included his bowing to the Saudi Arabian king [King Abdullah], a gesture interpreted in the Islamic world as submission. From that point it spiraled downward ..."

I agree with author John Myers. The debt that Obama has accrued is outrageous and no one has really questioned his actions, not Congress or our Free Press. Obama playing the race card as does his Attorney General Eric Holder is unfortunate because race is not the problem; rather it is Obama's incompetence.

No other President of the United States has ever bowed to another world leader, until Obama.

Obama's bows to Saudi Arabian King Abdullah:

Photo Getty Images – telegraph.co.uk/news/worldnews 08 04 2009

And Obama, bowing to Japanese Emperor Akihito:

LA Times photo of Obama bowing to Japanese Emperor Akihito 11/14/2009

And Obama bowing down to the Leader of Communist China, Hu Jinato:

freedomslighthouse.com/2010/04

All of which are unconscionable, a sure sign of weakness; an embarrassment to the United States; and unforgivable.

Rules of Engagement in Combat Zones: Obama has supported the Rules of Engagement [ROE] that have jeopardized our troops in Afghanistan whereby our soldiers in a combat zone are told to hold their fire unless there is evidence of hostile action or direct hostile intent. This, along with "COIN" [Counterinsurgency Strategy] also called "winning hearts and minds" adopted in 2009 favors our enemies.

How outrageous and yet there has not been a great opposition to Obama's orders from our Congress or Free Press that have put our military in a horrible position, along with Obama's cutting of military budgets and the reduction of our military to pre-World War Two levels.

Keystone Pipeline Delay: Why the delay? The ongoing delay in deciding to go ahead with the Keystone Pipeline is causing loss of jobs, jeopardy to our oil production/sales, and is affecting our national security.

The supposed reason – further studies. The real reason is Obama is catering to the environmentalists. We can become energy independent with the Keystone Pipeline, allowing further drilling in the United States and our waters that will also result in more jobs in the United States. This is *scary* allowing Obama to continue blocking our energy independence. Wake up America!

Veterans Administration [VA]:
What a disgrace! Obama while a candidate for President promised he would clean-up the VA. Aside from the fact that Obama has not cleaned-up the VA in the last five and three quarter [5 ¾] years, the VA has gotten worse!

I know of veterans who in the past related the delays in receiving treatment through the VA. Recently, a veteran advised me that he, along with many of his veteran friends absolutely refuse to go to a VA facility because of the constant delays. As I said, "What a disgrace!" And again, if the VA system does not work, how can ObamaCare? It cannot!

Excerpt from an article in "Newsmax" [www.newsmax.com] dated June 3, 2014: by Drew MacKenzie, titled: **"Poll: Most Americans Outraged by VA Scandal; Many Blame Obama."**

States in part, "An overwhelming number of Americans are outraged by the Veterans Affairs scandal, with many of them believing that President Barack Obama is clearly or partially to blame for the crisis, a new poll reveals.

The Washington Post-ABC News poll found that 97% of Americans described the falsified wait times and the long treatment delays for veterans as a serious problem, while 82 percent called it "very serious."

Asked whether they thought that Obama was "personally responsible" for the VA scandal, 19 percent said he deserved a "great deal" of the blame, while another 19 percent said he was a "good deal" to blame.

A further 41 percent said he was "just some" to blame, adding up to 79 percent of respondents who thought that the president is in some way responsible for the embattled department's problems.

The poll also found that 65 percent of Americans believe that VA Secretary Eric Shinseki was "right to resign" in the wake of the ongoing investigation. Twenty-two percent felt he should have kept his job."

And Obama had the guts to address the American Legion's Annual Convention on August 26, 2014 in Charlotte, North Carolina. I said "guts" because of what has and has not accomplished regarding "our" veterans. Well, watching Obama's speech, I, as I am sure many others, noticed the lack of enthusiasm and basically being ignored by those in attendance. Why? Because Obama has failed both "our" military, and "our" nation. He cut military budgets; cut the military size to pre-World War II levels; not cleaned up the Veterans Administration as he promised in the 2008 election; not wearing the American Flag lapel on his suits while campaigning for president in 2008; and the most insulting to "our" veterans, not saluting the American Flag when campaigning in 2008.

As I have said before, Obama is a total disgrace and I am ashamed to have him as president!

Other Obama Violations: Allowing Drone strikes on American citizens; four [4] Executive appointments when U.S. Senate 'not' in recess – 'Overturned' by the United States Supreme Court in June 2014; Obama took Chairmanship of U.N. Security Council; and declaring the "War on Terrorism" is over on August 6, 2009.

Economy: How can we not discuss the economy? Yes, when Obama took office, we had definite economic problems, but has Obama improved the economy? NO! The stock market is up, but for the majority of citizens in our country, the economy is worse. There are so many unemployed that many have given up looking for employment so the figures are not correct. So many businesses that have closed: strip malls have empty stores; shopping centers have store after store closing; and office buildings have many vacancies and there are so many empty buildings.

And gasoline prices coming down in late 2014, but had doubled during Obama's administration.

Security: Are you safer today? The majority of people in "our" country say NO! How can we be safer with ISSI and other terrorist groups wanting to destroy us? And, our borders are wide open. Of course, this has been a problem for years and belongs to Republicans and Democrats, but the climate is much worse now: Obama has not only allowed illegal immigrants, mostly children from South American countries, but has encouraged them; and these children are bringing diseases into the United States; and not being screened regarding their criminal backgrounds. And while our border guards are tendering to these minors, the borders are wide open for drug smugglers and terrorists. *Obama, "use your pen" and "SEAL 'our' borders NOW!*

EBOLA: Another example of Obama leading from behind. We are lucky that Ebola has not spread into the United States. Yes, they are now screening individuals at airports, BUT our borders are still wide open. Think about it, if terrorists are willing to strap bombs on their bodies to blow themselves up, wouldn't they be willing to get Ebola and come across our borders. Something is majorly wrong with Obama's thought process.

ISSI, ISSL & Radical Islam: Obama was made aware of the build-up of ISSI for over a year, yet he did nothing. As ISSI spread throughout Iraq, what did Obama do – nothing. And now what is Obama doing re ISSI: constantly saying we will not put boots on the ground; and airstrikes against ISSI, but only 5 a day. If you want to eliminate ISSI/ISSL, then have 200 airstrikes a day! And Obama refuses to call it what it really is: Radical Islam. We cannot win if we cannot even identify our opposition. If we do not stop them now, they will come to the United States and with our "open borders"; they are probably here.

Cuba: Another action by Obama not for the benefit of all United States citizens. Obama's announcement to overhaul U.S. policy toward Cuba because he said the U.S. policy has not worked. Sorry Obama, it has worked. Did you forget the missiles aimed at the United States; and the dictatorship and poverty that still exists in Cuba. Obama, your actions dishonor President John F. Kennedy who stood up to Cuba. Cuba must change before we renew relations and lift the economic sanctions, especially our trade embargo and travel ban.

Free Community College: Obama's proposal again not for the benefit of all U.S. citizens. Nothing is "free", so who will pay for this benefit? All of the rest of us.

Each topic on this list is significant and yet Obama states there are "no scandals" in his administration. This goes to my statement about Obama **"DoubleSpeaking."** Obama basically talks out of both sides of his mouth; he states one thing to one set of individuals and another to another set. It is time for America to wake up!

And let us not forget Obama's statement that the United States is no longer a Christian Nation, it is a Muslim Nation. This statement goes hand-in-hand with his support of Muslims around the world.

Chapter XVII
Dealing with the Taliban and ISIS

Prisoner Exchange of Bergdahl for five [5] Terrorists

We traded five Islamic terrorist generals that hate America for one American soldier that hates America. *Unbelievable!* Obama negotiates a deal with the Taliban for the release of Army Sgt. Bowe Bergdahl. Help me understand that deal. Obama just put five prisoners back into the field to fight again. That's *scary!*

Side bar note: In case you live in a cave... it has always been the policy of the United States of America to NEVER negotiate with the enemy. Obama sends out sound bites to make you feel good and to believe the war in Afghanistan is over. As some sort of "symbolic" gesture he wanted the *only prisoner of war in Afghanistan released*. Withdrawing our troops from Afghanistan is no indication that the war is over. The Taliban. ISIS, and other terrorists have not declared that war over, nor has anyone else.

Maybe ISIS doesn't represent every single one of the world's billion Muslims... but when you combine the thousands who follow ISIS, Boko Haram, Al Qaeda, Taliban, Al Nusrah, Hezbollah, Hamas, the MUSLIM BROTHERHOOD, Abu Sayyaf, and HUNDREDS of other terrorists groups, you get a pretty good representation of the population.

Obama had in-depth knowledge of the background of Sgt. Bergdahl being a "deserter" and/or "traitor" and/or a Taliban "collaborator," who left his post in Afghanistan by just walking away...! How dare you, Mr. president, to hold a press conference at the White House with Bergdahl's parents knowing he was a deserter. You just urinated on every Vet in America.

The Blaze on June 3, 2014 posted an article by Jason Howerton titled: *"The Simple Arabic Phrase Bowe Bergdahl's Father Said at a Press Conference with Obama That Has Sparked a Heated Debate".*

The phrase *'bismillah al-Rahman al-Rahim'* [spoken by Robert Bergdahl] is a common Arabic phrase, considered by some to be a major pillar of Islam and featured prominently in the Koran." The phrase means *"in the name of God, the merciful, the compassionate."*

"That's the simple phrase that Robert Bergdahl, father of freed Army Sgt. Bow Bergdahl, said in Arabic ... proceeded to speak in Pashtu, also known as Afghani, because he said his son might have difficulty understanding English after five years in captivity."

Furthermore, during the week before this exchange that Bergdahl's father communicated with the Taliban, "... As previously reported by The Blaze, Robert Bergdahl tweeted – and then deleted – the following message: "I am still working to free all Guantanamo prisoners. God will repay for the death of every Afghan child, amen!"

In an Email to me on June 5, 2014 from Keith Koffler, Editor of "White House Dossier" [www.whitehousedossier.com] titled: *"Obama: "No apologies" for Bergdahl"* he says in part, "... president Obama said today during a press conference in Europe that he had nothing to apologize for with respect to the release of five dangerous Taliban leaders in exchange for Sgt. Bowe Bergdahl.
Well, he's mistaken about that. ... "

This is because Obama has never apologized for anything or held anyone accountable, until he was forced to have the head of the Secret Service resign.

Significant, on August 21, 2014, as reported by: FoxNews.com in an article titled: *"Pentagon broke law with Bergdahl prisoner swap, government watchdog says."*

The article states in part: *"A nonpartisan government watchdog agency said Thursday that the Pentagon broke the law when it swapped five Taliban leaders for Army Sgt. Bowe Bergdahl earlier this year.*

The Government Accountability Office, in a legal opinion issued at the request of congressional lawmakers, said the Defense Department violated the law by failing to notify key Capitol Hill committees at least 30 days in advance."

Further, the report said the Pentagon broke another law by using funds that were not technically available.

... Sen. Lisa Murkowski, R-Alaska, among the lawmakers who requested the report, said Thursday that the president "clearly defied" the law.

"We have all seen the President decide to override the concept of checks and balances in many questionable executive actions, but the GAO opinion confirms that by doing so in connection with the release of Bowe Bergdahl, he engaged in a clear violation of the law," she said in a statement. I hope this opinion by the nonpartisan Government Accountability Office sends a clear signal to the President that his recent shift towards unilateral action is not consistent with this nation's principles and our carefully designed separation of powers." ...

I doubt president Obama will change anything in light of the opinion of the nonpartisan Government Accountability Office; so sad. Again, because Obama does what he wants and with a lackluster do nothing Congress and a Press that caters to him, he continues to violate everything.

There is no excuse permitting Obama in dealing with the Taliban; or his efforts to undermine the United States of America.

Obama completely disregards "our" U.S. Constitution; "our" Declaration of Independence; "our" Bill of Rights; "our" U.S. Congress; and "our" Laws.

Wake up America! Wake up "our" supposed "Free Press." America, stop making excuses for Obama! *Obama was never properly vetted!*

As I stated in 2008 and I stand by this statement today,

> *"Obama is a fraud, an imposter and a phony and has put forth the greatest 'HOAX' in the history of "our" country, in over 230 years!"*

Philip J. Berg

Impeachment or jail for treason would happen to anyone else that had defrauded the American people and government, as Obama has.

CHAPTER XVIII – TREASON
Has Obama committed Treason?

What a question – and *scary* – and frightening!

To think a President of the United States would commit Treason! But that has been and is transpiring. I will set forth the law and then various allegations of Treason that Obama has committed. The Conservative Tribune (http://conservativetribune.com) in an article dated 06/25/2014 titled: **POLL: Has Barack Obama Committed Treason?** Sets forth the following, "The Constitution of the United States in Article III, Section III defines the crime of treason stating,

"Treason against the United States, shall consist only in levying War against them, or in adhering to their Enemies, giving them Aid and Comfort. No Person shall be convicted of Treason unless on the Testimony of two Witnesses to the same overt Act, or on Confession in open Court.
"The Congress shall have Power to declare the Punishment of Treason, but no Attainder of Treason shall work Corruption of Blood, or Forfeiture except during the Life of the Person attainted."

Title 18 U.S. Code Section 2381 further defines "treason" as:
'Whoever, owing allegiance to the United States, levies war against them or adheres to their enemies, giving them aid and comfort within the United States or elsewhere, is guilty of treason and shall suffer death, or shall be imprisoned not less than five years and fined under this title but not less than $10,000; and shall be incapable of holding any office under the United States.'

And the article states in part, "... *some examples of actions taken*

*by the President or administration members under his direct control ....
Let it be noted that we consider violations of the oath he swore, to
preserve, protect and defend the Constitution and to faithfully execute
the laws of the nation,* **to be an act of levying war against the United
States."** *[emphasis added]*

*"It is our belief that, should it be found that the President is indeed
guilty of committing treason for any or all of the following crimes, he
should at the very least be impeached, if not imprisoned."*

I list some of the titles and specifics as set forth in the article with
bold added by me:

"NDAA – The indefinite detention ... provision of The National
Defense Authorization Act ... is a clear violation of the First, Fourth,
Fifth, Sixth, Seventh, Eighth and possibly even the Ninth Amendments
of the Bill of Rights.

NSA spies – The warrantless wiretapping and data-mining of
American citizens ... constitute a direct violation of the Fourth
Amendment, and has a distinct chilling effect upon the First
Amendment right of free speech.

IRS targeting of opposition – The President has used the IRS ... to
directly harass and impede the First Amendment protected rights of
free speech, religious liberty and political activity of conservative and
libertarian American citizens, in an attempt to silence dissent and
opposition. ... Could be construed as violations of a person's Fourth
Amendment right against unreasonable search and seizure and Fifth
Amendment right of due process and self-incrimination.

Benghazi – The President and members of his administration have
lied to the American people in their attempt to cover-up ... the terror
attack in Benghazi. His failure to protect American citizens serving the
U.S. overseas, and his failure to hunt down, kill, prosecute or
otherwise serve justice to the terrorists responsible for the deaths of
four Americans, can only be viewed as giving aid and comfort to the
enemies of the United States.

Fast and Furious – the botched gun-running scheme by the ATF and DOJ placed firearms in the hands of known criminals and drug cartel members ... and resulted in the death of hundreds of Mexican citizens and U.S. Border Patrol agent Brian Terry, which can be classified as giving aid to the enemies of the U.S. Furthermore, the underhanded goal of the operation was to implement further gun-control restrictions on law-abiding American citizens, which is an infringement and violation of the Second Amendment of the Constitution.

Arming Syrian rebels – The President's administration went to great lengths to secretly overtly arm and assist members of the Syrian opposition ... forces, many of whom were known to be Al-Qaeda affiliated terrorists. Once again, he has given aid and comfort to our enemies.

Undeclared war in Libya – president Obama ordered Naval and Air strikes on the sovereign nation of Libya, stationed a multitude of forces around the country ... and sent in covert and overt ground forces, in the attempt to overthrow the regime of Mohammar Gadhafi. This was all done without a formal declaration of war by Congress, or even an authorization of force, which is a violation of the Constitution, therefore a violation of his oath of office.

Unilateral Obamacare delays – Obamacare, as much as the American citizens may dislike it, it was duly passed by Congress and upheld by the Supreme Court, and is therefore the law of the land. The President has unilaterally changed or delayed ... various provisions and aspects of the law, without Congressional approval. This is a violation of his oath of office by failing to faithfully execute the Office of the President, which means to uphold the laws as they are written.

More failures to faithfully execute the law – The President and his administration have taken it upon themselves to decide which laws they will enforce and which ones they will ignore. Laws like the Defense of Marriage Act ... border security ... and immigration laws, work requirements for welfare ... and mandatory minimum drug sentencing laws ... have all been summarily ignored or changes by the administration, without the due process of Congress. Though some may agree with his intentions or even the outcomes, he has not followed the process as set out in the Constitution.

An executive action on gun control – The President has great disdain for the Second Amendment and his agenda to disarm law-abiding American citizens. When Congress failed to pass gun control measures, because the American people told them overwhelmingly not to ..., the President took Executive actions of his own to infringe upon our right to keep and bear arms. He has done this through VA regulations disarming veterans, EPA regulations attacking lead and ammunition, ATF regulations attacking gun manufacturers and dealers, and regulations aimed at broadening the definition of mental health in order to disqualify more Americans of their Second Amendment rights.

Promotion of known anti-American/Muslims - Brotherhood members in administration – president Obama has associated himself with, and given jobs in his administration to, people known to be anti-American, socialists, current or former terrorists, or members of terrorist affiliated groups like the Muslim Brotherhood. People like Bill Ayers, Eric Holder, Van Jones, Huma Abedin and Mohamed Elibiary are just a few from a long list.

Acceptance of Chairmanship of UN Security Council – president Obama became the first U.S. President to chair the UN Security Council. In the process of accepting this position, he has violated Article I, Section IX, Clause VIII of the Constitution, which reads:

No Title of Nobility shall be granted by the United States: And no Person holding any Office of Profit or Trust under them, shall, without the Consent of the Congress, accept of any present, Emolument, Office, or Title, of any kind whatever, from any King, Prince, or foreign State."

I believe the above article sets forth acts that Obama has committed, that do, if Obama is tried and convicted, would find him guilty of Treason. Time will tell if Obama is forced to resign; is impeached; or is tried for Treason. These several options await Obama, as he has truly succeeded in changing America, to "our" detriment.

Unfortunately, because of the actions of Obama there are many articles and lists' regarding Obama's alleged treason.

In an article in: The Jag Hunter found at thejaghunter.wordpress.com titled: *"Obama's Treason: A Partial, Not Exhaustive List of Obama's Acts of Treason with Links"* Wednesday, 28 November 2012 states in part, with **bold** added by me:

"... **ITEM:** Perpetrating acts of fraud, perjury and conspiracy in his refusal to confirm his local eligibility to serve as president under the U.S. Constitution Article II, Section I, constituting treasonous felony offenses of high crimes and misdemeanors in violation of our U.S. Constitution Article II, Section 4;

... **ITEM:** Making bribery attempts in word and in deed, as Obama administration offered bribes to at least three Federal candidates for office: Joe Sestak, Andrew Romanoff and Jim Matheson, in violation of U.S. Code Title 18, Section 201;

... **ITEM:** Defying a Federal Court Order by refusing to grant lawful deep water drilling permits, in violation of the U.S. Constitution Article II, Section 3, and Article III, Sections 1 & 2;

... **ITEM:** Executive Branch creation and implementation of regulations asserting unconstitutional force of Federal law on matters explicitly rejected by or contrary to the will and intent of Congress, specifically the EPA implementation of Cap and Trade, in violation of U.S. Constitution Article I, Section 1 and Section 8;

... **ITEM:** Refusing to secure our broken borders from illegal alien invasion, international criminal incursion, and terrorist cadre penetration, in violation of U.S. Constitution, Article III, Section 3 and Article IV, Section 4;

... **ITEM:** Executive Branch malfeasance and impeding the administration of justice by preventing U.S. Department of Justice from investigating crimes committed for the direct benefit of the

President by presidential associates including: voter intimidation at the hands of the New Black Panthers and ACORN election fraud, in violation of U.S. Constitution Article II, Section 3, and U.S. Criminal Code Section 135, (Comp. St. Section 10305); ...

The allegations of treason are up to Congress, if they are going to proceed."

How can Congress not proceed? The acts of treason as set forth in this article and the prior article are such that Congress must act. If not, we have become a nation of lawlessness, yes, lawlessness, by our president Obama. One of the principles of our country is that no one is above the law! Treason is defined in our U.S. Constitution and our U.S. Code sets forth specifics for acts of treason.

We must demand that Members of Congress fulfill their Constitutional responsibilities and try Obama for Treason.

CHAPTER XIX - Impeachment

Has Obama committed acts that he should be Impeached?

What a question – and *scary* – and frightening!

Impeachment? The U.S. Constitution provides in Article II, Section 4:

"The President, Vice President and all civil officers of the United States, shall be removed from office on impeachment for, and conviction of, treason, bribery, or other high crimes and misdemeanors."

Well, if the glove fits, you must impeach!

As reported in The Washington Times on 03/01/2014 with a caption: *"Steven Seagal: Obama would be impeached if the truth about Benghazi came out"* and quoting from the Independent Journal Review, Steven Seagal speaking at the Western Conservative Conference said: *"Never in my life did I ever believe that our country would be taken over by people like the people who are running it at this day. If the truth about Benghazi were to come out now, I don't think that this man would make it through his term. I think he would be impeached."*

Unfortunately, and I mean <u>unfortunately</u>, there is a great deal of talk about impeaching Obama based upon his campaign promises and the non-fulfillment thereof and other specific acts. I say this because Obama inspired the citizens of our country for hope for our country to move ahead for the benefit of all the citizens of our country; Obama stated that his administration would be the most open and transparent administration ever. Unfortunately, that did not occur, to the detriment of all the citizens of our country and the world.

I present the following reasons Obama could be charged with for impeachment, a drastic step, and with the current climate in our Congress, will not happen.

An article in Personal Liberty Digest titled: *"The Case for Obama's Impeachment"* dated June 9, 2004 by Bob Livingston states in part "with **bold/underline** added by me."

"There is clear and convincing evidence that President Barack Obama has on numerous occasions willfully committed treason and high crimes and misdemeanors and should be removed from office.

The 'crimes' that led to the impeachment of both Andrew Johnson and Bill Clinton and the resignation of Richard Nixon pale in comparison to Obama's. Johnson's 'crimes' were purely political. He favored a policy of benevolent reconciliation with the Southern States following the Civil War.

He issued a series of proclamations that directed the Southern States to hold conventions and elections to reform their governments; he attempted to veto a number of bills establishing military districts to oversee the new State governments; he vetoed an incumbent protection act called the Tenure of Office Act; and he fired Secretary of War Edwin Stanton, who was working against him at every turn.

Those moves were all contrary to the wishes of the Republicans who control both houses of Congress in the aftermath of the war. The impeachment vote in the Senate failed by one vote on all three counts to receive the two-thirds majority necessary to remove Johnson from office.

Clinton was impeached for perjury to a grand jury and obstruction of justice in the Paula Jones sexual harassment suit and the related independent counsel's investigation in the Monica Lewinsky affair and various other Clinton misdeeds. Forty-five Senators - all of them Republican - voted to remove Clinton from office over the perjury charge. Fifty voted to remove him for obstruction of justice. Though Clinton was clearly guilty, not one Democrat in the Senate voted to impeach. And, in fact, the Senate voted 100-0 to not hear any live witnesses in the trial.

Nixon, of course, resigned a couple of weeks after the House opened its impeachment hearings over his role in the cover-up of the Watergate break-in and other allegations of his misuse of office, the facts of which were just coming to light at the time.

"... Six years of this lawless regime is more than any sane person should be expected to endure. Even leftist legal scholar Jonathan Turley called Obama "the president Richard Nixon always wanted to be." "So here are my [Bob Livingston's] articles of impeachment - in no particular order - for the undocumented usurper currently despoiling the People's House: Barack Hussein Obama."

The following are excerpts from the list as set forth in the article.

"He provided aid and comfort to the enemy by releasing five suspected terrorists and former members of the Taliban who participated in or orchestrated attacks against Americans.

He violated a law he signed six months prior requiring him to notify Congress 30 days before releasing GITMO detainees.

He has willfully and repeated violated Article I, Section 1 of the U.S. Constitution by continuously amending the Affordable Care Act, aka Obamacare.

He knowingly and willfully violated Article I, Section 7 of the U.S. Constitution by signing the ACA [Affordable Care Act], knowing it was a bill for raising revenue that had originated in the Senate.

He engaged in fraud by repeatedly lying to the American people about the effects of the ACA by claiming that Americans could keep their current coverage and physicians if they chose.

He exercised an abuse of power by instructing, through his proxies, agents of the Internal Revenue Service to target conservative organizations and his critics for extra scrutiny and audits.

He participated in an obstruction of justice and a criminal conspiracy by hindering a Congressional investigation into the Internal Revenue Service targeting scandal and using Attorney General Eric Holder and the Department of Justice in that obstruction.

He provided aid and comfort to the enemy by ordering or allowing the sale of arms and ammunition to al-Qaida-linked terrorists in Syria and by dispatching agents of the government to advise and train in the use of those weapons and in military tactics.

He failed, despite repeated request by the U.S. Consulate, to provide the security necessary to ensure the safety of U.S. personnel and the Consulate in Benghazi, Libya.

He knowingly and willfully denied military assistant to Americans under attack at the Benghazi Consulate, resulting in the trashing of the U.S. Consulate building, the theft of sensitive documents and the deaths of four Americans: U.S. Ambassador Chris Stevens; Information Specialist Sean Smith; and former Navy SEALs Ty Woods and Glen Doherty.

He knowingly and willfully lied and ordered his proxies to lie about the circumstances surrounding the attack on the U.S. Consulate in Benghazi, thereby perpetrating a fraud on the American people in order to ensure his re-election and to cover-up his illegal gun running operation.

He has repeatedly violated the 4th Amendment by allowing agencies under his direction to continue to spy upon, wiretap and collect personal information of American citizens who are not criminal suspects.

He has repeatedly violated Article II, Section 3 of the U.S. Constitution by disregarding laws passed by Congress, including, but not limited to, U.S. immigration laws, civil rights laws and the Defense of Marriage Act.

He knowingly allowed the illegal sale of weapons to Mexican narco-terrorists that were later used to kill Americans, including border agent Brian Terry.

He obstructed justice by participating with Attorney General Holder in a cover-up of the Fast and Furious gun running scheme.

He knowingly and willfully violated Article IV, Section 4 by failing to protect the Border States against invasion, and in fact encouraged that invasion through his rhetoric and with the use of its executive orders *that contravened U.S. immigration law.*

He instructed his Interior Secretary to ignore the orders of Federal Courts to lift a moratorium on Deepwater drilling in the Gulf of Mexico, which denied oil workers an opportunity to earn a living and damaged the U.S. economy.

He broke established precedent and contravened established bankruptcy law, to the detriment of the bond holders and the advantage of his campaign contributors (auto unions) in the General Motors bailout.

In the auto bailout, he knowingly and willfully deprived numerous auto dealers of their dealerships for political reasons in violation of Amendments 4 and 14.

He repeatedly transferred funds from the U.S. Treasury to his cronies and campaign contributors for use in failing green energy schemes.

He violated Article II, Section 2 of the U.S. Constitution by appointing officers without first obtaining the "Advice and Consent of the Senate."

The author, Bob Livingston, continues:

"In his book **Faithless Execution, Building the Political Case for Obama's Impeachment**, Andrew C. McCarthy notes, 'Impeachment is a grave remedy on the order of a nuclear strike.' Obama's lawless Presidency has been nothing less than a nuclear strike on the U.S. Constitution, which now lies in tatters. 'Impeachment is a political remedy: even if palpably guilty of profound transgressions, a president will not be ousted without a groundswell of public ire.' McCarthy writes. **In his case for impeachment, McCarthy breaks Obama's high crimes and misdemeanors into seven articles**. [Emphasis and **bold** added by me]

They are:

Article I: The President's willful refusal to execute the laws faithfully and usurpation of the legislative authority of Congress.

Article II: Usurping the Constitutional authority and prerogatives of Congress.

Article III: Dereliction of Duty as President and Commander in Chief of the U.S. Armed Forces.

Article IV: Fraud on the American People.

Article V: Failure to execute the Immigration Laws faithfully.

Article VI: Failure to execute the laws faithfully: Department of Justice.

Article VII: Willfully undermining the Constitutional rights of the American people that he is sworn to preserve, protect and defend.

Without commenting directly on the above lists and Articles of Impeachment prepared by writer Bob Livingston and Andrew C. McCarthy, it shows numerous actions of president Obama that have hurt our country and deprived our citizens of all the protections that we are entitled to by "our" U.S. Constitution, Declaration of Independence and Bill of Rights.

I am not commenting specifically on each allegation as I set them forth for individual consideration so that you can and should advise your representatives in Congress to proceed to investigate and try Obama for his actions and inactions that have violated his oath of office.

It is a sad day for the citizens of our country!

There are so many comments at this time regarding impeachment, and I would like to relate a segment of remarks by Sarah Palin published July 11, 2014 on FoxNews.com titled:

"The case for Obama's impeachment: The Constitution's remedy for a lawless, imperial president," which reads in part

" ... No serious person who is paying attention can deny that

Obama and his administration have abused and violated the public trust and disregarded the Constitution. Let me count the ways.

Without notifying Congress as required by law, he set free terrorist prisoners at a time of war when they can return to the battlefield to kill our troops.

In violation of our Constitution, he regularly ignores court orders, changes laws by executive fiat, and refuses to enforce laws he doesn't like, including our immigration laws.

When Congress declined to pass amnesty for illegal immigrants' offspring, he unilaterally enacted his own version of it, which created the current crisis on our border as illegal youth pour into our country to receive what he legally promised them.

He committed fraud on the American people when he promised that if we liked our health care plan we could keep it.

He "went" to war in Libya without Congressional approval. When our ambassador begged for security at the consulate in Benghazi, he was ignored and then murdered when the consulate was attacked as predicted. Americans were left behind to die, as the president did nothing to rescue our people there. Afterwards, he helps spread the lie that a spontaneous protest over a YouTube video was to blame for this highly organized, premeditated terrorist attack.

Obama's IRS targeted his political opponents were harassment. Then the agency lied to and stonewalled Congress and likely destroyed subpoenaed evidence, while Obama falsely declared there's no corruption there, not even a smidgen. What about the hard-drive that was hidden from access that had the emails we have all been looking for!

From the VA scandal to his unconstitutional recess appointments, to his DOJ wiretapping reporters and giving guns to Mexican drug cartels, to violating religious freedom exercised by businesses and ignoring in-house illegal fundraising, the list of abuse goes on and on.

Barack Obama's administration is proving itself a festering boil of scandal. The Constitution is rock solid in holding the president responsible for the executive branch. He can't just vote "present" while shrugging and feigning ignorance about all these abuses of the public trust, any more than a mob boss can claim innocence because he didn't personally do the hit. The buck stops with the guy at the top.

Impeachment is the ultimate check on an out-of-control executive branch. It is serious, not to be used for petty partisan purposes; and it is imperative that it becomes a matter of legitimate discussion before the American people lose all trust in our federal government.

Impeachment requires moral courage to advance what is right, and it requires political will. A complacent or disheartened electorate may silently endure these abuses from the administration, the permanent political class is only too happy to maintain the status quo, and the mainstream media is not a fair watchdog. So, the nation's last line of defense is for 'We The People' to rise up and say, "enough is enough."

Obama's lawless encouragement of illegal immigration should be the tipping point for that political will because it impacts all Americans – native-born and legal immigrants of all backgrounds who followed the rules and now watch rewards go to rule breakers while they're forced to complete for limited jobs and resources. It's the tipping point because the forgotten working class is hurt most by this lawlessness; and these good Americans deserve the strongest, most effective tool to defend the livelihoods they've so honorably built.

The *"blind Steeple"* demand cautious inaction and dismiss even a discussion of impeachment. With Obama's poll numbers in the tank and his liberal policies exposed as failures, why rock the boat? But that argument misses the point.

The president is radically changing the way the executive branch does business. He is setting a dangerous precedent that will fundamentally change us. With his "pen and phone," he's abrogating Congressional authority in violation of the Constitution's separation of powers. He's making himself a ruler, not a president. We had a revolution back in 1776 because we don't like kings.

...The only thing necessary to transform America into something that is unrecognizable is for good men to do nothing! If not these violations and the president's promise to continue to "go it alone" in ignoring the separation of powers and rule of law, what will it take for you to take a stand? How bad does it have to get?

We live in America where the NSA spies on our communications, the IRS targets us because of our political beliefs, the border is overrun by foreign nationals, terrorist leaders are released to the battlefield, our health care is taken from us and we're forced to buy a plan we don't want and can't afford, Catholic nuns are targeted by the government simply because they adhere to their Catholic faith, the Justice Department arms Mexican drug lords, and the president keeps a "kill list" of people he's authorized to be executed on sight.

If you're comfortable with all that, then by all means sit back and hope for the best. Those concerned about America want change. That comes with healing the injuries done to society by an unchecked president; that starts with impeachment."

Again, the above article set forth many examples of what writer, Sarah Palin, feels are impeachable offenses.

As I've stated several times in this book, it is time that "We The People" wake up and do something now to stop Obama from destroying "our" country that we have loved.

CHAPTER XX
Freedompalooza

An Annual Festival on the 4th of July committed to the fight for Freedom.

And the truth prevails, year after year, at Freedompalooza, an annual festival on the 4th of July committed to the fight for freedom by exposing the truth by means of music, speakers and vendors.

In my speech on July 4, 2013 I read in part an article that appeared in Newsweek magazine June 2013.

A column by Matt Patterson stated in part: "… Unfortunately, minorities often suffer so that whites can pat themselves on the back. Liberals routinely admit minorities to schools for which they are not qualified, yet take no responsibility for the inevitable poor performance and high drop-out rates would follow. Liberals don't care if these minority students fail; liberals aren't around to witness the emotional devastation and deflated self-esteem resulting from the racist policy that is affirmative action. Yes, racist. Holding someone to a separate standard merely because of the color of the skin - that's affirmative action in a nutshell, and if that isn't racism, then nothing is.

And that is what America did to Obama. True, Obama was never troubled by his lack of achievements, but why would he be? As many have noted, Obama was told he was good enough for Columbia despite undistinguished grades at Occidental; he was told he was good enough for the US Senate despite a mediocre record in Illinois; he was told he was good enough to be president despite no record at all in the Senate. All his life, every step of the way, Obama was told he was good enough for the next step, in spite of ample evidence to the contrary.

What would this breed if not the sort of empty narcissism on display every time Obama speaks? In 2008, many who agreed that he lacked executive qualifications nonetheless raved about Obama's oratory skills, intellect, and cool character. Those people – conservatives included - ought now to be deeply embarrassed.

The man thinks and speaks in the hoariest of clichés, and that's when he has his Teleprompters in front of him; when the prompter is absent he can barely think or speak at all. Not one original idea has ever issued from his mouth – it's all warmed-over Marxism of the kind that has failed over and over again for 100 years. [An example is his 2012 campaign speeches which are almost word for word his 2008 speeches].

And what about his character? Obama is constantly blaming anything and everything else for his troubles. Bush did it; it was bad luck; I inherited this mess. Remember, he wanted the job, campaigned for the task. It is embarrassing to see a president so willing to advertise his own powerlessness, so comfortable with his own incompetence. [The other day he actually came out and said no one could have done anything to get our economy and country back on track.] But really, what were we to expect? The man has never been responsible for anything, so how do we expect him to act responsibly?

In short: our president is a small-minded man, with neither the temperament nor the intellect to handle his job. When you understand that, and only when you understand that, will the current erosion of liberty and prosperity make sense? It could not have gone otherwise with such a man in the Oval Office. "

This article in 2013 was one of the first, or the first, for a major publication to go after Obama for the lack luster president he was and still is. Matt Patterson from Newsweek went into depth about Obama's background and indicates to all of us why we should not be surprised about Obama's performance as president. And now, a year and a half [1 ½] later, Obama has continued as Matt Patterson described. How sad!

I proudly say that I have been a regular featured speaker with my last appearance this past July 4, 2014 during which time I addressed the group with the topics I cover in *ObamaScare*.

I am proud to say that I owe a special thanks to Paul Topete and his Pokerface Band that plays yearly at Freedompalooza and their band appeared for me in Washington, DC in front of the United States Capitol when I brought my message to Washington.

And thanks to the videographer, Vincent Mineo, for his very

professional work, year-after-year.

Philip J. Berg

CHAPTER XXI

Berg Helps Veterans

Protesting Jane Fonda a/k/a "Hanoi Jane"

I came to the aid of all United States Veterans when in 2013 I started a web site, ***fondaisatraitor.com***, to protest Jane Fonda [a/k/a "Hanoi Jane"] sitting on a tank facing our U.S. military while smiling as she was surrounded by Communist North Viet Cong.

During the Vietnam War, Americans demanded Jane Fonda be tried for Treason, but because of her father's status in Hollywood, it never happened. Instead she has lived a life of privilege, moving from one millionaire husband to the next, all the time enjoying the lavish lifestyle America afforded her; the country she hates.

Now at the ripe old age of 70, Fonda has decided to once again flip her finger to the American people. Hanoi Jane played Nancy Reagan in a movie called "The Butler."

A communist sympathizer, traitor and collaborator she now portrays the wife of one of America's most loved Conservative Presidents. Plus the irony is Ronald Reagan was a President who fought Communism on all fronts.

This is how the left spits on America and all our values. They look to the bottom of the communist barrel to come up with a disgraceful woman like Jane Fonda a/k/a Hanoi Jane.

We say no!!! I assisted Veterans demanding the theaters all across America "Just say No" to the distribution of the movie, "The Butler."

CHAPTER XXII
Illegal Immigration at Southern Borders

Children coming from South America with diseases and
What Obama, Congress & our Free Press Must Do

Wake up America – insist that politicians: the president, all members of congress – republicans, democrats and independents act "now." I set forth herein what must be done now by Obama, Congress and our Free Press.

OBAMA – Use *"YOUR PEN"* and issue an EXECUTIVE ORDER changing the law immediately so that illegal immigrants from countries other than contiguous countries, Mexico and Canada, are immediately deported!

Use "YOUR PEN" and "SEAL" "OUR" BORDERS!

Use *"YOUR PEN"* and issue an EXECUTIVE ORDER regarding the illegal alien crisis stopping "all aid" to Guatemala, El Salvador and Honduras until the flow of children stops! Obama, you met on July 25, 2014 at the White House with Vice President Biden and the Presidents of these South American countries: Guatemala President Otto Perez Molina; El Salvador President Salvadore Sanchez Ceren; and Honduras President Juan Orlando Hernandez. Apparently, nothing significant happened, as illegal children continued crossing "our" borders.

CONGRESS – Pass immigration legislation that is in line with our legal immigration policy that has existed over the years; that means illegal immigrants must be deported; immigrants must do what legal immigrants have done for years – follow our laws!

PRESS – Report the truth about the crisis along our southern border and all the scandals in "our" country! Be the "Free Press" you are supposed to be! STOP covering for Obama! You're covering for Obama and his administration is allowing the destruction of y[our] country!

In an article on Western Journalism [WJ] dated August 21, 2013 titled: *"Obama's 13 Impeachable Offenses"* by Jerry McGlothlin states in part, *"... June 15, 2012: The Obama administration announced it will stop deporting illegal immigrants under the age of 30 in a 'deferred action' policy to circumvent immigration laws. This comes after Congress rejected a similar measure about a year ago. Since then, more than 500,000 illegals have received the deferment and only 20,000 have been rejected. As for the law-abiding applicants who have been waiting in line, well, that Obama's idea of lawfulness."*

The article by Jerry McGlothlin indicates the specifics of the stoppage of deporting illegal immigrants, another example of Obama breaking the laws and Obama being out-of-control.

CHAPTER XXIII

Marine SGT. Andrew Tahmooressi

U.S. Prisoner in Mexico

Another nightmare for our country is the imprisonment of Marine Sgt. Andrew Tahmooressi, age 26, in Mexico. He was in prison since March 31, 2014, now over seven [7] months, until recently released, no thanks to president Obama. The Sgt.'s position is his non-intentional entrance into Mexico at the San Ysidro, California border entrance, when, according to Sgt. Tahmooressi, he drove his vehicle into the wrong lane and could not use the turn back lane to the United States, and therefore had to enter Mexico.

Upon his entry into Mexico, he immediately told the guards at the border station that he had three guns in his vehicle as it is a violation of Mexican law to bring any guns into Mexico. At the time of this border incident he was not on active duty or in a military uniform. He was in the San Diego area for medical treatment after his two [2] tours of duty in Afghanistan.

While I agree that the laws in Mexico are different than the United States as there is no prosecutor discretion to allow the disposition of charges by the prosecutor, there has been enormous pressure to the White House to do something: for Obama to make a telephone call to Enrique Pena Nieto, President of Mexico, to publicly ask for the release of the Sergeant. I know of no action taken by Obama so far; I say that because perhaps something has been done behind the scenes, and if it has been, to no avail.

The question becomes is why Obama has not made a public effort to call Mexican President Nieto to have the release of Marine Sgt. Tahmooressi. This is significant because under the allegations of Fast and Furious, our government gave weapons to the Mexican drug cartel which ended up costing the life of an American Border Control official. Also, with the current border nightmare of illegal children crossing our border from South America is the fact they are coming through Mexico. This should be a bargaining chip in the ongoing illegal border crossing.

It has been reported on several occasions the Obama has spoken to Enrique Pena Nieto, President of Mexico, but has not raised the issue of Marine Sgt. Tahmooressi.

Again, another example of Obama doing his own thing to the detriment of this United States Marine.

On August 26, 2014, Governor Jerry Brown had a state luncheon in Sacramento at the Leland Stanford Mansion honoring Mexican President Enrique Pena Nieto, and upon questions from the Press, Governor Brown indicated it was a federal problem, not his. How disgusting, Governor Brown had an opportunity to address the issue of Marine Sgt. Tahmooressi and failed to do so. What a lack of leadership!

CHAPTER XXIV

MALAYSIA MH17 - Obama could have Avoided the Destruction

The current situation in Ukraine where an airplane, a Malaysia MH17 was blown out-of-the-air on July 17, 2014 by a surface-to-air missile and 298 people died of which 80 were children. This was a result of the failure of Obama's foreign policy! I believe Obama could have taken steps that would have avoided this tragedy. He is all talk and no action.

When Putin attacked Crimea, Obama did nothing. However, the critical situation regarding Putin and others around the world began when Obama drew a "red line" in Syria, and then he failed to follow through and then Obama said he didn't draw the 'red line', someone else did. **DoubleSpeak** again, but this time with major detrimental results!"

I am sure Putin is shaking in his boots over the inaction of Obama. The Russian forces, "Pro Russian Rebels," around and in Ukraine are under the control of Putin. The missile that hit the plane would not have been in Ukraine if Obama did something at the time of the takeover of Crimea. Obama threatens and basically does nothing; oh yeah, he issues sanctions. The sanctions Obama placed against Russia have so far really had limited impact.

With a major world crisis occurring over the missile blowing a plane from 38,000 feet, what did Obama do? Not much; continued no leadership role. Obama's Representative to the United Nations, Samantha Power, delivered a much stronger speech at the United Nations than Obama at the White House.

We The People must do something to stop the outrageous conduct of president Obama. Obama has become a laughing joke, no leadership, **DoubleSpeak** and a total embarrassment.

CHAPTER XXV
Dictionary and Civil & Criminal Law

Words to Remove - "Conflict-of-Interest" & "Cover-up"

I mentioned in several chapters the following words:
"Conflict-of-Interest" / Chapter 7
"Cover-up"/ Chapters 11, 13, 15 & 17

And gave reasons why they must be removed from all dictionaries, regular and legal; and from all civil and criminal crimes.

I set forth what I believe is *"Conflict-of-Interest"* and *"Cover-up"* and these issues must be looked into, because unanswered, our country is in real trouble. Obama and his administration have, for the entire time of his administration, been doing their own thing, disregarding "our" U.S. Constitution, not following the laws of the United States and, as I set forth in other chapters, have major issues of "Conflict-of-Interest" and "Cover-up."

I set these words herein, as Obama and his administration have set new standards, to all of our detriment, and therefore, I felt it necessary to stress to you, the reader, to make sure you understand why I believe we must demand the truth or remove these words from all dictionaries, regular and legal; and from all civil and criminal crimes.

Briefly, I set forth the details of *"Conflict-of-Interest"* in Chapter VII called 'The "SEALED" Case – *Berg, as Relator v. Obama*.' In this case, a False Claim case, I alleged that president Barack Obama a/k/a Barry Soetoro was **not** a U.S. citizen, natural born or even naturalized and therefore served 'illegally' as an United States Senator for Illinois as an U.S. Senator must be a U.S. Citizen that I allege Obama isn't, and therefore the salary & benefits he received must be returned to the U.S. Treasury. The **"Conflict-of-Interest"** I alleged that the decision to proceed or not was up to the head of the Department of Justice and the head of the U.S. Attorney's Office, both heads being the **same** individual, U.S. Attorney General Eric Holder. The conflict was that Attorney General Eric Holder was so close to president Obama [details set out in Chapter VII] that Eric Holder violated Conflict-of-Interest as set forth in the Code of Federal Regulations and the United States Codes **and** the decision to dismiss my case was definitely a conflict.

Regarding the issue of **"Cover-up,"** I set forth in Chapter XI [Benghazi] and Chapter XV [Scandals – IRS] the facts that support my allegations of **"Cover-up."** The two [2] year delay in facts coming forth about Benghazi; the false assertions by Obama and his administration about the initial cause; and the ongoing denial of what actually happened versus the recently related facts from the personnel on the ground says **"Cover-up."**

Regarding IRS – the ongoing lies about the facts; the Emails, missing or not and why; the hard drives, destroyed or not and why; as well as the lack of credible testimony indicates **"Cover-up."**

Therefore, the words, **"Conflict-of-Interest"** and **"Cover-up"** must be removed from all dictionaries, regular and legal; and from all civil and criminal crimes.

I really do not want these words removed! I want "our" Congress and "our" Free Press to demand the truth about all of these scandals and disclose and prosecute the **"Conflict-of-Interests"** and **"Cover-ups."**

CHAPTER XXVI
Radio, Newspaper, Magazines & Internet Appearances

After I filed my first lawsuit against Obama, the interest grew quickly to become a major communications platform. My first major exposure was a ten [10] minute video interview that was taken in front of Independence Hall, Philadelphia, Pennsylvania in October 2008. The name of the video is *"October Surprise"* by Illuminati Productions. Molotov Mitchell interviewed me and as of Spring 2014, it had been viewed 4.3 million times. Episode 6 can be seen here: *https://www.youtube.com/watch?v=gA6_k3NtXZs#t=58*

I was on hundreds of radio shows; newspaper and magazine

articles; a lot of internet exposure; very little TV; and a great deal of YouTube. My website, **_Obamacrimes.com_**, became so popular that it was #7 in the world.

Radio: The following are a few of many radio shows that I have been a guest:

Michael Savage – the first time I was on, Savage kept asking me to stay on for the next segment and at the end of the show, Savage told me I was the guest with the longest time on his show... ever.

Webster Tarpley - World Crisis Radio - on a regular basis
Lou Vickery – Lou in The Morning – many times
Matt Ray – America's Morning News.
Alex Jones – many times
Rolleye James – many times
Bill Cunningham – many times
John Clark - many times
Fred Smart – many times
Peter Boyles' – KNUS, Denver, CO - many times
Roger Hedgecock's Show, San Diego, CA
Steve Malzberg
Coast To Coast AM
Wiley S. Drake
Lars Larson Show
Pastor James David Manning
Paul Price
Michael Volin
Geir Smith – Before it's News
Rose Colombo
Dr. Bill Deagle
Jeff Harrison
Lan Lamphere
Rumor Mill News Radio
Ian Punnet
and many others

Newspaper & Magazines – numerous including:
Globe Magazine - 01/12/2009 & others
Philadelphia Weekly – 08/09/2009

And a newspaper article by Jeff Schreiber, americasright.com on 08/23/2008, right after I filed the 1st lawsuit against Obama and it is important to read as the questions I raised then are still unanswered:

A Conversation with Philip J. Berg, Esq. (Obama birth certificate lawsuit)
americasright.com ^ | 8-23-08 | Jeff Schreiber

Posted on **Sunday, August 24, 2008 2:11:37 AM** by **Doug from upland**

A Conversation with Philip J. Berg, Esq.

Fairly late yesterday evening, I had the opportunity to speak with Philip Berg, the Philadelphia attorney who filed suit against Illinois senator Barack Obama in Federal Court in Philadelphia, questioning the constitutional eligibility of his candidacy for president.

I was fortunate enough to be in the right place at the right time to break the story, which only now is beginning to gain traction for a hopeful leap into the mainstream media. Berg, who served as Deputy Attorney General of Pennsylvania for eight years, ran twice for governor in 1990 and 1998 and once for the U.S. Senate in 2000, was former chair of the Democratic Party in Montgomery (PA) County and a former member of the Democratic State Committee, was more than happy to speak with me yesterday afternoon in the lobby of the courthouse following a hearing in the chambers of the Hon. R. Barclay Surrick.

Immediately, we established that we couldn't be more ideologically dissimilar. He believes that the United States government was behind the attacks of September 11, 2001; the very mention of such theories make me ill. He was an ardent supporter of Hillary Clinton's candidacy during the primaries; I sell tee shirts showing the former first lady and one of her quotes ("We're going to take things away from you on behalf of the common good," said in June 2004) juxtaposed under the words "RE-DEFEAT COMMUNISM."

Needless to say, Philip Berg and I are very different. I'm not sure that I completely buy into the various allegations made in the complaint filed late on Thursday afternoon, but I value more than anything other than my wife and child the United States Constitution and the ideas and ideals of those who wrote it here in Philadelphia so many years ago; for that reason, I firmly believe that Berg's action against Barack Obama must be given the full attention that it deserves, for the sake of America and everything for which She stands.

Philip Berg, from what I can tell, is not the stark-raving mad whack-job that people on the American political left are already portraying him to be. In our two discussions, he was rational, he was calm, he was congenial and showed a sense of humor -- something I thought inexistent in most liberals. I'm not afraid to say that I like the guy.

He found time to fit me in amidst an increasingly busy schedule. He had just completed a 20-minute live, drive-time radio interview with a San Diego, CA show, presumably Roger Hedgecock's show, but I don't know for sure. Earlier on Friday, he taped a 20-minute interview with Webster Tarpley, apparently an influential figure among those who, like Berg, feel that our federal government, incapable and cumbersome as it is, was able to organize and execute the 9/11 attacks and keep the conspiracy quiet afterwards. I didn't press on Tarpley; I'm like David Banner when I get angry, only with love handles. Berg also mentioned that he was to be on Coast To Coast AM early this morning from about 1:15 to 3:00 a.m., and on Monday was scheduled for another drive-time interview on a Mississippi radio station.

The mainstream press, once it does grab a hold of this story, will undoubtedly cast Philip Berg as either (1) a nutjob with a questionable past or (2) a low-level party operative retained by Hillary Clinton and her flunkies to do some dirty work in the days leading up to the nominating convention in Denver. I thought I'd tackle the latter issue first, perhaps to determine where his loyalties lie and how he feels about the candidates.

Being the natural skeptic that I am, Mr. Berg, I couldn't help but think that a relatively well-known and respectable local party operative such as yourself would be the perfect person to act as surrogate on behalf of Hillary Clinton and her campaign, only a matter of weeks after she somehow maneuvered her way into having her name included in the nomination. Care to comment?

I have had no direct or indirect contact with anyone on the Hillary Clinton campaign. Did I help her in the primaries? Yes. Was I in favor of her over Obama? Yes. What did I do? I contributed some money and made some phone calls to various states for her. Other than that, I attended one Montgomery County [PA] Democratic Committee dinner at which her daughter spoke, though for the record, Obama's representative was also at the same function. So, am I closely involved with them? No.

And as I told you this afternoon, even among those who helped me prepare for this case, while I know they may be against Obama's violation of the Constitution, I do not even know nor have I asked where they stand politically.

What was it that drew you to Hillary's candidacy in the first place?

I think that she is a remarkable woman. I think that over the years she has shown herself to be a leader. I was looking at everyone at the very beginning and I thought she really stood her ground. I think that we could use a woman in the White House, and I think she knows the issues, and the experience she had being First Lady helped, along with the experience gained in the Senate since then.

Throughout the past year, though, she and Barack Obama had shown themselves to be ideologically planting their flag on the same turf. Before you knew about all of this other stuff, before birth certificates, citizenship and eligibility, what was it that so turned you off to Obama?

Obama just never turned me on. There has always been something missing there, and as his various associations came out, the kind of people he was involved with, it really turned my stomach. I couldn't believe it.

That, and he had an excuse for everything. His phony responses to the Rev. [Jeremiah] Wright issue turned me off. He said "I never knew what he was like." He was a member of that church for twenty years. Twenty years! When the story first broke, he went on all of the television and cable stations and claimed he was never in the pew when Rev. Wright made any of these remarks. By the time he made his speech in Philadelphia days later—a speech that the mainstream media agreed might have been the best in the history of the world—he did a complete turnabout and admitted that he was in the pew at the time of the remarks. At what point is enough, enough?

It should be noted that Oprah joined that church in 1984 and left in 1986 because she felt that the viewpoint of Rev. Wright and that church could be detrimental to her television career. [I suppose he meant THIS --Jeff] Obama was somehow there for twenty years and did not know what Rev. Wright was like? Nobody can believe that.

And then it went on, issue after issue, association after association, Bill Ayers and so on and so forth. And the media let him slide. They let him slide on doing drugs. Cocaine, marijuana – some other candidate saying this would be hammered by the media.

Everything was overlooked. Look at the issue he's making now, about John McCain not knowing how many properties he owns.

The way it was phrased in the television commercial, it looked to me to be an obvious reference to his age. Don't you think?

That's right. Why can't we ask Obama about the time he said he had visited 57 states? If Hillary Clinton had stated that, you'd still be hearing about it today. If McCain had said that, you'd still be hearing about it. But Barack Obama says it, and it just disappears.

Not to mention that, in the weeks and months leading up to the 2004 election, the folks in your party were up in arms about any reference to the considerable wealth of Teresa Heinz Kerry. Now that it is Cindy McCain and not Ms. Imperceptible Accent, family wealth is fair game. Why is that?

I don't know. Listen, she's worth over $100 million dollars. They can have as many houses as they want. But I must give credit to McCain – he's never taken an earmark during all his years in the Senate for the state of Arizona. Now, the guy has crossed the line on a number of bills and I cannot say that I'm rooting for McCain, but he certainly has more pluses than Obama.

Obama is an empty suit. He's very good when he delivers a speech—I don't know if he writes them himself or has a team of speechwriters—but when he's off of the teleprompter, his oratory goes down the drain. That's why he didn't want to do all of these town meetings across the country with McCain, and the atrocious performance at Saddleback Church last week shows that Obama will likely falter in the three scheduled debates before the election.

I chalk much of his success up to the influence and agenda setting of the mainstream media. Speaking of which, are you happy with the coverage which the mainstream press has given your civil action?

Well, no. First of all, the mainstream media hasn't covered it yet. I'm doing an interview with a journalist tomorrow morning at 10:00 who says he'll be able to get it out into the mainstream media.

Well, once it bridges that gap for the first time, then it should spread just as the recent accounts of John Edwards' infidelity did. It took more than eight months for the story to reach a newspaper or television show of note.

Yes. I was talking to a producer from one of the Fox shows, and she said that until it appears in the mainstream press, we cannot cover it. The Times-Herald, out of Norristown here, they're airing a story here either Saturday or Sunday, and I have a feeling that they'll do a good job on it, seeing that they're pretty much my hometown paper.

I'm encouraged by the response over the Internet. I'm discouraged by the people in the mainstream press but I think we're going to crack it on this case. There are just so many people involved at this point ... people are sending out stories all over the place ... I've been involved in big cases over the years, and this is the single greatest initial response I've ever received in any case and I think it's because it's so significant – we're talking about a serious constitutional issue which has never been dealt with before. If we're right, which I believe we are, Obama really should be taken to task, because he knows that he violated the law. And I hope, if we're right, that someone brings criminal charges against him.

Criminal charges?

I think it's an absolute disgrace. If you go back to his record when he was running for the state senate, he threw off a competitor because he didn't meet the requirements. So I think this guy has got a lot of nerve, I really do, and I believe we're right, and I believe that action should be taken against him. He could cause, as I said to the judge today, irreparable harm to people in this country, and if it happens, there could be all sorts of bad stuff going on.

Is there any historical precedent for this? I'm not entirely positive, but I think that George Romney--Mitt's father--was deemed constitutionally eligible to run for president in 1968 even though he was born in Mexico.

I'm not sure about that, but if you remember [Thomas] Eagleton, he was forced out because of mental treatments--shock treatments-- and was replaced with Sergeant Shriver who, along with McGovern, lost.

A change of this sort is always detrimental, and that's why we believe the Republicans are aware of this, they're waiting, and they will bring it out in September or October and, at that point, would destroy the Democratic Party. Because of the backlash and the people who will be so disgusted, it will lose the presidency, and it could lose the Senate, the House, the governor races and other races across this country. I really think that Obama owes it to everyone to produce, right now, a vault birth certificate and proof of the oath of allegiance he took upon his return to this country from Indonesia, which I don't believe exists. If he has these documents, he owes it to everyone to bring them out right now.

I've written a lot over the past few months about race and

politics, and back in February and March warned of the potential for Barack Obama and his supporters to counter substance with charges of racism and cries of racial intolerance. What do you say to those people who inevitably will, perhaps looking at the underlying African story, call you a racist?

Of course some people might look at me and assume I'm doing this because he's black. I'm not. I'm Jewish, and I'm a life-long member of the NAACP, so people will be hard-pressed to confront me on any of those issues.

Rumors as to Barack Obama's citizenship have been swirling around the Internet for months. Why did you wait so long to file suit?

They asked me the same question when I was doing the radio interview for the San Diego station. I received a phone call about ten days ago, and someone said "you've got to do this." I explained that, before I went forth with it, I had to do due diligence, check all of the sources and check all of the information to find out if it was for real. And I believe it is for real.

Factcheck.org released a statement yesterday, including images showing an embossed seal and appropriate signatures, and maintained that after fondling the certificate they could attest to its authenticity. How satisfied are you with the independent forensic document experts cited in your complaint?

Well, I'm not familiar with that site [he asked me to spell it --Jeff] but I've seen documentation supporting our arguments just the same and I'm satisfied with that. Look, the truth comes down to this -- at this point in time, it's time to fish or cut bait, time to stop pussy-footing around. At this point in time, Obama owes it to people to produce the documents. If I'm wrong, even if he doesn't want to handle it himself and has the person in charge of his campaign communications come out and say, "here is the vault copy of the birth certificate, here is the certified copy of his oath of allegiance from when he came back from Indonesia, this issue should be put to bed and Mr. Berg should withdraw his suit immediately or we'll sue him to high heaven," then I'm wrong. If they do not do that within the next day or so, then I know we're right. If they let the case linger, then I believe we're right. The challenge I've made to them is that, if they don't produce these documents, then we know they're wrong.

Yes, but in a constitutional issue such as this one, wouldn't you carry the burden of proof, Mr. Berg?

Yes, it is on me, but what I am saying here is that I've created an issue which I'm sure will be all over the convention next week, whether the reporters want to deal with it or not. It should be brought up with the delegates; someone should bring it up and confront them with it. I'd like to go to Denver, and if I have the chance to speak in front of Obama delegates, I would explain that "if I'm wrong, I'm out of here – but it is incumbent upon you to ask your candidate to confirm that he is a citizen and produce the necessary documentation, and if he doesn't do it, then this party is going to go down the drain."

Switching gears now, the mainstream media has proven to be very protective of Barack Obama up to this point. I've even suggested that sitting on the John Edwards story in the weeks prior to the Iowa caucus was done not so much to protect Edwards, but to protect Obama from Hillary Clinton, who stood to benefit from Edwards' votes should he have dropped out early. Do you worry that you will be discredited as a result of bringing attention to the various issues, inconsistencies and unanswered questions surrounding the mainstream media's chosen candidate?

No. I'm not worried about that. I can handle myself in front of the media. If the media wants to confront me, I'll confront them. I'll ask them why I need to do this, why they didn't do this months ago. With the resources at their disposal, with the access and the ability to travel, it is incumbent upon them to have properly vetted Obama, and the fact that they have not done so is a disgrace.

A couple of years ago, in 2005, you were subject to sanctions and fines for reported ethics violations. A few years before that, there were the Federal Racketeering actions filed against President Bush and others suggesting prior knowledge and a cover-up of the September 11 attacks. And, of course, in the wake of the 2000 election, you called for the resignation of three Supreme Court Justices. You and I discussed, this afternoon, the effect of credibility on the authentication of rumor -- how do you transcend such issues with regard to this action?

The sanction and fines are on appeal.

The RICO action was withdrawn because we wanted to put together a more detailed RICO complaint, and that's why, when I represented Ellen Mariani she subsequently did not want to pursue the action. I got a second plaintiff named William Rodriguez, and things were moving along in the case, when he decided to withdraw for personal reasons. The case has put me into personal bankruptcy, but I plan to come back and proceed with the case.

And yes, I asked three Supreme Court Justices to resign because of their involvement with the 2000 election. I think what they did was improper. I spent three weeks down in Florida and, on the Saturday in question, I was sent out to a county in the panhandle and discovered, personally, white-out painted on ballots. Serving as a volunteer sent to check on things, I confronted the judge for that single county—I forget the name of the county at the moment—and some people say I was lucky to have survived, and only did so because an NBC affiliate was there filming and a reporter was there taking pictures which ended up running on the front page of the paper in that area. Other people said, "you know, you were ten miles from the Alabama border, and if those news media people hadn't been there, you might never have been heard from again."

See, I'm not afraid to come forth with issues which need to be exposed. Am I perfect? Of course not. In this case, however, I feel 99 percent that we're right on this particular case.

In terms of credibility, my very successful record in big cases shows some of that. I'm the only attorney in the country to defeat "cell phone" legislation in Hilltown Township, Bucks County, PA, meant to ban the use of hand-held cell phones while behind the wheel of a car, and did that pro bono. I have also represented PAWS—Performing Animal Welfare Society—in California, pro bono, protecting the rights of abused circus elephants, and was extremely successful in that case. My record, over the years, is such that I can stand on my own two feet in front of anyone.

This is also my 27th year as a member in the Barren Hill Volunteer Fire Company/Fire Police, where I have served as lieutenant, as sergeant, and just as a member. I average over 100 calls per year.

Regardless of credibility, how do you get past the circumstantial nature of the evidence cited in your complaint -- for instance, the account of Barack Obama's mother staying in Kenya and not flying back to Hawaii until after Barack's birth, all based on a custom at the time which prevented late-stage pregnant women from boarding airplanes?

Well, that's going to be tough, but the way around it is the grandmother—I'm not sure if she is still living—or the sister and brother who, according to reports, stated that they were at the Mombasa, Kenya hospital when Barack Obama was born. By subpoenaing records from that hospital, by subpoenaing the family members, we can obtain the evidence we need.

I think that, in this type of case, the burden of proof shifts. I think that Sen. Obama owes it to his party and to the citizens of this country to show that I am wrong. If I am, if he produces the documentation, the case will go away, I'll go away, and he can go forth and do what he can in the election. But if he ignores this topic, I believe it shows guilt on his part.

Now that Judge Surrick denied the temporary restraining order, where do you go from here?

We plan to wait until the various parties are served, and then I'll make the appropriate motion to the court for expedited discovery. At that point, we'll probably have a conference call with the judge to see where and when we will be proceeding, but this case, because of the nature of it and because the judge said he will make an effort to keep the case moving along, it needs an expedited track to overcome the normal time frame of six months to one year and beyond. This case cannot take that long.

This has to be brought to the forefront. That's why, again, Sen. Obama really owes it to everyone to confront this. He should threaten me. "Berg," he should say, "here are the documents and, if you do not withdraw the suit, I will sue you." Right now, he has no basis to sue me. If he does have the documents, he should show them, and I'll walk away. I'll withdraw the case. But, again, he must show me a certified vault copy of his birth certificate and must show me a certified copy of the oath of allegiance taken between the time he was 19 to 21 at a Consulate, U.S. Embassy or the like.

If those documents can be presented, again, I'm out of here. But I don't think he can, I don't think he will, and I think it is a total disgrace on his part.

Okay, in twenty seconds or less, why is it so important that these proceedings move forward?

It is important for these proceedings to go forward at this time because the later it goes on, the more disheveled the Democratic Party will look. If it is proven later on, or if it is otherwise not acknowledged until after he is elected, then procedural steps will have to be taken whether the news comes before or after January 20. Either way, we're looking at the destruction of the Democratic Party.

It is a disservice to every citizen of this country, especially those who donated hundreds of millions of dollars to his campaign. It is a disservice to the entire voting public, and indeed to the system as a whole."

Today, in 2014, I stand by my statements in the above article and I still question Obama, the Democratic National Committee and our supposed Free Press for not researching the still unanswered allegations

CHAPTER XXVII
American Politics – What is going on?

We, the American people must wake up to what is actually transpiring in American politics and government. From the president down throughout the Senate and House of Representatives, we are being misled. It is time to clean house. It is significant and to the detriment of all U. S. citizens.

president Obama disregards the sentiment and opinions of the American public as well as "our" U.S. Constitution. He acts as if he owns this country... wrong... "We The People" own it; Obama just has temporary control of it. His ratings are dropping as people become more aware of his underlying agenda and Socialist mindset. A poll in June 2014 confirms what I have said for months... Obama "is the worst President in history."

Additionally, the global opinion and respect of the United States dramatically dropped throughout the world as Obama has done significant things... *some by doing and some by not doing*, and that undermined our foreign policy. He has no foreign policy. This caused further problems for Israel and has deteriorated the efforts by undermining our efforts to curtail Iran's nuclear efforts by lessening sanctions on them without getting anything in return and by, unbelievable, negotiating with Iran; has caused Russia, China, Iran, North Korea and others to re-evaluate their positions around the world because of Obama's lack of foreign policy; his "Redline to Syria" and then his **"DoubleSpeak"** stating someone else set the "Redline"; his lack of stance against Putin's takeover of Crimea and Putin's recent buildup of troops along the Ukrainian border and insurgency into Ukraine at the end of August 2014; and loss of great portions of Iraq by ISSI, as Obama is always proceeding from behind – in August, 2014, six [6] months late in bombing ISSI in Iraq and his ongoing delay in going after ISSI in Syria – ISSI cannot be curtailed, they must be eliminated – they are a threat to the world, but especially to the

United States, because they stated so! In September 2014, it was disclosed that Obama had been receiving 'daily' briefings on ISSI for over a year. Obama's inaction was a crime against the world for allowing ISSI to grow and take land, money from banks and military equipment and become a monster group that murders at will, takes girls and women as hostages and rapes them. Our "Free Press" continues to *not* expose Obama. What a disgrace!

Congress should be ashamed of themselves as their ratings reflect an opinion of no confidence with eight [8%] to thirteen [13%] percent believe they are a *basically do-nothing Congress*. In 2014 they finally passed a budget, the first in five [5] years. Don't you find that *scary*! We hired them and now it's time to fire them, all of them! The entire Senate and House of Representatives as we all know what they do, which is basically nothing. People say... we do not know what we will get if we replace them, but we know what we have and that is not significant, not good for "our" country.

However, what takes place when the members of Congress go home; ninety-five [95%] percent of them are re-elected on a regular basis because of gerrymandering and more important, individuals at home feel that they know their member of the Senate or House and feel good because when they call the various offices and they are able to secure a congratulatory letter for their child, spouse or parent, as well as other services. The reason to re-elect should go to the work of these individuals for representing the people they represent, as the purpose for our representatives in Congress are to deal with national problems that exist, a function that is basically a failure.

CHAPTER XXVIII
U.S. House of Representatives to Sue Obama

House Speaker John Boehner is Suing.

Finally, some action by the U.S. House of Representatives. On July 24, 2014, the House Rules Committee by a vote of 7 to 4 voted to authorize a lawsuit against president Barack Obama. The next step was for the issue to be brought up by the full House of Representatives. On July 30, 2014, the full House of Representatives voted on party lines 225 to 201 to permit House Speaker John Boehner to sue. Senate approval is not necessary.

The lawsuit is necessary for one main reason; it is time some action is taken against Obama because he is out-of-control; doing his own thing; disregarding "our" U.S. Constitution, "our" Declaration of Independence and "our" Bill of Rights.

Obama has done more to hurt the United States of America, than every other President of the United States. Before I go into more details regarding the forthcoming lawsuit, I want to give everyone background on lawsuits against a President.

I have been told I am an expert in filing lawsuits against Presidents, because I filed lawsuits against two [2] sitting Presidents: President Bush and president Obama. I sued President Bush over the events of 911 and president Obama over his "Constitutionally Eligibility" to be President and over his illegal term as a United States Senator for Illinois.

The first issue that one must overcome is that of "Standing," that is the right to bring a lawsuit.

In my cases against President Bush, there was no question of standing as I represented two [2] individuals, both of which were injured, as one must show they were injured to proceed. In my first case that I filed, I represented Ellen Mariani, whose husband, Louis Neal Mariani, was on the second plane that hit the World Trade Center. The case against Bush (and many others), drew a tremendous amount of media attention in the United States and around the world, as people killed in the plane crash and subsequent building fires and building collapse wanted to know what really happened on 911.

I, with my client, Ellen Mariani's, approval, withdrew my original lawsuit against Bush for tightening-up my RICO complaint I had filed. During this same time, another person, William Rodriguez, was in contact with me to become a plaintiff in a case against President Bush and others, as he was aware of my initial case.

William Rodriguez was an interesting individual, as I learned he was a hero from 911, having helped others to get out of one of the buildings of the World Trade Center. Mr. Rodriquez was a janitor at the WTC and was late for work that day, 09/11/2001. If he had been on time to be at work, at the time the plane hit the building, he would have been in the Windows of the World restaurant, at the top of the WTC; and he would not be here today.

William Rodriquez & Philip J. Berg

Mr. Rodriguez was in the basement of the WTC and before a plane hit the building he was in, he heard and saw the effects of an explosion in the basement of the building he was in. He saw a worker coming from the area of the explosion with burns on his body and skin coming off his body.

Thereafter, Mr. Rodriguez became a hero after the WTC was hit by a plane, as he helped people get out of the building and he was the last person out of the WTC, actually diving under a fire truck to survive, and he was injured.

I traveled with Ellen Mariani to Boston, Massachusetts for a taping of an interview to be broadcast overseas on the 911 anniversary. Ellen promised prior to and at the taping that she would me a plaintiff in the re-filed case against Bush. Thereafter, something happened and Ellen decided not to go forth with her 911 case against Bush, etc. I respected Ellen so much and new how much she really wanted the truth about 911 that I wished her well.

So, when I re-filed the RICO case against Bush, it was with only one plaintiff, William Rodriguez. In both cases against Bush for 911, there was no question about "standing," as both parties, Mariani and Rodriguez, were injured.

Then, let's take a look at president Obama, who I sued several times for several reasons.

My first lawsuit, _Berg v. Obama_, I was the Plaintiff against Obama, was filed in August 2008, prior to Obama being nominated for President in Denver, Colorado.

My lawsuit was based upon my belief that Obama was, as I still believe, "Constitutionally Ineligible" to be President. Ultimately, Federal Judge Surrick dismissed my case stating that I, Philip J. Berg, did not have "standing" as I was not injured. How absurd! In my opinion, I, as all citizens of "our" United States have been and are affected by Obama and the words of "our" U.S. Constitution begin with the words, "WE THE PEOPLE." Judge Surrick stated that in the future, Congress can decide who has "standing" to sue a Presidential candidate or President.

Philip J. Berg

I filed several lawsuits against Obama and filed four [4] applications for Injunctions against aspects of the election process regarding Obama to the United States Supreme Court.

In one of my lawsuits against Obama, I was the Plaintiff in the United States District Court for the District of Columbia, as discussed in Chapter VII – The "SEALED" case – *Berg, as Relator v. OBAMA*.

The significance of this type case, a *Qui Tam* or False Claims Case is that the U.S. Supreme Court has ruled that the person bringing the case, the "Relator" has "Standing."

Now, let's look at what the United States House of Representatives plans on in their lawsuit against president Obama. I stated earlier that the House Rules Committee approved the legislation, followed by the approval by the full House of Representatives.

The basis of the lawsuit is that Obama has overreached his position as President by using executive powers to keep his Affordable Health Care plan [ObamaCare] going.

The first issue that will come up in Court, if the lawsuit is filed, is whether the parties bringing the lawsuit have Standing. I believe they do. The main reason, Congress makes laws, "not" the President. The President cannot change laws on his own, yet Obama has made over forty [40] changes in the law – violation of "our" Constitution. As I said, I believe the House of Representatives has "STANDING."

In an article by REUTERS, dated July 24, 2014 titled, *"U.S. House panel votes to authorize lawsuit against Obama,"* by Annika McGinnis, says in part, " … While the lawsuit would focus on Obamacare, Republicans have complained bitterly about the president's actions on several issues.

For example, House Speaker John Boehner wrote in June that Obama's use of executive orders, including raising the minimum wage for federal contractors and stopping deportation of undocumented youths brought to the United States by their parents, risked giving him a 'king-like authority.'

But Boehner has tamped down calls from some fellow Republicans for impeachment proceedings against Obama, which would be a first step toward removing him from office.

The lawsuit would focus on Obama's implementation of his landmark healthcare law, known as 'Obamacare,' which Republicans have been trying to repeal for years. Republicans claim Obama went beyond his legal authority and bypassed Congress when he delayed healthcare coverage mandates and granted various waivers."

The above comments summarize the basis of the forthcoming lawsuit. The lawsuit is necessary to bring specific attention to a major violation of the U.S. Constitution, Obamacare, by an out-of-control president Obama.

An article in CNN Opinion dated July 7, 2014 titled: *"Boehner: Why we must now sue the President"* by John Boehner says in part, (CNN) – "Every member of Congress swore an oath to preserve protect and defend the Constitution of the United States. So did President Barack Obama.

But too often over the past five years, the President circumvented the American people and their elected representatives through executive action, changing and creating his own laws, and excusing himself from enforcing statutes he is sworn to uphold – at times even boasting about his willingness to do it, as if daring the American people to stop him.

That's why, to file suit in an effort to compel president Obama to follow his oath of office and faithfully execute the laws of our country.

The president's response. 'So sue me.'

What's disappointing is the President's flippant dismissal of the Constitution we are both sworn to defend. I know the President is frustrated. I'm frustrated. The American people are frustrated, too.

… I don't take the House legal action against the President lightly.

…

In the end, the Constitution makes it clear that the President's job is to faithfully execute the laws. And, in my view, the President has not faithfully executed the laws when it comes to a range of issues, including his health care law, energy regulations, foreign policy and education.

There must be accountability. We have a system of government outlined in our Constitution with the executive branch, the legislative branch, and the judicial branch. Congress has its job to do, and so does the President. When there are conflicts like this – between the legislative branch and the executive branch – it is my view that it is our responsibility to stand up for this institution in which we serve, and for the Constitution.

... Over the last five years, starting – not coincidentally – when his political party lost the majority in the House of Representatives, the President has consistently overstepped his authority under the Constitution and in so doing eroded the power of the legislative branch.

The legislative branch has an obligation to defend the rights and responsibilities of the American people, and America's constitutional balance of powers – before it is too late."

Speaker Boehner says it like it is; and the arrogance of Obama saying, "So sue me." It just confirms that Obama believes he is above the law. I support Speaker Boehner's efforts to sue president Obama. The lawsuit will indicate to the world that "our" government works!

CHAPTER XXIX
Israel and Hamas Conflict

United States must take a stronger position for Israel
and stop negotiating with Iran.

Major conflict because Hamas is determined to destroy Israel; and they have so many tunnels into Israel, that bring Hamas troops with guns and apparatus to kill or kidnap Israelis; and shooting missile after missile into Israel.

Can you imagine missiles being shot daily at seventy-five [75 %] percent of the cities in the United States? Americans would not accept that for one minute. And where is the United States? Not supporting Israel as strongly as they should. It still goes back to Obama's first trip to the Middle East on his "apology tour" to all of the Arab nations, and NO stop in Israel! Israel has an absolute right to defend itself and to do everything possible to stop Hamas; the best way is to destroy Hamas.

Hamas has no ability to build missiles; the missiles are coming from Iran; and what is Obama doing – negotiating with Iran regarding nuclear missiles. How outrageous! Can we really believe Iran? I do not think so, yet Obama is still negotiating with Iran.

president Obama and Secretary of State John Kerry are wrong!

The United States has allowed money to flow to Iran, with no benefit in return to the United States – Iran should not be trusted in any manner. We must stop "negotiating and any dealings with Iran.." And what just occurred, negotiations with Iran were extended four [4] more months.

Regarding Israel – by seeking a truce with no benefit to Israel; by the U.S. Senate placing funding for the "IRON DOME" anti-missile system attached to a bill for immigration reform – changed on July 28, 2014 by separating it; and Secretary of State John Kerry slipped with microphone on saying how Israel has pin point shooting ability.

Philip J. Berg

Further, John Kerry's attempts at a quick cease-fire with apparently treating both parties, Israel & Hamas, equally. Hamas is a terrorist organization, like ISSI, determined to destroy Israel.

The demands by Israel & Hamas for a cease-fire appear irreconcilable with Israel wanting Hamas in Gaza to be weapon free, while Hamas wants a lifting of the Israel-Egypt blockade.

"Several cease-fires were agreed to with Hamas breaking each one. However, a cease-fire was reached on August 26, 2014 and has been holding. Time will tell if it holds." The United States must support Israel one hundred [100 %] percent and must demand a weapon free Gaza!

Chapter XXX
Missing Link – Proof Obama Born in Kenya

My Interview with Bettina Viviano About Bill Clinton's Remarks That
Obama Ineligible to be President
October 26, 2014

I always knew there was a missing link regarding the question that was always asked of me – "If you have the truth about Obama being born in Kenya, how come Hillary Clinton does not have the information?" and my response was, "I'm sure that Obama has something on Hillary." I was right and the following interview with Bettina Viviano gave me my answer.

Over the years I had spoken with Bettina many times about Obama and her movies as I am a member of SAG [Screen Actors Guild] but never in depth like this interview with Bettina Viviano, a film producer from California, on October 26, 2014.

Bettina Viviano began, "Until 2008, I had never thought much about politics. I have been in the film business since I was 19, having been a Production Executive for Steven Spielberg, a Literary Agent and for the last 20 years a Literary Manager/Film Producer. So, how I ended up here is just a strange, bizarre journey that all started with a random phone call about producing a documentary film for the 2008 Hillary Clinton Campaign.

In 2008, my literary client and best friend, Gigi Gaston, received a phone call from the Clinton Campaign, asking her if she would be interested in directing/producing a documentary film on the voter fraud being committed against Hillary by the Obama Campaign. Gigi then called me, and asked if I would be interested in producing the film with her. I stared at the phone and thought to myself, 'Why on EARTH would I care about voter fraud in a Democratic Primary?' At that time, I didn't even know what a Caucus was, or for that matter really what went on with a political Primary. But, for some reason I said yes, and from that moment on my life has changed in ways I never thought could happen. I wake up every day terrified for my country, whereas before I thought America was so strong, proud and indestructible that I didn't even need to show up to vote. In fact, I never voted and was never registered to vote until 2008 when I immediately registered Republican and voted McCain. I was so scared for my country, after what I had seen, that I was the first person in line to vote in 2008.

Once we decided to make the film, which by the way NO political party paid for, and we paid for out of our own pockets, the floodgates opened up and we were literally bombarded with stories about ACORN and Obama voter fraud. There were over 2,000 complaints in Texas alone. What we witnessed and documented were the most egregious stories of document fraud, death threats, vandalism, threats of job loss, threats of being banned from the Democratic Party, you name it. Anyone and everyone who didn't immediately toss their Hillary vote for an Obama vote received some sort of threat."

The interview was flowing so well, I didn't want to interrupt Bettina. She continued,

"Meanwhile, the other forms of fraud included the Democrats busing school kids into distant precincts they didn't live in, giving them steak dinners, a day off school, and handing them an Obama ballot. Or, the Democrats taking vans and going to Skid Row, picking bums off the street, giving them $20, a bottle of Vodka, and some cigarettes, handing them an Obama ballot, driving them to vote, then dumping them back on the street. They did the same thing in retirement homes and mental institutions, where the prospective "voters" were usually completely unaware of what they were doing, and why they were being taken to vote. They actually got caught and reprimanded for this action.

As we were witnessing this hideous fraud unfold, we of course got into investigating who Barack Obama was, and why the DNC and Democrats were so desperate to make him the candidate, over Hillary. It would have seemed to me that the Democratic Party voters should choose, and Hillary had the most popular votes of any candidate in history. We had a Democrat consultant on our film, from Houston, who was incredibly high up in the party and in politics in general. I asked him WHY there was this huge push for Obama over Hillary.

He was the first person to tell me about Billionaire George Soros, who pumps Billions of Dollars into Anti-America, globalist, open borders, foundations. He also basically owns the Democrats. Our consultant told us all about Soros, what he did to aid the Nazis as a teenager, and how he met with both Hillary and Obama, choosing Obama because Obama was much more compliant with the plan to weaken and diminish America. His exact quote was "Hillary might be as far to the left as Obama is, but she loves her country. Obama has no love for America and has no problem with Soros' plan to destroy us."

That was of course not the most troubling thing about Obama. I was immediately confronted with truth and facts about him that the media refused to report. The real Obama was absolutely nothing like what the media portrayed him as."

At this point, I was in total shock about the facts that Bettina was telling me, and I asked her to continue without me interrupting her with questions. Bettina continued,

"Never mind that he had absolutely zero qualifications or experience that would cause anyone to believe he could run our country. But, it was worse. He was clearly a pathological liar from day one (as we now see, having an almost impossible time keeping up with his lies.) And, his associations, both personal and political, were so radical, so Anti-America, and in the case of Bill Ayers and Bernardine Dohrn, etc., so criminal that they would preclude this man from even being giving FBI clearance. As I dug and dug and found all of Obama's specious friends and colleagues, I became aware that this man would be on a mission to belittle, humiliate, embarrass, degrade and ultimately totally weaken America. Why couldn't everyone see this? It wasn't hard to find if people just did the smallest amount of research.

Then there were other criminal acts. He went to Kenya to campaign for his Radical Islamist cousin, Raila Odinga. He used his U.S. Senator letterhead, cell phone, computer, travel, etc. to interfere in another country's elections, and in this election to help a seriously radical Islamist to become President of Kenya and to install Sharia Law. This is not someone who should be U.S. President, but it is also from what I can tell a clear violation of the Logan Act. I wrote letters to Senator Feinstein about it, but of course got no response.

When Odinga lost the Presidential race, Kenya became a "killing field" of Christians being murdered and burned alive. Churches were burned down, and as Christians tried to flee, the Islamists would throw them back into the Churches to be incited and encouraged. Why on earth would America elect this man?"

I said to Bettina," This is unbelievable!" and she responded, "There is more as she continued,

"There were then the FEC violations, and Obama accepting campaign cash from overseas donors in Gaza, etc. What kind of President of the U.S. receives donations from terrorists? That of course also led us to the Rashid Khalidi, PhD, Edward Said Professor of Arab Studies and other associations of Obama, radical Anti-Israel activists, and Khalidi was just one step short of being a PLO terrorist. His views on Israel are what we are seeing now with Obama. In 2008 I picketed the LA Times for the notorious "Khalidi Tape" which exists as proof of Obama's Israel hate. He was at a dinner for Khalidi, and proceeded to call Israel's actions towards Palestine "acts of genocide." I tried to alert every Jew I could about this. I knew that Obama's foreign policy would be radically Pro-Islam and Anti-Israel. I was right. I called people like Ed Koch and every Jewish leader I knew. It all fell on deaf ears. Obama was the Messiah. I was just being crazy. Most of those people have since apologized to me and said they should have listened, but of course it's too late.

Every single thing Obama had done in his political career had now become clearly the act of an amoral, unethical and in my opinion, criminal Marxist whose only goal would be to trash my country. He wasn't hiding it from anyone when he went on the "America Sucks World Tour," giving speeches in foreign countries apologizing for, and humiliating America and Americans. Again, what kind of American "President" does this? I was appalled.

Of course, one of the biggest red flags was that Obama refused to document himself. I want to reiterate that it was the Clinton people who first brought up Obama's birthplace and questionable qualification to be President. I had never heard of the Natural Born Citizen clause of the Constitution, but I was immediately surrounded by the Clintons and their supporters who were loudly claiming that Obama was not eligible. There were no Republicans in my life at that time. My only political friends and allies were Clinton Democrats, and there was no such thing as the Tea Party. Everything I know about Obama's lack of eligibility to be President came from my experience with the Clinton Campaign. Everything!

During the Democratic Primary, it couldn't have been more obvious that the Clintons and Obamas absolutely hated each other. Obama called Bill Clinton a "racist" and he never forgot it. It was so awful that on the daily campaign phone calls, some people stopped getting on them because it ended up being a Bill Clinton hate fest towards Obama. I was asked by a delegate to get on one of those calls, and did in fact hear Bill Clinton screaming about Obama. He also referred to him as the illegal, or the immigrant, or something to do with his eligibility. At the time, I didn't think much of it, because literally everyone I was surrounded and involved with believed Obama was not eligible to be President. Whether it was the Birth Certificate, now proven to be a total fraud and forgery, or his Indonesian citizenship, or the fact there is endless proof he was actually born in Kenya. An innocent man doesn't hire attorneys to the tune of millions of dollars to hide who he is, as Obama has. And, as we all know,

Obama has sequestered any and all documents relating to who he is: no passport, health records, no high school, college, and Occidental, Columbia or Harvard records. He never wrote anything for the Harvard Law Review, the man is a cipher, yet he holds the highest job in the world.

I can't express how disgusted and appalled I am that even the Republicans won't challenge this fraud. Obama was never properly vetted by anyone, and if he were, he wouldn't be in the job. It's that simple.

When it was clear that the Clintons knew Obama wasn't eligible for the job, I continually asked delegates and Clinton friends WHY the Clintons wouldn't come forward and tell the truth. Over and over again I was told that Bill was planning on coming forward and spilling all the truth about Obama. Every single day I would ask "when" because I couldn't stand the thought of Obama winning. It was doomsday and crunch time for our country. There was even a point when Bill Clinton was interviewed and asked if Obama was "qualified" to be President. He smirked and said "If he's over 35 and a U.S. Citizen, then I guess he is." That was apparently a shout out to the people who knew that the citizenship was certainly questionable, and Clinton supporters knew Bill would do it.

Back in 2011, our documentary ran on Fox and Friends for several weeks, in fact longer at the time than any story had ever run consecutive weeks on their show. They would not allow me to be on the show, because I had run and registered Republican, after the horrors of the Democratic Primary. But my partners and the delegates for Hillary, etc. were all still registered Democrats. Fox loved that the fraud was committed by Democrats on a Democrat. Gloria Allred was in our film, and went on Fox and Friends for us.

I was interviewed to be on Fox, but as I said, they didn't want Republicans anywhere near the story. However, they did ask me to get in touch with a member of the Hillary Campaign and ask her to do the show. She was a woman who had been incredibly important to us in evaluating exactly how many delegates and votes were stolen by the Obama Campaign, and Fox really wanted her on the show. I called her, and she had become a very scared, terrified, isolated woman, who password protected her blog, and refused to speak to anyone about the Primary. I remembered a story she told me about Bill Gwatney, who was murdered by a random gunman, and who was a close Clinton friend and ally, and Chairman of the Arkansas Democratic Party. There was no reason for Gwatney to have been sought out and shot, and the motive was never discovered. This woman told me that it was a "warning" to Bill Clinton to shut up about Obama.

However, Bill isn't the kind of guy to be told to shut up, so he kept telling people he would expose Obama. Then, she told me, they threatened his daughter Chelsea, and Bill never opened his mouth. She told me this story word for word the same way she had told me years earlier. Considering all of the dead bodies that piled up around this mess, I am not surprised. One of the first was the man who broke into the passport office and got Hillary and Obama's passports. It just got worse from there.

It's been a horrifying six and one-half [6 ½] years watching Obama do exactly what those of us who knew the truth said he would do. He is America's enemy, the enemy within, and it will be very difficult to turn around the damage he has done, intentionally. I have over 200,000 documents dating back to 2008 documenting all of this disgrace. I plan to write my own book as well, hoping that this never happens again, and that people wake up."

I said to Bettina, "Wow, unbelievable, but very believable. This is the missing link. I always knew there was something that prevented the Clinton's from exposing Obama."

Bettina then said, "I will send you a photo that was taken from a screen shot of an interview by the BBC with Sara Obama, Obama's step-grandmother, in her home with a calendar on the wall with Obama's picture with the title, "THE KENYAN WONDER-BOY IN THE US" – "YEAR 2005" with notation under the photo, "Illinois Senator Barrack Obama."

This link is worth visiting to learn more of Bettina's own words. *http://www.wnd.com/2012/04/hollywood-producer-heard-bill-clinton-say-obama-ineligible/*

And, as I have said since 2008 and I stand today by my original statement:

"Obama is a fraud, phony and an imposter and has put forth the greatest 'HOAX' against the United States of America in over two hundred and thirty years."

Wake up America! Wake up Free Press!

CHAPTER XXXI
Can America Survive?

Only if We Take Action!

America cannot survive the way it has for the past two hundred thirty-eight [238] years where people legally came to the United States through immigration. The legal immigrants made sure their children were educated; the legal immigrants worked jobs to enhance their families so that their children and grandchildren could go forth with a better education, better jobs, better homes, and a better life in our country.

Obama and his administration have sent our country on a downward spin. We must take action because we are losing the rights and privileges our forefathers, grandparents, fathers, mothers, sons and daughters fought for to preserve; and those that survived enacted the Declaration of Independence, the U.S. Constitution and the Bill of Rights that we are in the midst of losing those rights and privileges. Obama has done more to the detriment of the United States than all of our prior Presidents together. We must stop Obama by a concerted effort.

The following article must be read as it goes into detail about Obama's proposal for ISSI, but really Obama trying to save his presidency, which is doubtful:

"NEW YORK POST – September 14, 2014
MORE FROM
Michael Goodwin

The rising clamor over the beheading of two Americans, and rapidly sinking polls, forced president Obama to reassure the nation last week he had a plan to deal with the Islamic State. He did some of what he had to do, but only some, and so most military analysts believe the expanded airstrikes will not be a sufficient match for the size and weaponry of the terrorist army.

They miss the point. The disjointed speech wasn't really about terrorism and launching a new war. It was about saving Obama's presidency.

He is sinking fast and could soon pass the point of no return. In fact, it may already be too late to save the SS Obama.

The whole second term has been a string of disasters, with the toxic brew of his Obamacare lies, middling economic growth and violent global breakdown casting doubt on the president's stewardship. Six years into his tenure, nothing is going as promised.

Earlier on, he could have trotted out his teleprompters and turned public opinion his way, or at least stopped the damage. But the magic of his rhetoric is long gone, and not just because the public has tuned him out.

They've tuned him out because they've made up their minds about him. They no longer trust him and don't think he's a good leader.

Most ominously, they feel less safe now than they did when he took office. Americans know the war on terror isn't over, no matter what their president claims.

Those findings turned up in a tsunami of recent polls that amount to a public vote of no confidence. They shook up the White House so much that the plan to grant amnesty to millions of illegal immigrants was put on hold to try to protect Democratic candidates from voter wrath in November.

That was a necessary tactical retreat, but it doesn't change the - basic calculation. The president's problem is that he has been wrong about virtually every major issue.

His worldview, his politics, his prejudices, his habits — they've been a mismatch for the country and its needs. He has been a dud even in the one area where he seemed a lock to make things better, racial relations. Only 10 percent believe race relations have improved under him, while 35 percent said they are worse, according to a New York Times survey. The remainder said there wasn't much change either way.

That's shocking — but not surprising. Barack Obama was not ready to be president, and still isn't. It is a fantasy to believe he'll master the art in his final two years.

The lasting image will be his yukking it up on the golf course minutes after giving a perfunctory speech on the beheading of James Foley. It revealed him as hollow, both to America and the world, and there is no way to un-see the emptiness.

That means, I fear, we are on the cusp of tragedy. It is reasonable to assume the worst-case scenarios about national security are growing increasingly likely to occur.

Obama's fecklessness is so unique that our adversaries and enemies surely realize they will never face a weaker president. They must assume the next commander in chief will take a more muscular approach to America's interests and be more determined to forge alliances than the estranged man who occupies the Oval Office now.

So Vladimir Putin, Iran, China, Islamic State, al Qaeda and any other number of despots and terrorists know they have two years to make their moves and advance their interests, and that resistance will be token, if there is any at all.

Throw in the fact that Europe largely has scrapped its military might to pay for its welfare states, and the entire West is a diminished, confused opponent, ripe for the taking. Redrawn maps and expanded spheres of influence could last for generations.

Of course, there is a possibility that America could rally around the president in a crisis, and there would be many voices demanding just that. But a national consensus requires a president who is able to tap into a reservoir of good will and have his leadership trusted.

That's not the president we have."

This article by Michael Goodwin is right on point about president Obama and reinforces what I have said about Obama for six years. Obama had no experience to be President; he was great with his teleprompter; he spoke a great game plan; and the DoubleSpeak set in early on. I feel Obama is on the path of what he set out to do, to destroy the United States of America that most of the citizens in the United States loved. What has occurred is that Obama actions and inactions have caused a total lack of support by "our" citizens; Democratic candidates are ducking him, trying to claim they do not support Obama's agenda, although Democratic U.S. Senators up for re-election in 2014 voted in the high ninety [90%] percent on all of Obama's issues.

How can we stop Obama? We, U.S. citizens must demand accountability by "our" Congress and "our" Free Press. Do your part now because not doing will be the downfall of the United States of America that we have known, respected and loved."

CHAPTER XXXII
What the American People Must Do Now!

Red, White and Blue Fest

American People Demand Action Now!

1) *Demand Sealing of Southern Border & Change Amnesty & 2008 Law.*
2) *Repeal / Major Changes of ObamaCare [Affordable Health Care Act].*
3) *Treat "our" Veterans the way they should be - Excellent*
4) *Demand a stronger Foreign Policy – Have the United States Be a Leader again.*
5) *Abolish IRS to a "Flat Tax" and/or "National Sales Tax" & Tariffs & Lower Corporate Tax Rates.*
6) *Stand Up to Federal Government - Like Clive Bundy situation.*
7) *Demand 'Free Press' do their job.*
8) *Review Acts of Impeachment & Treason of Obama.*
9) *Enforce Litter Laws.*

It is time for the American people to take a look at what has been transpiring in our country; to take from the time that they're spending on their jobs; their families; their children; with sports and recreation; to decide what to do so that our children and grandchildren and future generations are able to enjoy the rights and privileges that have come forth in the past two hundred thirty-eight plus [238+] years.

It is time therefore, for a real third party and/or for people to demand that the major parties, Democrat and Republican, put forth candidates who will work to restore the rights and privileges that our forefathers gave us. With the Election results of November 2014 with the Republicans gaining in the U.S. House and taking control of the U.S. Senate, hopefully a change will occur.

We must demand that Congress, that has been a do nothing Congress for years, start being caring and productive. At this point, Congress, yes, the Senate and House are overpaid; they should be ashamed to receive the salary they do. Presently, all of them work part-time in terms of time spent in Washington and what they accomplish; hardly doing anything beneficial for "our" country. Congress finally passed a budget for the first time in five [5] years; we, their constituents cannot do that. Get real.

Congress can redeem themselves right now. Forget your political parties and do right for "our" country – start by straightening 'our" country out; cross party lines and work together to protect our country and:

1. **Demand Sealing of Southern Border & Change Amnesty & 2008 Law.**

As I stated in detail in Chapter XXI, it is imperative that Obama, "our" Congress and "our" Free Press take immediate action to stop illegal immigrants, especially the children from Guatemala, El Salvador and Honduras entering our Southern Border, as they are bringing diseases into our country, burdening our school systems and are potential security risks."

2. **Obama must Use his Pen and issue EXECUTIVE ORDERS to:**

Immediately change the law so that illegal immigrants, including the children from countries other than contiguous countries are immediately deported!

Immediately Seal "our" Southern Borders!

Immediately Stop "all aid" to Guatemala, El Salvador and Honduras until the flow of children stops!

3. Repeal / Major Changes of ObamaCare [Affordable Health Care Act]:

Repeal ObamaCare! It is a total mess as reported from doctors all across the country. How can anyone create a healthcare program like ObamaCare without the input and direction of healthcare providers? From the outset, it was designed for failure. Insurance reform and Healthcare reform are two different things. It does not solve the major problems with healthcare in our country: forty [40] million not insured; and the high costs of Emergency Room care.

Please do not forget the stupid words of Congressperson Nancy Pelosi [D-CA]. *"… let's pass ObamaCare so we can read it and find out what it says! …"*

The numbers put forth by the Obama Administration were not believable.

And what has Obama done? Violated "our" U.S. Constitution again!

Obama has made over forty [40] changes in ObamaCare [Affordable Health Care Act]. It must be repealed or major changes!

3. Veterans:

Treat "our" Veterans as they should be – Excellent - as the men and women who have served and protected us deserve:

It is a disgrace how we treat, [do not treat] "our" Veterans. Anyone who has served "our" nation in the military should have the finest medical and psychological treatment and all the support they need. We should provide it immediately… without ANY delay. How can

ObamaCare work if our veterans can't get proper healthcare. The VETS already paid their premiums! Our government gives billions away to foreign countries. Some are not even our allies and want to destroy us. I suggest we take care of "our" Veterans the way they should be. I say this while advising you that I never served in the military, as I was medically barred.

A good friend of mine, Specialist E5, Leo G. ["Pete"] Peters, brought to me a major problem with the VA, that being the lack of credible counseling/advice regarding proper diet, especially with diabetics. Pete had practical experience being hospitalized several times for conditions other than diabetes. While hospitalized, a complete lack of care from the dieticians regarding food being served to him or diet to follow when released; a total waste of government resources, that you and I pay for. And without proper diet to diabetics, down the road can be loss of limbs, aside from the tragic loss, additional expenses for artificial limbs and physical therapy. What a loss!

I am concerned when organizations like Wounded Warrior Projects [WWP], (an excellent program), cannot provide sufficient special services because of funding. While I admire and support all programs that assist our wounded veterans, WHY do we have to have any of them? These brave men and women served "our" nation and we should support them one hundred [100%] percent. We send billions of dollars around the world for many reasons. Our top reason must be to support our veterans! With Obama, it is not going to happen.

Obama campaigned in 2008 to straighten out the VA, however... it got worse, not better and the problems still exist. Obama said the right words in order to get their votes, then forgot about them. Here is another *scary* event... bonuses were given to VA administrators and other personnel from thirty [30%] to forty [40%] percent. How disgusting!

4. Demand a stronger Foreign Policy – Have the United States Be a Leader again:

We must restore our place in the world. The United States of America has been the shining star in the world until Obama has taken down the path of destruction. Obama's plan to lead by being the nice guy has not worked and cannot work. In the world that has and exists, one leads by strength and Obama has taken that away. We must demand a stronger Foreign Policy, but first we need a Foreign Policy!

5. Abolish IRS and implement a Flat Tax and/or National Sales Tax and Tariffs and Lower Corporate Taxes:

The current tax structure is wrong! There are too many exemptions under the tax code. Corporate taxes, the highest in the world are too high. We must make changes!

Abolish the IRS! A Flat Tax would be fair to everyone. Take away all the loopholes and exceptions and the 73,954 pages of the IRS Code, as of 2013; have the same exceptions for everyone at the low end of income; and eliminate tens of thousands of IRS employees.

A National Sales Tax on all sales to all products sold in the United States would eliminate all other taxes.

Tariffs on all products coming into the United States would increase and equalize our production in the United States.

Lower Corporate Tax Rates would keep corporations in the United States and would stop the exodus taking place; would result in more jobs in the United States. Make the United States "friendly" to corporations!

6. Stand Up to Federal Government – Like Clive Bundy did.

An example of the people standing up to the Federal government. A civil matter regarding Bundy's cattle grazing on public lands [Bundy ranch has been in family for more than a century, 100+ years, and owned the land since 1887], that brought in the BLM [Bureau of Land Management] with guns. The government claimed they were protecting the desert Tortoise and the environment of 150,000 acres of desolate country. How dare the government!

If someone breaks the law, the BLM has no lawful authority to enforce the law; the Sheriff has the responsibility.

Then, U.S. Senator Harry Reid declares the Bundy's "Domestic Terrorists" and brings in Home Land Security. Something is wrong here. [As I stated earlier in this book, compare this to Ft. Hood, Texas where murders occurred and Obama refused to call the shooter a terrorist, but called it "Work Place" injury. What a disgrace!

7. Demand 'Free Press' do their job:

And we, yes, *"WE THE PEOPLE,"* must demand truth investigative journalism and reporting... and not party line support. Stop buying their papers, stop buying their advertisers products, stop watching or listening to their stations and see how fast they begin to do a better job.

The Press must report accurately and fairly all the news. Stop being favorable to Obama and his administration; yes, Obama and his administration have failed the citizens of the United States. The Press bent over backwards for Obama; the Press never vetted Obama.

My demand of the Press: Do right for the citizens of "our" country; they deserve it; show you can put aside your favoritism and expose Obama for the fraud he is; expose his administration for the fraud they are; expose the scandals for what they are – scandals. "Our" United States Press – the world knows you have covered for Obama and his administration; it is time to change – to help the United States survive based upon the principles of "our" forefathers, "our" U.S. Constitution; "our" Declaration of Independence; and "our" Bill of Rights!

Congress must:

Immediately pass immigration legislation in line with our legal immigration policy that has existed for years; and deport illegal immigrants.

Press must:

Report the truth about the southern border; be the 'Free Press' you are supposed to be – expose Obama for the fraud he is and report the scandals of the Obama administration.

8. Review Acts of Impeachment and Treason of Obama:

Because Obama deserves it. Obama has desecrated "our" U.S. Constitution. Obama is "Constitutionally Ineligible" to be President. Obama has usurped the Office of President. Obama changes laws as he sees fit; declared Congress as irrelevant; decides what laws to enforce and which laws to disregard; destroyed our respect from individuals and leaders around the world; caused chaos with our foreign policy; curtailed our space program; and overall has become the worse president in the history of the United States.

Does Congress have the guts to proceed with Impeachment and/or Treason? *I doubt it.* As of October 15th, 2014, American citizens do not want Impeachment. However, "We The People" must demand a realistic look at what Obama has done and take appropriate action as directed in "our" Constitution.

9. Enforce Littering Laws:

It is a disgrace how Americans litter; it is ugly the mess along sidewalks, streets in neighborhoods, in our towns and cities, and our country.

Littering shows a lack of feeling good about our great nation. Each of us must do better and for those that don't, they should be cited and the penalty should be hours of community service picking up litter! Let's show we care!

I, Philip J. Berg, am proud that I am a citizen of the United States of America. All citizens of the United States and our Press – wake up; stand up; we can do better!

And as many of you that can, please attend the following. I will be there:

Red White and Blue Fest:

(http://constittutionalpatriots.org) is a national patriot rally to be held in the Spring of 2015 in Sunny Hills, Florida, north of Panama City, to plan a major annual event on 9/11 in Washington, DC. The founder of the event is Zeeda Andrews who was the founder of the October 2013 Trucker's Ride for the Constitution. The event is being produced by Zeeda's group, ConstitutionalPatriots.org and also Advance America Foundation. Steve Gronka is the Chairman of both groups.

Timing is everything. *ObamaScare* has been delayed because of many additions that I have included.

On October 6, 2014, I received a telephone call from Michael Henning, michael@sovranfilms.com from Dallas, Texas, who had previously interviewed and filmed me regarding my efforts to expose Obama. We discussed Obama's current situation with crisis after crisis and I told Mike that I was about to release *ObamaScare* and the contents thereof. Mike said he would help promote my book. He called me to advise that Steve Gronka would be calling me regarding the *Red White and Blue Fest* national patriot rally that he was coordinating and he wanted me to be involved.

Steve Gronka called me in the evening of October 6, 2014 and we had a detailed conversation of his plans and he asked me for my thoughts and for my participation at his event. He then stated that Mike had told him about my forthcoming book and he said it was vital to explain to the citizens of the United States the entire background of Obama and his scandals. Steve explained to me that the purpose of **Red White and Blue Fest** is to unite all of the numerous groups that want the truth from our government and the troubles we are in because of Obama and all progressives and to teach participants how to effect change.

Steve said the teaching event is to explain citizen grand juries and warrants as well as other legal remedies and how common law and founding documents validate the legality of citizen grand juries and other legal remedies; as people want to do something the founders predicted we would need the power to do, to take back our country from corrupt bureaucrats.

I asked Steve what this patriot rally wants to accomplish. Steve replied they want to educate as many patriots as possible to: go back to their states and do citizen grand juries and citizen warrants, as well as pursue other legal actions; find contacts to get CSPOA [Constitutional Sheriffs and Peace Officers] or Oath Keeper to help with enforcement; have workshops on common law courts, the Constitution and Federalist Papers; and start We The Kids History Clubs for kids in their schools; and more.

I asked Steve who the participants will be. He said groups that have held various rallies, concerts and events, but this gathering is to bring all together, especially the leadership of the various groups so that they can meet, get to know each other, and get some confidence about working together.

The groups include bikers, truckers, farmers, veterans, hunters, law enforcement, militias, patriot groups, and patriots from all backgrounds.

Steve said plans are underway to have all enjoy learning how to take back our country and also have some great entertainment! These include a Biker Rodeo, Trucker Rodeo, Law Enforcement and Veterans Marksmanship Competition, Civilian Marksmanship Competition, three nights of country music concerts having three acts per night, exhibitors and food concessions.

Steve was so excited in discussing this event saying this is the ultimate Patriot Rally to learn how to take action. He stated that a Camping Village will be available for tents, Coaches and RVs!!!

Steve said the goal is to have on 9/11 citizen warrants and citizen grand jury verdicts to take to Washington, DC for the 9-11 biker ride which is going to become a Patriot Ride including bikers, truckers, veterans, hunters, law enforcement, farmers, and every patriot and patriot group that will join the ride.

Steve stated the purpose is to call out and arrest if possible all of those in government who have violated their oath of office and committed other crimes against the people; doing this under the statutes regarding sedition and seeking a court or courts that would hear the cases.

Steve felt this gathering could be greater than the original ride idea started by Top Fuel Bill and his 2 Million Bikers to DC for which he got the National Coalition of Motorcyclists Silver Spoke Award, the bikers' version of a Nobel Prize.

Steve said the 9/11 event will be different; instead of riding through DC there will be one stop, with two [2] parts. We will surround the United States Capital Building and the White House with all of our patriot riders from all groups and additionally have CSPOA and Oath Keepers with us to enforce the Citizen Warrants resulting from the verdicts of the Citizen Grand Juries.

Steve and others planning the 9/11 event point out it will take on the aspects of the citizen revolt in Iceland (http://www.knowledgeoftoday.org/2012/05/iceland-news-icelandic-revolution.html) a few years ago where the citizens rose up; marched into their national capital and surrounded the parliament building; and threw stones at the building until the members of parliament surrendered (David and Goliath). Last, but not least, they arrested the Prime Minister and top three bankers and charged them with over 200 crimes and held elections to replace members of parliament !!!

Steve concluded by saying, "We know it is unlikely that the 'pres' would ever be turned over for arrest, but at least the statement will have been made. We may actually be able to arrest some Senators and Representatives and other bureaucrats. The main thing is that this needs to get done! The press will have a feeding frenzy and that won't be such a bad thing!

Steve Gronka

M. Steven Gronka
Fearless Leader
Advance America Foundation
Sea Quest Kids
Kids Broadcasting and Boating Networks
KBN Sea Action News
KBN See Action News
Advance America Foundation Film and Television Division

6 South Dillwyn Road
Newark, DE 19711-5544
USA
www.seaquestkids.org
stevegronka@seaquestkids.org
Phone: 404-434-0660

This gathering is a must for all that want change. We The People can change the direction of our government peaceably!

Philip J. Berg

CHAPTER XXXIII
Conclusion

I have fully explained the "Constitutionally Ineligible" person in the White House. Obama who "couldn't" care less about "y[our]" U.S. Constitution. He has done everything in his power to undermine the greatness of our country. He has urinated all over... the "Greatest Generations and what they fought for and tried to convince us it is roses.

Obama will go down, in my opinion, as the worse president of the United States. His values are frightening, and *scary*. Obama has no foreign policy and is the laughing stock around the world regarding his foreign policy.

Benghazi should have been Obama's downfall and still might be, as it is one thousand [1,000] times worse than Watergate. If there was ever a major "Cover-up," it is Benghazi. The American people must demand the truth and those responsible for Benghazi should be removed from office and tried criminally for their actions/inactions that resulted in the death of an U.S. Ambassador and three [3] others.

The Mideast has turned into a total nightmare. Obama has no foreign policy; has lost the respect of leaders throughout the world; has hurt Israel and other Mideast countries with his positions with Syria, not following through after he drew his "red line," Iran and now Iraq and the Radical Islams.

Obama's efforts to eliminate ISSI/ISSL are questionable, and time will tell. Obama is a year late in even acknowledging the seriousness of ISSI/ISSL and his coalition efforts that began in late September 2014 have been a slow start. We need "boots on the ground" by someone, as Obama has stated the U.S. will not put "boots on the ground." Also, if an air attack is going to work, do a massive airstrike, 200 or more strikes a day, every day, not the limited airstrikes that have taken place.

I am sure Putin is shaking in his boots over the comments that Obama has made regarding the takeover of Crimea and the invasion of Ukraine.

Obama has stated publicly that he is reducing our military to a pre-World War II level and he has called Russia a "Regional Power" with Putin's moves from weakness. What a joke!

Obama has the United States positioned as one of weakness with no backbone and we are no longer the major power in the world. Currently China, Japan, North Korea, Iran and Russia are reassessing what position they should take around the world with our no follow through and lackluster president Obama.

It is time that the national Free Press, Members of Congress and the American people do everything in their powers to stop the downward spin that Obama and his administration have caused.

Obama has destroyed our space program, has undermined our military, has hurt our foreign policy, has destroyed our health care system, was about to give away control of the internet, and hurt our economy and I cannot think of one major accomplishment that Obama has accomplished that will benefit all of the citizens of the United States.

Obama is not only *scary*, but frightening. Let us not be like individuals in Germany in the 1940's, who did not want to be involved, until there was a knock on their door and they were taken away.

Obama must be stopped because he will be in office until January 20, 2017 which is a period of time that he can continue his efforts to undermine the United States of America, and as he said, "...I've got a pen, and I've got a phone. And I can use that pen to sign executive orders and take executive actions and administrative actions...."

And I conclude by saying:

Change! It is time to make it happen!

Appendix I

References

"Attorney Phil Berg Demands Disbarment of Justices O'Connor, Scalia, and Thomas". Archive.democrats.com.

"Rodriguez RICO complaint". 911review.com.

"Wake Up, Anti-War People!: Phil Berg". Video.google.com.

Bravin, Jess (January 29, 2014). "Supreme Court Ousts Attorney Who Sued to Oust Obama". Wall Street Journal.

"Rodriguez v Bush Lawsuit Docs From PACER".

"Rodriguez Complaint from PACER".

"Order Granting Motion to Transfer from PACER" (PDF).

"Order Dismissing Complaint against USA, DHS, and FEMA" (PDF).

"Order Dismissing Complaint against Balance of Defendants from PACER" (PDF).

"Berg v. Obama", No. 08-1256 (E.D. Pa. Oct. 24, 2008) 574 F.Supp.2d 509 at 521, aff'd 586 F.3d 234" (PDF). Retrieved 2010-12-03.

"Judge rejects Montco lawyer's bid to have Obama removed from ballot,"[dead link] Philadelphia Daily News, October 25, 2008.

Kevin Amerman, "Supreme Court won't hear Berg's appeal," The Morning Call (Allentown, Pa.), January 16, 2009.[dead link] http://origin.www.supremecourt.gov/docket/08-570.htm

http://en.wikipedia.org/wiki/Barack_Obama_presidential_eligibility_li tigation

Index

www.ingramcontent.com/pod-product-compliance
Lightning Source LLC
Chambersburg PA
CBHW030819090426
42737CB00009B/793